Raising Healthy Kids

MICHIO KUSHI
AVELINE KUSHI
WITH EDWARD ESKO & WENDY ESKO

Avery Publishing Group
Garden City Park, New York

The procedures in this book are based upon the personal and professional experiences of the authors. Should the reader have any questions regarding the appropriateness of any procedure or material mentioned, the publisher and authors strongly suggest consulting a health care professional.

Because any material or procedure can be misused, the authors and publisher are not responsible for any adverse effects or consequences resulting from the use of any of the preparations, materials, or procedures suggested in this book. However, the publisher believes that this information should be available to the public.

Cover design: Ann Vestal
In-house editors: Linda Comac, Cynthia Eriksen, and Karen Hay
Typesetter: Bonnie Freid

Library of Congress Cataloging-in-Publication Data

Raising healthy kids : a book of child care and natural family health
    care / Michio Kushi ... [et al.].
        p. cm.
    Includes index.
    ISBN 0-89529-578-4
    1. Macrobiotic diet. 2. Children—Nutrition. 3. Child care.
    4. Health. I. Kushi, Michio.
    RM235.R35 1994   93-46170
    613.2'6—dc20   CIP

Copyright © 1994 by Michio Kushi, Aveline Kushi, Edward Esko, and Wendy Esko

Printed in the United States of America

10 9 8 7 6 5 4 3 2 1

Contents

Acknowledgments

We would like to take this opportunity to thank everyone associated with this book. We thank Michio and Aveline Kushi—on whose lectures and writings this book is based—for their love and compassion for children everywhere. We also thank Lawrence H. Kushi, Sc.D., now at the University of Minnesota, for writing "Growing Up With Macrobiotics" and for his ongoing research on diet, health, and nutrition. We thank Rudy Shur, Cynthia Eriksen, Linda Comac, and the staff of Avery Publishing Group for their support, encouragement, and guidance.

A Word About Gender

The chances are just about equal that your child is a boy or girl. Unfortunately, the English language does not have a singular pronoun that includes both genders. We did not wish to refer to children as "it," and we find "he/she" too awkward. To give equal time to both sexes, we have, therefore, used the feminine "she" and "her" in even-numbered chapters and the masculine "he," "him," and "his" in odd-numbered chapters.

Preface

Since the beginning of history, parents the world over have known that when caring for children, every day brings new challenges and new rewards. Our experience caring for children dates back to 1974 when the first of our seven children (five boys and two girls) was born. Even after twenty years of experience in this area, we feel that our learning is just beginning.

For all parents, the health of their children is a primary concern. We have been fortunate in that all of our children were breastfed and raised on a diet of whole grains, beans, fresh organic vegetables, sea vegetables, and other whole natural foods. This has meant that their basic dietary foundation has been sound, and that in their early formative years, they did not have to cope with the hazards of the modern high-fat, highly processed diet.

In our family, we have tried to educate our children about the importance of eating well, and about simple natural methods of caring for their health. We have also encouraged them to learn how to cook basic daily foods. As our children became teenagers, they occasionally experimented with foods we do not normally serve at home. During these times, we tried not to be judgmental by labeling their dietary experiences as "good" or "bad." We encourage our children to think for themselves and, hopefully, discover how their eating habits affect their health and behavior. We have found that the best dietary teaching comes from the example provided by both parents, especially in the daily preparation of healthful home-cooked meals.

On the infrequent occasions when our children have experienced minor health problems, we have, fortunately, been able to solve them without the assistance of a doctor. Simple dietary changes plus rest and basic home care, including the preparations described in this book, have been sufficient to deal with minor problems such as upset stomach, mild headache, simple fevers, or colds. As much as possible, we have encouraged our children to learn about and utilize simple home remedies such as a cabbage leaf plaster, mild carrot daikon tea, a tofu plaster, hot apple juice, ume-sho-kuzu drink, lotus root tea, and others. However, we would like to emphasize that the advice in this book, including the advice on home remedies, is not a substitute for qualified medical care. Parents have the responsibility to seek appropriate medical assistance in an emergency or if they suspect a serious health problem in their children.

Together with teaching our children about food and health, we have tried to inspire them with a dream of health and peace, and instill in them a spirit of endless discovery and adventure. As when conveying the importance of proper diet, this has resulted more from the example of daily life than from formal teaching. From time to time, we have taken the older children on lecture tours of Europe and the United States, and have encouraged them to travel and become citizens of the global civilization of the future. As teachers of macrobiotics, we have frequently invited students from other countries to live in our home. We have managed macrobiotic student houses where as many as twenty people, mostly young students at the Kushi Institute, have lived and studied. This has allowed our children to be exposed to people from a wide range of cultures and backgrounds, and has, hopefully, broadened their outlook and horizons.

Michio and Aveline Kushi, our teachers and coauthors, have had a lifelong interest in children's education. Michio has lectured frequently on this topic as well as on the topic of children's and family health. Aveline is a mother and grandmother. She has personally guided hundreds of families, including our own. A graduate of teacher's college in Japan, Aveline taught in an elementary school before coming to America to teach macrobiotics. In her writings, she has stressed the need for education to help children develop on the human as well as technical level:

The most important principle of education is not teaching children to memorize facts and figures, but guiding them in the development of a well-rounded personality. This includes the capacity to judge and figure things out for themselves, the capacity to love others and relate to a wide variety of people, and the willingness to assume responsibility for their health and behavior. Helping a child develop as a whole person is more important than providing information to remember.

In the future, I hope that education will include practical training to help children develop as whole persons, rather than offer only technical training. A more holistic approach to education is vital if children are to be able to relate to the rest of humanity and contribute to world peace.

She has also called for the adoption of healthful natural-food meals in schools:

I hope all public institutions, and especially schools, will discover the importance of daily food in creating health and happiness. Childhood is the foundation for future life, and should be something that everyone has happy memories of. Making each child's school experience healthful and rewarding is an important element in this. One of the goals of macrobiotics is to make the highest quality education available to all children. In this way, we can make a direct contribution to a healthy and peaceful world.

Aveline's words are especially important today. In this era of MTV, compact discs, computer games, VCRs, and fast foods, children are exposed to an incredible array of dietary and electronic stimulation. In many ways, they grow up much more quickly than in the past. However, the stress of modern living is causing families to fragment and exposing children to new challenges and difficulties. In the 1950s, the heyday of the nuclear family, the vast majority of children were raised by both parents. During the 1990s, about a third of all American children will be raised in single-parent households.

Macrobiotics offers a powerful alternative to the collapse of the family. The macrobiotic way of life embraces extended, nuclear, single-parent, and other models of family life. By emphasizing home cooking, macrobiotics can help restore a biological center to every family. A diet based on whole grains, fresh local vegetables, beans, sea vegetables, and other complex-carbohydrate foods helps secure the health of each family member.

When the members of a family share healthful, home-cooked meals, they begin to share the same healthy quality of blood. Sharing the same blood and spirit is what a family is all about. Macrobiotic eating can also reverse the trend toward declining fertility by strengthening reproductive health and vitality. In traditional cultures, cereal grains (the principal foods in a macrobiotic diet) are associated with fertility and abundance. That is why rice is thrown at the bride and groom at weddings.

In the natural macrobiotic family, love and harmony are the goal of family life. This goal is symbolized in the Japanese concept of *Wa*, which can be translated as "peace" or "harmony." The character for *Wa* is made up of symbols that represent cereal grains and the mouth. The ancient people who formulated this character were leaving behind an important message for our time: A diet based on whole cereal grains and other plant foods promotes social harmony and peace.

As families adopt a grain-based diet, their members will come to live in harmony with each other and with our natural environment. As the number of strong and healthy families increases, we envision a time when families and children throughout the world share a sound and healthy quality of blood, a dream of health and peace, and a sense of connectedness to the planetary family of humanity.

Edward and Wendy Esko
Becket, Massachusetts

Growing Up With Macrobiotics

Growing up with a macrobiotic diet has been an experience shared by few. While attending public schools in New York City, the Greater Boston area, and Los Angeles, I was always acutely aware of the differences between the food my family prepared at home and the lunches served in the school cafeterias or brought to school by my classmates. These differences were further highlighted when I visited my friends' homes. While my family might snack on brown rice or noodles with vegetables, theirs would have baloney sandwiches on white bread, or store-bought cookies and crackers.

It does not take much imagination to envision the difficulties these dietary differences could have on young children who strive for acceptance among their peers. We often hear of the social pressure involved when adolescents experiment with their first cigarette, or beer. Important as these experiences are for socialization, they generally represent a minor part of daily life. Food and food choices, on the other hand, are an integral part of human existence, and the obvious differences in this area between my family and others were a continued source of anxiety.

Early in my elementary school days, my parents would prepare rice balls—called omusubi—for my siblings and me to take to school for lunch. I remember how they were made—of brown rice, flavored with a touch of umeboshi and covered with nori sea vegetable. They were then wrapped in aluminum foil and placed in the paper bags we carried to school. Had we lived in Japan, such lunches would have been common; one can purchase similar lunches, though made with white rice and umeboshi with food coloring, on the "bullet" trains that run from Tokyo to Osaka, and elsewhere throughout Japan. Even in Gay Head on Martha's Vineyard, where we attended school for a few months, these lunches were accepted, with some curiosity, by our classmates. On one occasion, my mother prepared such rice balls for all fifteen of the pupils who attended our one-room schoolhouse. They were a great hit.

Outside of such rare experiences, however, the usual reaction to these rice balls was negative and critical. "What's that?" my classmates would ask. In response to my explanations, they would contort their faces and exclaim, "Yecch, seaweed! How can you eat that stuff?" They would then watch with horrified fascination as I would self-consciously try to eat my lunch. It was not much help that the teachers would have similar reactions to my eating habits, though without the caustic remarks. But it was also not difficult to detect their concern and fascination with the food I was eating. Thinking back on those experiences, I wonder if they knew that every bite of commercial ice cream they ate contained some of that infamous "seaweed."

My eventual response to such experiences was to stop bringing lunch to school. I developed the habit of sitting and socializing with my friends–but not eating– during lunch periods. After school, I would return home for a mid-afternoon meal. Initially, this did little to allay my teachers concerns, since all they could see was that one of their pupils was not eating lunch. Nevertheless, in due time they came to accept my not eating school lunch as part of my lifestyle. This was not without incident, however. The first day that I attended elementary school in Brookline, Massachusetts, I did not have a lunch, having already developed the habit of not eating at school. Nor did I wish to purchase the school lunch–they were serving hot dogs. My teacher was concerned, not having encountered such a situation before, and failing to understand my reluctance to buy lunch in the cafeteria. In final frustration, the school's principal was summoned to deal with this unique situation. She marched down from her office and forced me to stand in line for lunch at her side. I cried, hoping for sympathy, but eventually acquiesced to her demands by somehow managing to be served peanut butter in a hot dog roll–minus the hot dog, of course.

Nonacceptance of macrobiotics also led to my experimenting with the food that makes up the mainstream American diet. Clandestine favorites included Snickers and peanut M&M's candy. I luxuriated in the cool, smooth taste of vanilla ice cream with jimmies. I tried bananas for the first time at a high school graduation potluck party, and sampled pineapples when I was off on my own in college. I discovered the therapeutic value of late night discussions– and parties–fueled in part by mushroom pizzas. The foods that had not been available to me at home were the illicit drugs of my youth. I did draw the line, however, at red meat, which I have knowingly tasted three times in my life–twice by accident; poultry, which I have yet to consume knowingly; and artificial sweeteners such as cyclamates or saccharin, which I may have unknowingly eaten.

The first realization I had that macrobiotics reached beyond my family's immediate experience came early in the ninth grade, when someone in my history class, whom I did not know, mentioned macrobiotics. This was the first time I met someone who knew of macrobiotics in a context outside my family's network of friends and acquaintances–truly a historic moment. Soon after- ward, I discovered that my English teacher frequented the Seventh Inn restaurant, which my parents had just recently opened, and my history teacher shopped regularly at Erewhon, a natural foods store owned by my parents.

Eventually, these discoveries became so commonplace that, in college, I was sometimes sought out because of my experience with macrobiotics. The growing acceptance of alternative eating patterns was evident in the vegetarian dining option at the college I attended. Out of a population of about 1,400 students, 150 to 200 would choose the vegetarian meal during any given evening. While many of these students ate "vegetarian" simply because the usual fare was less appetizing, a substantial proportion was dedicated to this lifestyle. Although other students at the college deserve the credit for organizing and overseeing the vegetarian dining hall, I did play a small role in influencing the food choices that were available. Partly through my suggestion, the college decided to order some food items from Erewhon, and the head chef at the Seventh Inn restaurant volunteered his time so he could demonstrate preparation methods for brown rice, miso soup, and simple steamed or sautéed vegetables to the kitchen staff at the college.

You, the reader, are probably a parent or parent-to-be. As you adopt a macrobiotic lifestyle, your concerns may include the consequences of such a change for your children—for their health, their socialization, their overall well-being. Although each family and child is unique, some words of encouragement and advice apply to most anyone. This book can be a source of such advice, as well as of common-sense suggestions for dealing with specific situations.

Elements of my youth and adolescence probably strike chords of familiarity with your experiences and those of your children. At a recent macrobiotic summer camp, one teenager remarked that, with his macrobiotic practice, he had felt like a real outcast among his friends, and had not until then understood the significance of macrobiotics for him. In a society in which the vast majority of people have little dietary consciousness, such feelings can be common for children who are raised in the minority of families who do care about the quality of their food.

Solutions to this type of problem are as varied as the families that wrestle with it. Some have attempted to create communities in which all families share the same philosophy of life, so that the social circles the children grow and play in do not have the conflict of experience familiar to me and my siblings. Others have attempted to accomplish the same goals by simply refusing to send their children to public—or private—schools, even if this deprived their children of playmates within their age group. Another approach is exemplified by the mother who has made a point of taking her children to McDonald's and other bastions of the American diet, so they would experience those foods and not feel any guilt about eating them. The former approach might be characterized as a "search for utopia," while the latter might be thought of as a "promotion of the inevitable."

In the United States of the 1990s, promoting macrobiotic dietary habits in the face of social pressures is much easier than it was twenty-five or thirty years ago. Many of the foods that are an integral part of macrobiotic practice have only recently become widely available. Basic items such as organically grown whole grains, beans, and seeds could not be had when I attended elementary school. The only whole grains one could readily purchase in food stores were oatmeal, Wheatena, hot cereal, and shredded wheat cereal. Brown rice was sold as a gourmet item at some stores, but the price was a few dollars a pound. My family sometimes shopped for sesame and sunflower seeds at pet stores, where they were sold as feed for parakeets and canaries.

The availability of many of the food items that many of us now take for granted can be directly traced to people such as Paul Hawken, one of the first presidents of Erewhon, who took it upon himself to search out farmers who would be willing to grow organic rice. He and my parents committed themselves to developing such sources of good-quality food by guaranteeing purchase of these crops. This commitment was instrumental in creating our current food supply. Dotted throughout the countryside are organic farms and small tofu and tempeh producers; sometimes there are also bakers of sourdough bread. Almost all major cities in this country, and most of western Europe, have outlets that sell good-quality whole grains and fresh vegetables. In some of these cities, such as Boston, Los Angeles, and Minneapolis, many of these food items are sold in the supermarkets. Some of these cities also have restaurants that cater primarily to people interested in macrobiotics, serving little, if any, red meat, poultry, or dairy food, and including such menu items as bean or sea vegetable of the day. We can be grateful for all of the heralded and unheralded people responsible for these and other related accomplishments.

All these recent developments can only serve to appease the acceptability of your child's macrobiotic eating habits to his peers. My nephew was recently attending the same elementary school where I ate my first—and only—peanut butter "hot dog." At least two of the teachers there have been interested in macrobiotics, and several of the other children who attend the school are from macrobiotic families. With these small but significant changes in society, concerns about protecting children from dietary extremes, or about how to deal with awkward social situations, start to diminish. Rather than searching for utopia or promoting the inevitable, you can find a middle ground.

As I reflect on what my parents must have gone through with five children, I sometimes wonder what their thoughts might have been about our food encounters. I doubt that any of my siblings or I could have secretly savored ice cream or cookies without our parents' knowing about it, yet I do not remember them ever punishing me or becoming hysterical for my having eaten foods not on the macrobiotic diet. Perhaps my older siblings bore the brunt of punishment for trying these foods, and my parents simply tired of dealing with it when it was my turn to experiment with other foods; however, I suspect their responses had more to do with their philosophy of life. Obviously, my parents did not attempt to create a utopia where we would be shielded from the temptations of society. Neither did they push us to experience as many delights as we could. What they did do was create a home environment that was as comfortable and as "macrobiotic" as possible. Many of the food items that are occasionally found in some macrobiotic households–like dairy foods or tropical fruits–would seldom, if ever, be seen at our house. My parents never prevented us from trying other foods, though they would be quick to point out the relationship between our physical health and the food we had recently eaten. Fevers, stomachaches, swollen lips, or runny noses could all be traced to recent patterns of eating or specific food items.

Many people who come to macrobiotics also seem to be concerned about implications for their children's health. High among these concerns is the possibility of various nutrient deficiencies. Does a macrobiotic diet provide enough protein, calcium, and vitamin B$_{12}$? These questions are especially acute for those with infants and children, as it is the practical responsibility of parents to ensure the health of their young children. During his lectures, my father sometimes proudly proclaims that while they were growing up, none of his children were hospitalized, except at birth, or had ever taken any medications for ailments. By and large, this apparently miraculous feat in this age of pill-popping is true. I was admitted overnight to a hospital once, for observation after I suffered a concussion and was somewhat amnesiac. I also did take aspirin once, and penicillin once, when I developed some sort of gastrointestinal upset when I was in South Asia. Otherwise, his tale is true for me, and probably similarly so for my siblings.

Such experience notwithstanding, it is important to realize that following a standard macrobiotic diet does require a bit more knowledge about nutrition than simply following the four food groups. I am aware of infants who have been hospitalized for vitamin B$_{12}$ deficiency whose parents have been faithful, perhaps too much so–such that their diets were too narrow or rigid–in their *practice of macrobiotics. I am also aware of other macrobiotic infants with cases of calorie malnutrition and vitamin D deficiency (rickets) that may have resulted from similar practices. Although these cases have been few, their occurrence is reason enough for increased levels of awareness about diet and nutrition. These cases also serve as evidence that such increased awareness can be beneficial.*

There is sometimes a tendency for people in macrobiotics to ignore such warnings, believing that following macrobiotics in a dogmatic way will ensure freedom from illness. In its extreme, this tendency can lead to individuals closing their minds to such seemingly negative experiences, dismissing them as cases in which the people involved "obviously didn't know how to practice macrobiotics." A case in point is the experience of some students at the Kushi Institute that was recounted to me recently. One of the instructors spent part of his class discussing the possibility of vitamin deficiencies. The students then proceeded directly to another class, in which the instructor told them, "One of the other teachers here is spreading rumors of nutrient deficiencies in the macrobiotic community. Don't you believe a word of it!" Although one might argue from a practical and public relations standpoint of the advisability of discussing nutrient deficiencies with students learning macrobiotics, it is clearly simplistic to dismiss the possibility altogether. Indeed such dismissal is contrary to the curiosity and search for understanding that is the macrobiotic spirit.

Generally, the way to raise healthy children, as is mentioned throughout this book, is to follow your intuition and use common sense. The best barometer of your infant's or child's well-being is your observation of his growth, physically, mentally, and spiritually. Does he react quickly to different stimuli? Does it seem that he is growing and developing with a natural inquisitiveness and an explorer's heart? Watch for infants who are overly quiet (oh, how well-behaved he is!) or extremely aggressive. And, of course, do not be afraid to seek out opinions about the health of your children from others, within and without the macrobiotic community. In your search for information, it can be useful to follow the advice of many health care practitioners: Take charge, be on top of things, be voracious in your appetite for knowledge, and do not ever give away your freedom to choose. In short, take responsibility for your children's lives until they are able to take responsibility themselves.

It is important to keep these health and illness concerns in perspective, recognizing that occurrences of nutrient deficiencies are few. Advice about some of these concerns is contained within these pages. Otherwise, it bears mentioning that it is best to eat a variety of foods, as much of a cliché as that may be, and use some common sense instead of following recommendations blindly. Although soy milk may look like breast milk, and have similar organoleptic properties, the two are not nutritionally equivalent. Kokoh is also not similar to breast milk, and neither kokoh nor soy milk should be used as a sole source of infant nutrition. While trying not to foster a "food as nutrients" perception, it can be helpful to incorporate into your diet beans, bean products, and sea vegetables on a daily or every-other-day basis. Eat fish if you desire, and do not feel guilt over an occasional dietary transgression. Much more importantly, use macrobiotics as a basis for enjoying life, of discovering the infinite variety of experience that unfolds daily around us and within us.

More representative of the norm for macrobiotic children are the comments often heard at macrobiotic summer camps. At these gatherings, hardly a day or hour goes by that someone does not remark how beautiful and bright the children are, and how healthy and inquisitive they appear. As a father of one and an uncle of ten, I can readily appreciate these comments, and be grateful that I know of macrobiotics, for myself and for the children in my life. I am certain that my brothers and sister would echo these sentiments. Although we all drifted away from macrobiotic "practice" at some point and to some extent in our lives, we have all returned to the spirit of macrobiotics–in our diet, our way of life, and our commitment to a better world. Indeed, we never left that spirit, being nourished by our parents' quiet example and spiritual guidance. I am truly grateful to them for the experiences that being their son has brought.

The adventure that is macrobiotics can be infinitely rewarding, providing life with great insights and insolvable enigmas. Those of us with children have the additional benefit of a shared adventure. Children can help us reflect on our lifestyles, appreciate our ancestors, and experience further dimensions of the human condition. While periods of anxiety and worry occur as part of the rhythm of life, these can also be turned around to become opportunities for self-reflection and growth. This book can assist you as a guidepost to help you understand and pass through some of these periods that are a part of family life. Please enjoy these pages, and accept, adapt, or reject the thoughts and practices they bring to you. Most of all, pursue your dreams so that your development and that of your children can reach its fullest potential.

In Peace,

Lawrence Haruo Kushi, Sc.D.

Introduction

The family is humanity's oldest and most natural institution. It is a miniature version of the order of life itself. The family is the place where human life comes into physical being, where it is loved and nourished, and where it receives the orientation for sound physical, mental, and spiritual growth. Long before the ancient civilizations of Sumer, Egypt, and China flourished, the family provided the thread from which the fabric of human culture was woven.

The family has survived repeated natural catastrophes and the rise and fall of countless civilizations. Of all our social structures, it has proven to be the most durable and flexible. It is an often overlooked fact that strong and healthy families are the cornerstone of a healthy and prosperous society. When the family is strong, so is society and the individuals that comprise it. When the family becomes weak, society as a whole begins to suffer.

There is no reason why the family cannot continue indefinitely, as long as the earth is capable of sustaining human life. However, of all the challenges—both natural and manmade—that the family has met and adjusted to during its long history, perhaps none are as great as those which confront it at this point in history. The very continuation of the family as we know it is now being challenged on many fronts, and as a consequence, civilization itself is in danger of degenerating.

THE INDUSTRIAL REVOLUTION AND THE FAMILY STRUCTURE

The decline of the family in the twentieth century is often attributed to economic and social changes that occurred as a result of the industrial revolution. During the later part of the nineteenth century, for example, millions of people left their ancestral homelands and migrated to the rapidly industrializing cities. Until about 1920, the majority of Americans lived in rural areas. Just sixty years later, however, in 1980, more than 80 percent of the population was living in cities.

The Extended Family Versus the Nuclear Family

This mass migration is associated with the decline of the extended family—in which three or four generations plus assorted relatives live together in the same house, farm, or village—and the rise of the nuclear family—in which a husband, wife, and children form the central unit. In the nuclear family, grandparents or other relatives usually do not live in the same house or meet daily with their children, grandchildren, or kin. Contact with relatives outside the nuclear family is often very limited.

One of the few groups today who have kept the extended family alive is the Amish of Pennsylvania. The Amish believe that relatives "should live close enough to see the smoke from each other's chimneys." The extended family is also strong among people in Asia, Africa, Latin America, and other less industrialized parts of the world. Even with industrialization, the extended family is still strong in Japan, although recently it has begun to weaken there also.

In modern America, however, even immediate family members are often separated by thousands of miles. In such cases, phone calls, letters, and occasional visits cannot substitute for the benefits of daily interaction. Aged parents are frequently sent to retirement communities or nursing homes rather than being invited to live with their grown children. This practice is recent and contrasts markedly with traditional expressions of respect and gratitude toward parents and elders, including the desire to care for them under any circumstances.

The extended and nuclear families represent opposite poles of family life. While the extended family emphasizes the place of the individual within the larger unit and cooperation for the common good, the nuclear family is identified more with the pursuit of individuality, often without consideration for, or in some cases, at the expense of, the larger family unit. With a rural agricultural base, the extended family tended more toward production and self-sufficiency. Children were viewed as contributing to the overall productivity and prosperity of the family as a whole. A large family was considered a sign of wealth.

The nuclear family, on the other hand, is oriented more toward consumption and dependence on others. From a consumerist point of view, children are often seen as liabilities. Couples often feel the need to limit the number of children or hesitate to have any at all because of economic considerations. This way of thinking has led to a trend toward zero growth and low fertility rates among married couples. Some of the tendencies of the traditional extended family and the modern nuclear family are summarized in Table 1.

These tendencies are of course relative and interchangeable. Some extended families embody characteristics of nuclear families and vice versa, while people within each type of family frequently have different tendencies.

Changes in Dietary Patterns

The development of industrial technology, the migration to the cities, and the rise of the nuclear family occurred together with another profound change in the nature of family life. While these changes were occurring on the surface, more fundamental biological changes were taking place at a deeper level. As people moved to the cities, they abandoned not only their rural lifestyle, but their more traditional, natural diet as well. In East and West, North and South, since the beginning of civilization, families nourished themselves with whole cereal grains, beans, fresh local vegetables, and other products of their regional agriculture. From the pioneer families who crossed the Great Plains to the Imperial Household of Japan (the family of the Japanese emperor), whole cereal grains and other complex carbohydrate foods were revered as staples of the diet. Countless families throughout history sat down to eat with the prayer, ". . . give us this day our daily bread."

However, from 1910 to 1976, during which time the divorce rate increased nearly 700 percent, the per capita consumption of wheat fell 48 percent; corn, 85 percent; barley, 66 percent; buckwheat, 98 percent; rye, 78 percent; beans and legumes, 46 percent; fresh vegetables, 23 percent; and fresh fruit, 33 percent, according to calculations based on United States Department of Agriculture surveys. During the same period, in which the average number of children per family dropped by half, beef intake rose 72 percent; poultry, 194 percent; cheese, 322 percent; canned vegetables, 320 percent; frozen vegetables, 1,650 percent; processed fruit, 556 percent; ice cream, 852 percent; yogurt, 300 percent; corn syrup, 761 percent; and soft drinks, 2,638 percent. The

Table 1 The Extended and Nuclear Family: General Tendencies

Characteristic	Extended Family	Nuclear Family
Period	Preindustrial	Industrial
Environment	Rural	Urban
Lifestyle	Agricultural	Industrial
Orientation	Time	Space
	Tradition	Fashion
	Unity	Fragmentation
	Solidarity	Individuality
Reproductive Ability	Toward increased fertility	Toward diminished fertility
Tendency	Toward stability, integration, and growth	Toward instability, dissolution, and decay
Economic Function	Production	Consumption
	Self-sufficiency	Dependency
Outlook	Cooperative	Competitive
	Spiritual	Materialistic
	Intuitive	Analytical

consumption of chemical additives and preservatives is also relatively recent: the amount of artificial food colorings added to the diet increased 995 percent since 1940, the first year that records were kept.

During the twentieth century, the emphasis shifted from a diet based more on the complex carbohydrates found in whole grains, beans, and vegetables, to a diet centered around animal protein, fat, and refined carbohydrates. At the same time, naturally fertile plant and animal species were replaced by infertile, artificially fertilized, or, more recently, genetically manipulated species. The vast majority of eggs now consumed in the United States, for instance, are unfertilized, while 95 percent of the beef cattle are now produced through artificial insemination. Many species of plants—including cereal grains—have been genetically manipulated to conform to modern agriculture and marketing practices.

Not only are the types of foods on the family table different, but so is the place where they are eaten. Until the middle of the twentieth century, people usually ate at home, together with their families. In the early part of the century, restaurants were found mostly in the larger cities and tended to cater to a small urban clientele. According to John C. Maxwell, Jr., however, this practice had changed by 1965. In *Advertising Age*, Maxwell wrote that the average American ate about one meal in four outside the home. By 1973, one in three meals were eaten in restaurants or cafeterias. Fewer families today eat together as their parents, grandparents, and ancestors once did. The trend toward eating out parallels the decline of the extended family and the decomposition of the family in general. (Table 2 summarizes the differences in dietary patterns between the extended and nuclear family.)

The Growth of Single-Parent and Single-Person Households

The twentieth century model of the nuclear family, in which a working husband supports a wife and two or more children reached its zenith in the middle of this century. However, it too is now in the process of disappearing, and currently makes up a minority of the households in the United States. In addition, a growing percentage of families are headed by a single parent, most often a woman. There are now about 9 million single parent households in the United States. About a third of all American children will be brought up in single parent families during the 1990s.

The number of people living alone is also increasing rapidly. Single person households totaled fewer than 10 percent of all families in the 1950s. By 1984, nearly a quarter of all households were made up of people living alone. Like single parent families, the number of single person households is expected to increase in the years to come.

If current fertility trends are not reversed, the twenty-first century could witness the dawn of the "artificial family," in which children are produced through artificial insemination, in-vitro fertilization, or other artificial techniques due to the decline of reproductive ability. The genetic engineering of the human species could also become widespread. If this *Brave New World* scenario comes to pass, it could mean the end of the family as we think of it, with the extinction of the natural human species.

EATING TRENDS AND TOGETHERNESS

In the past, family life centered around the hearth or kitchen where food was prepared and served. Traditionally a woman would put her time, energy, and love into making delicious and nourishing meals for her family. Mealtime was the time when the family would meet and discuss the day's events, resolve problems, make plans for the future, and share love, warmth, and good spirit. Mealtimes also offered a woman the opportunity to observe the members of her family. Based on her observations, she could adjust her cooking and selection of foods on the following day to meet their changing conditions.

Table 2 The Extended and Nuclear Family: Differences in Dietary Patterns

Extended Family	Nuclear Family
Centered around complex carbohydrates (whole grains, beans, vegetables, etc.)	Centered around protein, fat, and refined carbohydrates
Whole	Processed
Natural	Artificial
Organic	Chemical
Unrefined	Refined
Locally grown	Transcontinental
Seasonal	Nonseasonal
Prepared and eaten at home	Prepared and eaten outside the home
Influenced by tradition	Influenced by advertising
Naturally fertile plant and animal species	Infertile, artificially conceived, or genetically manipulated species

A woman who cooks for herself and her family not only brings family members together for meals but also determines the state of their health. When a man eats food prepared by his wife, his daily physical and mental condition are created by her. Both his sperm quality and the quality of her reproductive cells are determined by the food they share. Then, when the couple has intercourse, the woman receives sperm, the quality of which she helped to create. If she becomes pregnant, she then nourishes not only herself and her husband, but her baby as well. Her emotions, thoughts, and dreams affect the baby both directly and through the influence they have on her cooking. After giving birth, she then nourishes her baby with her milk, the quality of which is also directly influenced by her cooking and emotions. After weaning her baby, she prepares baby food and then meals for her children until they leave home many years later. Children who are raised in this manner naturally experience a strong physical, emotional, and spiritual bond with their mothers, fathers, and other members of their families.

Today, however, this natural pattern is frequently disrupted. Consider the case of John and Mary, a fictional couple who exemplify the lifestyle and dietary patterns of many couples today. Mary has an active career outside the home and is too busy to cook. Because she frequently works late, she usually stops for dinner at a restaurant near the office. The dinner chef is overweight and suffers from diabetes and high blood pressure. He works at the restaurant not so much because he enjoys cooking or out of love for his customers, but simply because he needs to earn a living.

The chef's physical and emotional condition directly affects the quality of the food he prepares. He frequently becomes upset and tends to handle the food in a rough, sloppy manner. As she eats there so often, Mary has surrendered her biological quality to an unknown chef. Because his food influences the condition of her blood, and through it her entire body, this chef is actually the hidden director of her life.

John has also gotten into the habit of stopping off at a diner on his way home from work. A female cook usually works in the kitchen during the dinner shift. Like the chef, she is overweight and suffers from a variety of physical and emotional problems. She is not particularly fond of cooking. Since her shift begins early in the morning, she is usually exhausted by the time John comes in for dinner. Because John eats there so often, his physical and emotional conditions are greatly influenced by her temperament and state of health.

The quality of this couple's reproductive cells—John's sperm and Mary's egg—is influenced not by Mary, but by these restaurant cooks. When their reproductive cells combine and a baby begins to develop, the male chef continues to have a decisive influence on the unborn child, since Mary keeps working and eating at a restaurant until just before delivery.

When John Jr. is born, rather than nursing the baby herself, Mary chooses an infant formula. As soon as he is old enough, she begins feeding him processed baby foods. The restaurant chefs—and the cows who provide milk for John Jr.'s formula—are the baby's source of nourishment, and, as such, have a primary influence on who he is and on his condition.

As soon as John Jr. is old enough, he is dropped off at a day-care center and introduced to the world of institutional and fast foods. It is rare for the family to eat at home with everyone present. Since John, Mary, and John Jr. eat separately more often than together, they do not get the opportunity to show their love, warmth, and support for one another. Because they so seldom see each other, communication becomes difficult and John and Mary's relationship becomes strained. The couple often quarrels, and, like many who have become estranged, eventually separate. As John Jr. grows older, he begins to feel closer to his friends who join him at the fast food restaurant or in the school cafeteria than he does to his parents. He spends more time in front of the television than he does with either parent. As he grows older, communication and understanding become increasingly difficult. Like many other children, John Jr. begins to feel isolated from his parents.

When children brought up this way begin their own families, they often do so independently of their parents. They may move to another city and visit their parents only on holidays or special occasions. When their parents retire, they may send them to an old age home, retirement community, or some institution rather than care for them in their own homes. As we can see, the patterns of isolation begun in childhood often last throughout life, so that sadly, many people today finish their lives alone, abandoned by their families and loved ones.

Although imaginary, the story of John, Mary, and John Jr. resembles the lifestyle of many modern families, and indicates the path down which numerous other families are headed. Although simplified, it underlines the direct and decisive influence that daily food has on physical health and emotional and mental orientation. Clearly, the well-being of individual family members determines the quality of a family's life together.

The factors that produce a healthy, well-balanced life will be our next topic of discussion.

RESTORING FAMILY HEALTH

What distinguishes a family from society as a whole? Once it was understood that the members of a family had a similar quality of blood, hence expressions such as "bloodline" and "blood relatives" came into being. These expressions symbolize the fact that the members of a family share a quality that is unique and distinct from that of other families and individuals in society.

Where do blood and biological quality come from? Daily food and drink are the primary factors in the creation of blood, body fluids, and cell quality. Families are united because their members share the same or a similar quality of food. When the members of a family eat differently, they lose their underlying unity. Because the foods they eat affect both their state of health and emotions, family members eating different meals may not be in synch with one another. One member's diet may cause him to experience headaches, and he may become moody. Another member may experience low energy levels.

The first step in restoring harmony to the family is to begin eating together; however, simply eating together is not enough. If people eat poor-quality foods, or if their diets are excessive or inadequate, they risk the eventual decomposition of their family due to cancer, heart disease, or some other degenerative illness.

Family disharmony frequently begins with discord between a husband and wife. Sexual disharmony, frustration, and unhappiness are the frequent cause of conflict among couples and thus are at the root of many family problems. Love and sex are the natural means to create offspring. Love and sexual attraction result from the complementary natures of men and women. The male reproductive organs, for example, are complementary to those of the female. The ovaries, Fallopian tubes, and uterus are held deep within the body in an upward position. The testes, scrotum, and penis have a more downward position outside the body.

YIN AND YANG ENERGIES

These differences are reflections of the two complementary energies that produce and animate all things on earth—yin and yang. Although the bodies of both males and females are charged by these two energies, they are present in different degrees. In the male body, descending, centripetal forces that come from the cosmos predominate. These are the yang energies, and include stellar, solar, and galactic radiation; cosmic particles; solar and galactic winds; and a variety of high-frequency waves. In the female body, rising, centrifugal forces generated by the earth's rotation are stronger. These are the yin tendencies. Hence, the classical association of paternal or masculine energy with heaven and maternal or feminine power with the earth.

The forces of heaven and earth continuously supply the body with life energy and animate all of its functions. The rhythms of the body—sleeping and waking, appetite and fullness, sexual desire and satisfaction, movement and rest, and the expansion and contraction of the heart, lungs, stomach, and digestive organs—reflect the alternating pulse of these primary energies. (Because these energies are found in different degrees in plants, foods, and individuals, they will be discussed more thoroughly in the chapters of this book.)

A man and a woman exchange these energies during intercourse. Orgasm can be likened to the spark of lightning that passes between the atmosphere and the ground during a thunderstorm. The buildup of excessive energy is neutralized in a flash of lightning. Similarly, a man's excessive charge of heaven's energy and a woman's excessive charge of earth's energy are momentarily neutralized when they unite during intercourse.

If the exchange of energy is smooth, both partners enjoy a healthy sex life and a mutually satisfying relationship. Naturally, they then relate to each other and to their children in a more loving and flexible manner. In order for a relationship to work smoothly, however, the couple's physical quality needs to be compatible. If they dine separately, and if their eating habits are chaotic, their physical and mental qualities become dissimilar. This may put a strain on their relationship. The couple's energy and biological qualities no longer match.

EFFECTS OF DIETARY IMBALANCES ON THE BODY

Diet also affects a couple's sexuality in another important way. When your partner eats excessive amounts of cheese, milk, butter, eggs, meat, poultry, and other foods containing heavy, saturated fats, his or her body begins to lose its natural conductivity to environmental energies. Deposits of hard fat begin to form in the arteries, blood vessels, and in and around the organs. The tissues themselves become more rigid and inflexible, and the skin becomes hard, tough, and insensitive. Nine out of ten adults have this condition to one degree or another. To find out if you have it, simply lie on your back with your knees raised and feet flat on the floor. Slowly breathe out and push your lower abdomen deeply but gently with the extended fingers of both hands. If you feel hardness or tightness here, or if you feel pain, the tissues in this region have already become tight and hard. Hardness or rigidity in the abdominal region is practically universal among adults. This condition interferes with the normal flow of environmental energies throughout the body, particularly in the region of the sexual organs.

Tightness or stiffness in the muscles and joints and hardening of the blood vessels accompany abdominal hardening. They are the result of a diet rich in cholesterol and hard, saturated fats, together with the consumption of foods such as refined sugar, tropical fruits, and oily or greasy dishes. Love and sexuality depend on our sensitivity to environmental energies, including the energy of our partner. If our body becomes hard and inflexible, our sensitivity, and therefore our sexuality and capacity to love, diminishes.

Effects on the Reproductive Organs

Dietary imbalances can directly hamper the normal functioning of the reproductive organs. In men, for example, the excessive intake of fatty, oily, or greasy foods, together with the overconsumption of protein, especially from animal sources, causes excess to build up in the prostate gland. The first signs of accumulation are often small microscopic nodules, known as prostatic concretions, that appear in the more alkaline fluid secreted by the gland. If plenty of hard fats are consumed—especially those contained in cheese, butter, ice cream, and other dairy products—and iced or chilled foods or drinks are taken frequently, the concretions may harden and calcify in a manner similar to the formation of kidney stones. Prostatic concretions may accumulate in the tissue of the gland in the form of cysts.

In many cases, the accumulation of fats and other types of excess causes the prostate to enlarge. Enlargement is further aggravated by the intake of sugar, alcohol, tropical fruits, honey, fruit juices, coffee, spices, and drugs and medications. Benign prostatic enlargement has become nearly universal among men: it is estimated that 10 percent have some form of enlargement by the age of forty, and practically 100 percent experience it by the age of sixty. Enlargement of the prostate produces a variety of symptoms, including difficulty in starting the flow of urine, dribbling of urine after urination, and increased frequency of urination, especially at night.

The prostate gland has a compact, tight structure and is located below the bladder. It surrounds the urethra, the tube that conveys sperm and urine to the outside via the penis. It also surrounds the ejaculatory ducts through which sperm travel en route to the urethra. During ejaculation, the prostate contracts and aids in the transport of seminal fluid. As we can see, the prostate is directly connected to male sexual functioning. If it becomes swollen, enlarged, or filled with calcified cysts, sexual ability and enjoyment decrease. Many cases of impotence, unsatisfactory sexual relations, or diminished vitality can be traced to problems in the prostate gland. (The relationship between diet and female reproductive disorders is discussed in detail in our other family health book, *Macrobiotic Pregnancy and Care of the Newborn.*)

Effects of Physical Health on Mental Condition

Physical hardness and rigidity lead to a variety of psychological problems, including feelings of separateness from one's environment and from friends and family. Children, and especially babies, do not usually experience these feelings. They normally sense that they are very much a part of what is going on around them. This is because their physical conditions are soft and flexible, thus allowing the unrestricted flow of energy through their bodies. This healthy conductivity to environmental forces creates the relatively high rate of physical and mental activity found in children. Flexibility in body and mind is associated with such positive attributes as imagination, creativity, playfulness, open-mindedness, curiosity, resiliency, optimism, and honesty.

Feelings of isolation from one's social and physical surroundings usually begin after childhood, as stagnation and hardness begin to appear in the body. As our physical condition becomes more rigid, our thinking and outlook come to reflect this change. Creativity and originality are replaced by imitation and lack of imagination. Instead of being open-minded and full of curiosity, our outlook becomes narrow and closed to new ideas, while optimism and honesty may be replaced by negativity and habitual repression of our thoughts and feelings. All to often, love and warmth are replaced by coldness and detachment as well.

Physical and mental inflexibility cause expression to become increasingly harsh and critical. A more peaceful, gentle, or subtle manner of expressing ourselves is difficult when our physical condition becomes hard and inflexible. In such cases, even when we wish to show love or affection, our expression often takes the form of criticism, scolding, or belittling others. Frustration builds as we lose the ability to freely express ourselves through words, actions, or creativity. Frustrations can be pent up for only so long before they erupt destructively, especially when they are fueled by an unbalanced diet.

Abusive behavior is occurring widely between husbands and wives, and parents and children. All too often, the dinner table, traditionally a place of togetherness and love, becomes a battleground, with loud and abusive behavior being served as the main course. The relationship between diet, physical condition, and abuse and neglect is summarized in Table 3.

The problems that confront the family today—from divorce and child abuse to infertility and juvenile delinquency—can be traced directly to individual imbalances in daily diet, mental attitude, and way of life. In the following chapter, we introduce a simple, common sense approach to health for the whole family through balanced diet, a natural daily life, and the recovery of love and understanding. By creating healthy and happy families, we are planting the seeds of peace and prosperity for generations to come.

FAMILY SPIRIT

The members of a family share a similar origin. Webster's Dictionary, for

Table 3   The Relationship Between Diet, Physical Health, and Abuse and Neglect

Type of Abuse or Neglect	Related Emotional Disturbance	Related Organ Dysfunction	Primary Influences (when consumed excessively)	Secondary Influences
Physical Abuse: A sudden outburst of anger in which a parent strikes or hits a child, sometimes producing injury.	Anger, short temper, impatience.	Liver and gallbladder.	Meat, poultry, eggs, red meat or blue-skinned fish, oil, fat.	Sugar, alcohol, drugs, medications, hard salty cheese, salt, chemical additives, pesticides, air pollution, overeating, lack of exercise, lack of outlet for creative expression.
Verbal Abuse: Shouting, screaming, or talking to children in an offensive or hysterical manner.	Excitability, excessive talking or laughing, shouting, feelings of "stress."	Heart and small intestine.	Saturated fats, dairy, sugar, spices, tropical fruits, alcohol, coffee, fruit juice.	Meat, eggs, poultry, insufficient activity, lack of discipline in daily life, chemicals, drugs.
Calculated Abuse or Neglect: Punishments such as locking a child in a dark room or tying a child to a bed; scolding or belittling a child; abandonment of children.	Irritability, suspicion, cynicism, lack of warmth or kindness.	Spleen, pancreas, and stomach.	Milk and other dairy, sugar, oil, fat, soft drinks, chemicals.	Animal food, poultry, eggs, spices, radiation, lack of contact with nature, tropical fruits and vegetables, stimulants, drugs, insufficient mental stimulation.
Passive Neglect: Failure to protect a child's physical welfare, for example by disregarding avoidable hazards in the home or leaving children under the care of an inexperienced person; failure to properly dress, clothe, or feed a child; lack of concern about children.	Depression, sadness, frustration, extreme self-centeredness, laziness.	Lungs and large intestine.	Dairy, oil, fat, sugar, white flour, animal food.	Flour products, fruit, spices, coffee, baked goods, alcohol, excessive fluid, soft drinks, air pollution, overeating, eating prior to sleeping, insufficient physical activity, isolation from society.
Sexual Abuse: Inappropriately touching a child's genital areas, or asking or forcing a child to touch the genitals of another person.	Fear, insecurity, depression.	Kidneys, bladder, and endocrine glands.	Fats, oil, meat, dairy, sugar, soft drinks, alcohol, coffee, excess fluid in general.	Salt, cold or iced foods or beverages, fruit, chemicals, drugs, insufficient activity, social or physical isolation.

Multiple Abuse or Neglect .... Any combination of the above ....

example, defines the family as "descendants of one common ancestor." Brothers and sisters share the same parents, and parents in turn have their respective parents and ancestors. Children are the most recent links in an ancestral chain that stretches back thousands of generations to the origins of humanity itself. We exist because of our ancestors. We cannot deny them nor can we separate ourselves from them.

In most traditional societies, people were deeply aware of their relationship to their ancestors. Love and respect for one's parents and ancestors was seen as being the same as love and respect for oneself. Love and respect for parents, elders, and ancestors was considered one of the most fundamental virtues.

America is young in comparison to the cultures of Europe and the Far East. When people immigrated here, they often lost contact with their families back home, and their awareness of their ancestors also diminished. Many people are not aware of their family histories for more than several generations, while people in other parts of the world frequently can trace their family histories back hundreds of years.

Our family has lived in a village in southern Japan for many centuries. There is a temple in the village that our ancestors have helped to maintain for nearly 1,200 years. Within the temple grounds is a cemetery where, for several hundred years, our ancestors have been buried. Whenever we visit this place, we feel deeply inspired. It evokes feelings of gratitude toward our ancestors and gives us a clearer sense of the continuity of existence.

Establishing Family Awareness

One way to affirm continuity with your ancestors is to visit their graves from time to time in order to extend your appreciation. Bring your children along so that they can also develop a sense of family history. If your family's ancestors are not buried in one place, think about establishing a central location in the future so that this tradition can continue among future descendants.

What are the most important things to give to future generations? Some might answer money, property, titles, stocks, or a bank account. Actually, material things are relatively insignificant when compared with intangibles such as a long, healthy life. One of the most valuable things to leave for future generations, aside from the knowledge of how to maintain their health, is the dream of establishing a healthy and peaceful world, together with love for all people. Money, titles, fame, and wealth come and go like tides in the ocean, but the dream of health and peace is imperishable.

A family record is also invaluable. It can include information such as your parents' names, where and when they were born, and what they did during their lives. Information about uncles, aunts, grandparents, and other relatives and ancestors can also be included, together with a history of your own life and activities.

Parents whose families do not yet have a family record may want to begin one. Make a set for each child. Ask them to add information about their lives when they get older, and to make copies to give to each of their children. Grandchildren can continue to add information and eventually pass copies on to the next generation. A family record will come to have great meaning for your descendants. It can serve as a source of continuity for centuries to come.

After experiencing many ups and downs and successes and failures in life, you can write down your conclusions, perhaps summarizing them in ten or twenty key points. Your philosophy of life can be given to your children along with your family record. Advice and wisdom about spiritual matters and about life in general is actually far more important than a will in which your estate is divided among relatives.

These records were known in the Orient as *Ka-kun*, or "family teachings." Many traditional families accumulated wisdom from generation to generation in this form. In some cases, the family teachings contain practical recommendations for daily living, such as "get up early in the morning" or "study for several hours every day," while others deal with broader ethical, social, or spiritual questions. When we compile our teachings, we should try to present a summary of our life experience so that our descendants may benefit from it.

As we have seen, educating ourselves and our children about food is very important. Respect and gratitude for ancestors complements a balanced, natural diet. If either of these aspects is missing, a family faces eventual collapse. Both are needed for the health and well-being of the family and society at large.

Today, people often marry without knowing much about their partner's family history or their own. Some marriages result from attraction based on superficial appearances. Most marriages are built on a shaky foundation. Small problems are often enough to destroy the marital relationship. The tendency today is for both partners to give up and say good-bye rather than try to solve their difficulties. If a couple is childless, the effects of divorce or separation are not as serious or long lasting. However, once a couple has children, the effects are much more serious. Although they may not be able to express it, the children of divorced parents frequently feel deeply disappointed and resentful. They sometimes become depressed and distrustful of other people. The breakup of a family is a very unhappy experience for a child.

Parents naturally place their children at the center of their universe. Their health and well-being come first. Proper nourishment of children—through diet and spiritual awareness—is the parents' primary concern. The well-being of their children comes before other considerations. Parents continually pour their love and energy into nourishing and guiding their children, even changing their job, place of living, lifestyle, or method of cooking for their benefit.

Love and care for children are the strongest human instincts, even stronger than the instinct of self-preservation. They develop quite naturally when the family achieves harmony and balance through a diet of grains and vegetables. In contrast the modern diet creates imbalances in the body that lead to illness and mood changes. The modern trend to eat meals separately also leads to feelings of isolation.

Separation is the hallmark of our modern age: separation between man and nature, husband and wife, parents and children, and body and mind, and between neighbors on the same street and neighbors in other parts of the globe. If we are to continue on this planet in an age of nuclear weapons, then separation, conflict, and isolation must be transformed into unity, harmony, and cooperation. Family health is the key to world peace.

Establishing a planetary commonwealth of humanity—a kind of global extended family—offers a clear alternative to present destructive trends. It will come about when the members of the human family begin to eat according to universal principles and establish a similar quality of blood and a common dream of health and peace. Chapter 1 will help you decide what foods to include in your family's diet and how to prepare nutritious, varied meals that your family will love.

CHAPTER 1
The Way to Better Health

While it is important for families to eat together, it is equally important that the meals they share consist of good-quality foods. If not, the family will eventually experience physical and mental disorders, and ultimate decomposition. To secure the long-term health and well-being of the entire family, we recommend basing the family's daily diet around such natural and traditional foods as whole cereal grains, fresh local vegetables, beans and bean products, and other complex carbohydrates. When animal foods are desired, white-meat fish and other low-fat seafoods may be eaten occasionally. Your foods *can* have a deliciously natural flavor without strong spices or artificial seasonings. Cereal grains, beans, and vegetables such as carrots, squash, daikon (long white radish), and cabbage are all naturally sweet and can be emphasized in cooking. Natural seasonings such as sea salt, tamari soy sauce (shoyu), miso (fermented soybean paste), umeboshi plum (salted pickled plum), and others can be used moderately to create genuinely flavorful dishes and to enhance the sweetness of your foods.

We recommend that all members of the family eat a macrobiotic diet. However, the general suggestions that follow are not meant to be used rigidly or interpreted dogmatically. Everyone has different needs based on factors such as age, sex, type of activity, physical constitution, present condition, and other characteristics. Your children's dietary needs are especially different from your own. For example, you need to pay careful attention to the amount of salt that your children use.

Adults can generally use a larger—but not excessive—volume, while it is better for babies and small children to avoid salt entirely, at least during the first year or so. The seasonings and condiments that are recommended for moderate daily use can be introduced gradually as children grow. Milder condiments can be prepared for children until they are grown.

Please always keep the uniqueness of each child in mind. As an aid in judging the particular needs of a child, mothers can reflect on their own dietary practices and experiences during each pregnancy. This will help when making adjustments for individual children. Since children's needs and desires differ from those of adults, the proportions outlined in the standard macrobiotic way of eating can be modified at each stage in the developmental process. General suggestions for adjusting the standard recommendations for children and older members of the family are discussed in Chapter 3. For additional suggestions and information, we recommend contacting a qualified macrobiotic instructor.

Our diets also need to be adjusted in response to the changing conditions in the environment, such as variations in season and climate. General recommendations for modifying the standard macrobiotic way of eating to suit particular environments are included in our other

---

On Children's Portions

The way in which you feed babies and small children is very important. Serve small portions instead of giving them too much food or too many dishes at once. When they have cleaned their plate and want more, then give them a small amount again. In this way, children do not waste food, the table is never messy, and they learn to always finish what is on their plate without parents' having to use discipline. Often mothers put too much food on children's plates. When children are eating, watch them and help or correct them if necessary. It is better not to habitually give between-meal snacks, if possible. When children are really hungry, serve them rice balls or other healthful snacks. Sometimes children crave fruit, and when this happens, try to keep their intake moderate. If we watch them carefully, we can really guide and manage our children's conditions.

—Aveline Kushi

Figure 1.1 The Standard Macrobiotic Diet

Whole Cereal
Grains 50–60%

Soups
5–10%

Vegetables
25–30%

Beans and
Sea Vegetables
5–10%

Plus Supplementary Foods

Fish and Seafood

Snacks

Seasonal Fruits

Condiments and
Seasonings

Beverages

books listed in the Recommended Reading List. These books are also recommended for further study.

In general, an optimally balanced diet consists of: 50–60 percent whole grains and whole grain products; 25–30 percent locally grown vegetables; 5–10 percent beans and sea vegetables; 5–10 percent soups; and 5 percent condiments and supplementary foods, including beverages, fish, and desserts. (See Figure 1.1 for proportions of foods in the macrobiotic diet.) The staples of the macrobiotic diet are discussed according to the volume of food consumed. In each of the food sections discussed in this chapter, the proportions of food given are for those living in a temperate, or four-season, climate.

WHOLE CEREAL GRAINS

We recommend that cooked whole grain cereals comprise at least half (50 percent) of every meal. Whole grains are grains that are eaten intact—that is, none of the edible portions of the grain (the bran, germ, and endosperm) have been removed. In terms of their nutritional value, whole grains are superior to cracked grain or flour products due to nutrient losses during the latter's processing, transportation, and storage. Cooked whole grains are also preferable to flour products because they are easier to digest.

Whole grains are composed of complex carbohydrates, proteins, vitamins, and minerals in proportions that ideally suit the needs of the human body. Grains in their whole form impart the most healthful, balanced, and peaceful energy. They are an excellent source of energy, providing about seven times more complex carbohydrates than protein. Whole grains are an excellent source of fiber, B complex vitamins, vitamin E, and phosphorus as well.

Whole grains for daily use include brown rice (short grain is preferable in temperate climates), millet, barley, corn, whole oats, wheat berries, and rye. Table 1.1 provides a more complete list of whole grains and grain products. In general, it is better to keep the intake of flour products, flaked cereals, and products such as couscous and grits below 20 percent of the daily proportion of whole grains.

Adjustments for Babies and Children

Whole grains are normally the first solid foods for babies. When making cereals for infants and small children, use more water than you normally do for adults.

Table 1.1   **Whole Grains and Grain Products**

For Regular Use	For Occasional Use	To Avoid
Whole barley	Buckwheat	Baked goods containing
Whole brown rice	Buckwheat noodles	dairy products
(short grain)	(soba)	Refined grain cereals
Whole brown rice	Corn grits or cornmeal	White flour products
(medium grain)	Couscous	Yeasted breads, crackers,
Whole corn	Cracked wheat (bulgur)	cakes, cookies, and
Whole millet	Pounded sweet brown	so on
Whole oats	rice (mochi)	
Whole rye	Rice cakes	
Whole wheat	Rye flakes	
Other whole cereal	Somen (sifted whole wheat	
grains	noodles)	
	Steel-cut or rolled oats	
	Sweet brown rice	
	Udon (whole wheat noodles)	
	Unleavened whole wheat or	
	rye bread	
	Unleavened bread made from	
	other whole grains	

If children are under the age of one, it is better to cook their grains with no salt; a one-inch piece of kombu (a sea vegetable) can be used instead. If they are under two, a very small amount of sea salt (several grains of salt for one or two cups of grain) can be added. Adults can use condiments to adjust the flavor of their grain dishes. Children may also enjoy using condiments. If so, condiments can be made from plain roasted seeds, such as sesame or sunflower, or a small amount of roasted sea vegetable combined with sesame seeds. Salt should be omitted when appropriate.

VEGETABLES

About one quarter (25–30 percent) of each meal may include vegetables prepared in a variety of ways, including steaming, boiling, and pressure cooking. Vegetables consumed as part of the macrobiotic diet should be organic, locally grown, and eaten in the season in which they were grown. Your meals can offer a variety of colors, tastes, and textures if you include many different kinds of vegetables. It is very important to consume vegetables to meet your body's requirements for the broad spectrum of vitamins and minerals we need for good health. Garden vegetables are typically classified into three groups: green leafy vegetables, root vegetables, and ground vegetables. Others have been classified according to their origin in the tropics. (See Table 1.2 for inclusion of various vegetables in the diet.)

In general, up to one third of your daily vegetable intake may be eaten in the form of macrobiotically prepared pickles or salads. We recommend avoiding commercial dressings and mayonnaise.

Green Leafy Vegetables

Green leafy vegetables like watercress and kale are an ideal source of nutrients, providing more vitamins, minerals, and proteins pound for pound than meat does. They are also considerably less costly. Raw vegetables are the most nutritious. If you are not accustomed to eating fresh greens, you may begin by adding them to soups or to sautéed vegetables. Eventually you may also enjoy them cooked separately, and served with other macrobiotic foods like beans.

Because of their high chlorophyll content, leafy greens are important for the health of red blood cells. They are also high in vitamin C and calcium. Greens contain alkaline minerals as well, which help to neutralize excess acidity in the blood.

Root Vegetables

Root vegetables such as carrots and radishes grow beneath the ground and generally supply greater energy than other types of vegetables. They are high in complex carbohydrates and a good supply of vitamins and minerals. They generally require greater effort to digest than the leafy greens, and consequently promote warmth as blood flows to the abdominal region to aid digestion. Because root vegetables can be kept for a long time without spoiling, they are a good choice for use during the cold winter months.

Ground Vegetables

Ground vegetables include round, stem, and climbing varieties that grow near or slightly above the surface of the ground. Nutritionally, they fall midway between the root and leafy green varieties. Like the roots, they are rich in vitamins and minerals and are an excellent source of complex carbohydrates. They do not need to cook as long as the root vegetables, and they can keep for a while but not indefinitely. See Table 1.2 for the recommended frequency of use for different vegetables.

Vegetables to Avoid

While tropical and semitropical vegetables may be enjoyed in their native setting, they are best avoided in temperate, four-season climates. They are generally too extreme in their energy and their effects on the mind and body for even occasional use. Vegetables in this category include asparagus, avocados, bamboo shoots, eggplant, green and red peppers, plantain, potatoes, spinach, sweet potatoes, tomatoes, and yams. Some vegetables like spinach are also high in oxalic acid, which interferes with calcium absorption.

It is best to avoid vegetables that have an acidifying effect on the blood when consumed on a regular basis. These include avocados, eggplant, potatoes, zucchini, and various edible weeds.

Adjustments for Babies and Children

When cooking vegetables for young children, remove their portion before adding sea salt or other salty adult seasoning. After removing your children's vegetables from the cooking pot, place them in another pot and, when necessary, let them cook a little longer, as children's vegetables need to be softer than those eaten by adults. Older children can eat adult-style vegetables. Boiled salads can be cooked a little longer for children. Vegetables can also be prepared using the nishime style of cooking, also known as "waterless cooking." With this method you can use kombu instead of salt for babies. Children over two can have very mild seasoning in their nishime dishes. Vegetables can be introduced with the eruption of baby teeth, usually after the baby has been eating grains for about a month.

SOUPS

One or two cups or small bowls of soup may be included daily. We recommend seasoning soups with a moderate amount of miso, tamari soy sauce, or sea salt, so that they taste neither too salty nor too bland. Soups may be prepared with a variety of ingredients including seasonal vegetables, sea vegetables—especially wakame and kombu—and grains and beans. Barley miso, also known as mugi miso, is generally better

Table 1.2   Vegetables in the Diet

	For Regular Use	For Occasional Use	To Avoid
Green and White Leafy Vegetables			
Bok choy	√		
Broccoli	√		
Brussels sprouts	√		
Carrot tops	√		
Celery		√	
Chinese cabbage	√		
Chives*	√		
Collard greens	√		
Daikon greens	√		
Dandelion greens	√		
Endive		√	
Escarole		√	
Green cabbage	√		
Iceberg lettuce	√		
Kale	√		
Leeks*	√		
Mustard greens*	√		
Parsley	√		
Romaine lettuce		√	
Scallions*	√		
Sprouts		√	
Turnip greens	√		
Watercress	√		
Ground Vegetables			
Acorn squash	√		
Buttercup squash	√		
Butternut squash	√		
Cauliflower	√		
Cucumbers		√	
Green peas		√	

	For Regular Use	For Occasional Use	To Avoid
Hokkaido pumpkin	√		
Hubbard squash	√		
Kohlrabi		√	
Mushrooms		√	
Pattypan squash		√	
Pumpkin	√		
Red cabbage		√	
Shiitake mushrooms		√	
Snap beans		√	
Snow peas		√	
String beans		√	
Summer squash		√	
Yellow wax beans		√	
Stem/Root Vegetables			
Burdock*	√		
Carrots	√		
Daikon	√		
Dandelion root*	√		
Jinenjo* (mountain potatoes)		√	
Lotus root*	√		
Onions	√		
Parsnips	√		
Radishes	√		
Rutabagas*	√		
Turnips	√		
Tropical/Semitropical Vegetables, etc.			
Asparagus			√
Avocados			√
Bamboo shoots			√
Eggplant			√
Fennel			√

	For Regular Use	For Occasional Use	To Avoid
Ferns			√
Green peppers			√
Okra			√
Plantain			√
Potatoes			√
Purslane			√
Red peppers			√
Shepherd's purse			√
Sorrel			√
Spinach			√
Sweet potatoes			√
Taro (albi)			√
Yams			√
Zucchini			√

*The starred vegetables are generally not recommended for babies. Their flavor is generally too strong for small children, and children often refuse to eat them.

for regular use, while soybean (hatcho) and rice (kome) miso may be used on occasion.

Adjustments for Babies and Children

Babies can have simple, unseasoned vegetable broth soups. Before seasoning the adult soup with sea salt, miso, or tamari, remove a small portion of the unseasoned broth and vegetables for babies. For older children, remove their broth and season it lightly. After removing the children's portion, season the remaining broth to taste for the adults in the family. Children usually do not like garnishes such as parsley or scallions in their soups. A piece of cooked green vegetable or a few strips of toasted nori, a sea vegetable, can be used instead. Soups may be introduced after about six to eight months of age.

BEANS, BEAN PRODUCTS, AND SEA VEGETABLES

About 5 to 10 percent of your daily diet may include cooked beans, bean products, and sea vegetables.

Beans and Bean Products

Beans have been cultivated around the world since ancient times. Along with vegetables, they are a traditional complement to whole cereal grains. Beans that are more northerly in origin, smaller in size, and contain less fat and oil than other varieties, such as azuki beans, lentils, and chick peas, are consumed most frequently. Medium-sized beans, like kidneys and pintos, can be used occasionally.

Although soybeans may be difficult to digest, they may be processed into tofu, tempeh, and natto. Tofu, which is processed from soybeans and then pressed into cakes, has been used since ancient times in China and then Japan before it came to the United States about a century ago. It has become increasingly popular over the last two decades. Although tofu does not have much taste by itself, it enhances the taste of foods that it is combined with, absorbing their flavors. This important food contains a higher proportion of usable protein than chicken.

Tempeh, an Indonesian fermented soybean product, is also high in protein. Its consumption may be favorable for those in the transition from animal foods because it tastes somewhat like pork and chicken, although it does have its own unique flavor. Natto is a fermented soybean product.

Soy foods are a good source of quality proteins and easy to digest. Bean products may be eaten on a regular basis, are easy to cook with, and provide a variety of different tastes. (See Table 1.3 for recommended consumption of beans and bean products.)

Adjustments for Babies and Children

Children do not need to eat beans until they are about two years old, although a small volume can be introduced earlier. It is difficult for babies to digest beans.

Children under two can have tofu, dried tofu, and tempeh. These can be introduced after ten months. Cook thoroughly, use little or no seasoning, and serve in small amounts. When beans are introduced, be sure to cook them until they are quite soft. The cooked beans can then be mashed and given in small amounts to your children. Tofu and tempeh can be introduced around the age of ten months.

Table 1.3   Beans and Bean Products

For Regular Use	For Occasional Use
Azuki beans	Black-eyed peas
Chick peas	Black soybeans
Dried tofu	Black turtle beans
Lentils	Great northern beans
Natto	Kidney beans
Tempeh	Lima beans
Tofu	Navy beans
	Pinto beans
	Split peas
	Whole dried peas

Sea Vegetables

There is a bounty of nutritious foods in the vast seas. For thousands of years, marine algae have been harvested for use as food by different cultures. There are four varieties of sea vegetables: green algae, brown algae, red algae, and blue and green algae. Extracts from sea vegetables are most frequently used as additives in food items such as ice cream, cheese, and salad dressing, just to name a few. The list of foods containing them is seemingly endless. In fact, any food product that uses thickeners or stabilizers most likely contains carrageenan, agar, or algin—all sea vegetable extracts.

Sea vegetables are an important part of the macrobiotic diet. They are among the most nutritious food groups on earth. For instance, they generally have a much higher mineral content than garden vegetables. We suggest that sea vegetables be eaten every day, so that they comprise about 5 percent of daily intake. Sea vegetables can be prepared in a variety of ways: in soups, with beans (kombu is especially recommended), or as side dishes with vegetables, such as carrots or onions, or with the soybean products already mentioned.

Sea vegetables that can be eaten regularly include kombu, wakame, nori, hijiki, arame, dulse, Irish moss, agar agar, and mekabu. Kombu, a brown algae, has many uses. It accentuates the flavor of the other ingredients it is used with. Kombu or wakame can be used for soup stocks, as a side dish, or in condiments. Wakame is particularly tasty in miso soup. You may wish to use nori as a garnish, as a condiment, or in rice balls. Hijiki, arame, and mekabu are good choices for side dishes. In addition, agar agar can be used for gelatin molds. (See Table 1.4 for a complete list of recommended sea vegetables.)

Table 1.4   Sea Vegetables for Regular Use

Agar agar	Kombu
Arame	Mekabu
Dulse	Nori
Hijiki	Wakame
Irish moss	

Adjustments for Babies, Children, and Seniors

Adults can enjoy more strongly seasoned sea vegetable dishes. Children may have very mildly seasoned or unseasoned sea vegetables. Their sea vegetables can be cooked until they are very soft. Babies under a year do not need any seasoning, so simply cook the sea vegetables until they become very soft. Sea vegetable side dishes, such as those with hijiki or arame, can be introduced after a baby is one-and-a-half to two years old, although wakame, kombu, nori, and other varieties can be used in the preparation of other dishes or for occasional consumption from the first introduction of solid foods.

SUPPLEMENTARY FOODS

Fish and Seafood

Depending upon your age, condition, and type of activity, a small amount of fresh white-meat fish or seafood may be eaten once or twice a week. Suitable varieties include carp, chirimen iriko (tiny dried fish), chuba (small dried fish), clams, flounder, haddock, halibut, oysters, scallops, shrimp, smelt, sole, and trout.

Fish is generally not necessary as a regular part of a baby's diet.

Snacks

A small volume of roasted seeds, lightly seasoned with sea salt or tamari, may be enjoyed as snacks by adults and older children. Suitable varieties include pumpkin, sesame, squash, and sunflower seeds.

It is better to minimize the use of nuts and nut butters, as they are high in fats and often difficult to digest. However, less oily nuts such as almonds, walnuts, and chestnuts—preferably roasted and lightly seasoned with tamari or sea salt—may be enjoyed on occasion by adults and older children.

Desserts may be enjoyed now and then, generally about two to three times per week. Unsweetened, cooked fruit desserts are preferable; however, small amounts of high-quality natural grain sweeteners, such as rice syrup, barley malt, or amazaké (slightly fermented sweet brown rice) may be added occasionally. Dried and fresh local fruits in season may also be enjoyed from time to time by those in good health. The regular consumption of fruit juice is not recommended, although it may be enjoyed periodically by those in good health, including children, especially during warm weather. Only locally grown fruits are advisable; therefore, it is better for persons living in temperate climates to avoid tropical and semi-tropical fruits and their products.

Fruit desserts are not necessary until after a child is one year old. It is important to note that small children and the elderly should be careful not to eat desserts that make them feel cold, such as kanten or chilled custards. Serve desserts at room temperature or warm them instead. Children should also avoid eating too many desserts made with a lot of oil or flour. (Table 1.5 lists fruits, vegetables, and concentrated sweeteners that may be eaten occasionally.)

BEVERAGES

The beverages most often consumed by Americans are soft drinks, orange juice, tea, coffee, beer, wine, whiskey, and milk. Studies conducted on consumption of these beverages implicate them in a number of health problems. Reports on the ill effects of caffeine bring into question consumption of tea, coffee, and cola. Use of flavored soft drinks and juices is also being questioned due to their sugar content and additives. Allergic reactions have been reported by orange juice drinkers, and its acidity is disagreeable. Drinking beer and alcoholic beverages is not recommended either because they contain additives, preservatives, and alcohol. And finally, milk consumption is implicated in heart disease due to its high cholesterol and fat content. Instead of these beverages, the macrobiotic diet recommends a number of special teas.

Whereas black teas have a high caffeine content, the teas used on the macrobiotic diet do not. Compared with processed brands, these teas contain considerably lower quantities of caffeine, because they are not processed to increase their caffeine content. They contain only minute quantities of caffeine. The benefits of macrobiotic teas are discussed more thoroughly in Chapter 6.

Table 1.5   Recommended Sweets

Vegetables	Concentrated Sweeteners	Temperate Climate Fruits
Cabbage	Amazaké	Apples
Carrots	Apple cider	Apricots
Daikon	Apple juice	Blueberries
Onions	Barley malt	Cantaloupe
Parsnips	Chestnuts	Cherries
Pumpkin	Raisins	Grapes
Squash	Rice syrup (ame or yinnie syrup)	Peaches
	Dried, temperate climate fruits	Pears
		Plums
		Raspberries
		Strawberries
		Watermelon

It is recommended that spring or well water be used in preparation of teas and other beverages. Mu tea is made from a variety of herbs. (Refer to Table 1.6 for recommendations on beverage consumption.) It is better to drink as thirst requires rather than out of habit.

Adjustments for Babies and Children

Babies may have spring or well water that has been boiled and cooled to room temperature, bancha twig tea, cereal grain teas, apple juice (preferably warmed or hot), and amazaké that has been boiled with twice as much water and then cooled.

CONDIMENTS

Condiments may be used in moderate amounts to add a variety of flavors to foods and to provide additional nutrients. Please remember that these condiments contain salt or minerals. Adults and older children can use them in moderation. Infants and small children need not use them. Please refer to Chapter 3 for recommendations for introducing condiments to children.

The following may be used by adults and older children:

- *Tamari Soy Sauce.* Use mostly in cooking. Please refrain from using tamari on rice or vegetables at the table.

Table 1.6 Beverages

For Regular Use	For Occasional Use	For Less Frequent Use	To Avoid
Bancha stem tea	Dandelion tea	Apple juice or cider	Alcohol
Bancha twig tea	Grain coffee	Fruit juice (temperate	Black tea
(kukicha)	Kombu Tea	climate)	Coffee
Boiled water	Mu tea	Green magma	Commercial
Roasted barley tea	Umeboshi tea	Nachi green tea	beers
Roasted rice tea		Naturally fermented	Decaffeinated
Spring or well		beer	coffee
water		Sake (rice wine)	Distilled water
		Vegetable juices	Herb teas
			Juice drinks
			Municipal or
			tap water
			Soft drinks and
			artificially
			flavored
			beverages
			Wine

- *Sesame Salt (Gomashio).* For adults, use eighteen to twenty parts sesame seeds to one part roasted sea salt. (When making gomashio for children, use a larger proportion of sesame seeds.) Wash and dry-roast seeds. Grind seeds together with sea salt in a small earthenware bowl called a suribachi (a serrated clay bowl), until about two thirds of the seeds are crushed.

- *Roasted Sea Vegetable Powder.* Use either wakame, kombu, dulse, or kelp. Roast the sea vegetable in an oven until crisp (approximately 350°F for 10 to 15 minutes) and crush in a suribachi.

- *Sesame Seed Powder.* Use four to eight parts sesame seeds to one part roasted sea vegetable (kombu or wakame). Prepare according to the directions for sesame salt. On the average, about one-and-a-half teaspoons for the above powders may be eaten daily by adults.

- *Umeboshi Plum.* Plums that have been dried and pickled for over one year with sea salt are called *ume* (plum) *boshi* (dry) in Japanese. On the average, adults may eat two to three plums per week. Umeboshi stimulates the appetite and digestion and aids in maintaining an alkaline blood quality. Older children may enjoy these plums on occasion.

- *Shio (Salt) Kombu.* Soak one cup of kombu until soft and cut into one-quarter-inch-square pieces. Add to a half cup of water and a half cup of tamari, bring to a boil, and simmer until the liquid evaporates. Cool and put in a covered jar to keep several days. One to two pieces may be used by adults on occasion as needed.

- *Nori Condiment.* Cut or tear sheets of nori (a sea vegetable) into one-inch squares. In approximately one cup of water, simmer until the texture is that of a thick paste. Add enough tamari soy sauce for a moderately salty flavor. Adults may eat a teaspoon of nori condiment together with a meal on occasion.

- *Tekka.* This condiment is made from minced burdock, lotus root, carrot, miso, sesame oil, and ginger. It can be made at home or bought ready-made. It is recommended that adults use it sparingly due to its strong contracting nature. Children normally do not require it.

- *Sauerkraut.* Traditional sauerkraut is made from cabbage and sea salt. A small volume may be eaten occasionally with a meal by adults and older children. (Please rinse sauerkraut and pickles under cold water if they are too salty.)

Other condiments for occasional use include:

- *Pickles.* Adults or older children may enjoy a small amount of pickles on a regular basis. Quicker and less salty pickles are generally preferable for children. Pickles are not necessary for children before the age of two. An occasional small volume of very mild tasting pickles may be introduced after this. Light, mild pickles are also better for older people. If they are in good health, the elderly can be served pickles made with tamari and ginger on occasion.

- *Vinegar.* A moderate amount of brown rice and umeboshi vinegar may be used from time to time. Other vinegars are best avoided. Vinegar is generally not recommended for babies.

- *Ginger.* A small quantity of ginger may be used occasionally as a garnish for adults or older children, or as a flavoring in vegetable dishes, soups, pickled vegetables, and especially with fish and seafood. Ginger is generally too strong for babies and small children.

OIL AND SEASONING

It is best to use only a moderate amount of high-quality, cold-pressed vegetable oil in cooking. It is generally advisable to limit the intake of sautéed vegetables and other dishes that contain oil to several times per week, and to use only a small amount of oil when preparing those dishes. Oil may be used occasionally in deep-frying grains, vegetables, fish, and seafood.

Adjustments for Babies and Children

It is not necessary for babies to have oil. Oil cannot be digested properly without using salt to balance it. Do not include oil in your children's diet until salt is introduced, and then in small quantities only. It is important for older adults to take a little more oil than young people, but it must be well balanced with the proper amounts of seasoning. Oils for regular use include corn, sesame, and dark sesame.

Naturally processed, unrefined sea salt is preferred over other varieties of seasoning. Miso and tamari soy sauce, both of which contain sea salt, may also be used. It is recommended that only naturally processed varieties—without chemical additives—be used, and even these are best used only moderately in daily cooking. These seasonings are best omitted when preparing food for babies. Please refer to Chapter 3 for recommendations for introducing them to children as they grow older.

Seasonings that can be used regularly by adults and older children include miso, rice or other grain vinegars, tamari soy sauce, umeboshi plum or paste, umeboshi vinegar, and white sea salt.

It is better to avoid artificial seasonings and those with added sugars or chemicals.

FOODS TO REDUCE OR AVOID

Many types of animal products, dairy products, fish, processed foods, sweeteners, stimulants, fats, and tropical fruits and vegetables should be reduced or eliminated from the diet. These foods are unbalanced and, as such, have adverse effects upon your health. (See Table 1.7 for a complete list of food items to avoid if you live in a temperate climate.)

BALANCED COOKING METHODS

When you cook or process food in some way, you change the quality of its energy. How the food is cooked determines the way in which its energy changes.

Fire and water are the primary influences used in cooking. Each of these factors changes food in a way that is opposite to the other. Fire has a more contracting effect. If we place a food over an open flame,

Table 1.7 Foods to Reduce or Avoid in Temperate Climates

Animal Products
Beef
Eggs
Wild game
Lamb
Pork
Poultry
Other red meats

Beverages
Cola
Soda
Other artificial beverages

Dairy Foods
Butter
Cheese
Cream
Ice cream
Kefir
Margarine
Milk (buttermilk, skim milk)
Sour cream
Whipped cream
Yogurt

Fats
Lard or shortening
Margarines, soy
Vegetable oils, processed

Fish
Bluefish
Salmon
Swordfish
Tuna
Other fishes with red meat or blue skin

Nuts
Brazil
Cashew
Hazel
Pistachio

Processed Foods
Canned foods
Foods processed with
    Additives
    Artificial coloring
    Chemicals
    Emulsifiers
    Sprays or dies
    Stabilizers
    Preservatives
Frozen foods
Instant foods
Polished (white) rice
Refined (white) flour

Stimulants
Alcohol
Coffee

Ginseng
Herbs
Spices (cayenne, cumin, etc.)
Teas, commercial, dyed
Teas, stimulating, aromatic

Sweeteners
Carob
Chocolate
Corn syrup
Sugar (white, raw, brown, turbinado)
Honey
Maple syrup
Molasses
Saccharin and other artificial sweeteners

Tropical Fruits
Bananas
Coconuts
Figs
Grapefruit
Kiwi
Mangoes
Oranges
Papayas
Prunes

it becomes drier and more contracted, and eventually turns into ashes. Water has the opposite effect. It draws the minerals out of foods, causing them to become softer and more expanded.

If we roast grains, beans, or seeds in a dry skillet, they become harder, drier, and darker in color. When fire is the only factor used—as in dry-roasting—the food becomes more contracted. On the other hand, soaking a food in water will change it in the opposite way. It will expand and eventually decompose.

In cooking, we balance these opposite energies. Cooking can be thought of as a form of predigestion in which food is energized and partially broken down, so that we are better able to extract energy and nutrients from it.

Methods such as boiling, steaming, and pressure-cooking combine these opposite energies to varying degrees: the drying and contracting effects of fire are somewhat counterbalanced by the expanding effects of water or steam. Fire energizes food by accelerating the movement of atoms and molecules, so that cells break down and recombine in more concentrated form.

The crispness or hardness of raw plant foods is caused by water pressure inside the cells. This pressure causes the cellulose that makes up the outer cell wall to assume a more rigid structure. Heat causes these water molecules to expand and rupture the outer cell wall and coagulates the protein molecules in the cells. The cells become softer and more contracted, like a balloon does when the air is let out of it. Meanwhile, water offsets these contracting effects by keeping the food moist. It prevents food from becoming dried out or burnt.

The skillful cook stops the cooking process at just the right time, before the water evaporates and food becomes burnt and contracted, but not before it is adequately softened, broken down, and condensed. Here we can see that the amount of time that something is cooked influences its quality. The longer we cook it, the more concentrated it becomes. So, quickly boiled or steamed greens still retain freshness and crispness, while those that are cooked for a longer time become softer and less crispy.

Pressure-cooking, which is the most common method of cooking brown rice in macrobiotic households, is a more concentrated form of boiling. It reduces the loss of minerals and other nutrients that would escape in steam during the boiling process. Pressure cooking is a more contracting factor, squeezing moisture from foods and making them more concentrated.

A pinch of sea salt, or a small amount of miso, tamari soy sauce, umeboshi plum, or other natural seasoning is usually added during cooking. The minerals in sea salt cause foods to contract, somewhat counterbalancing the expanding effects of water or steam. Methods of cooking that combine the contracting effects of fire, salt, pressure, and time with the expanding effects of water are generally more balanced than methods like dry-roasting or grilling. Vegetable foods become sweeter, softer, and more energized when cooked in a more balanced manner.

Baking is also a more contracting method of cooking. When grains are baked, they are first crushed into flour. This fragments and disperses their energy. Then, water is added to make dough, further adding to the expansive quality of the flour. However, the dough is then placed in an enclosed oven and baked until it hardens. Baking causes the flour to become harder and drier, and accelerates its contracting energy. That is why overintake of baked flour products can make someone become drier, stiffer, and thirstier.

Drying or pickling foods also accelerates their contracting energy. If we compare fresh and dried apples, we see that the dried apples have lost much of their moisture, and their sweetness has become more concentrated. If we compare fresh daikon with daikon that has been combined with rice bran and sea salt and aged for several years, as it is in takuan pickles, we see that pickling makes the daikon become harder, drier, saltier, and more contracted. On the other hand, oil creates expansive and upward energy. Only a small amount is needed from time to time to conduct heat and release the energy in food. On average, high-quality sesame oil is used in sautéing two to three times per week in most macrobiotic households.

Variety, not only in the foods you cook, but in the methods you use to cook them, is an important element in a healthful way of eating. During the course of a day, we recommend that you use a variety of cooking methods. For example, you may wish to pressure-cook your main brown rice dish; use both quick and slow boiling for soups, beans, and vegetable dishes; blanch or steam your greens; and serve fermented pickles, pressed vegetables, or occasional raw salads. Moreover, condiments such as gomashio and sea-vegetable powders are prepared by roasting and crushing the ingredients. A wide range of cooking styles helps each person receive a well-balanced mix of food energies.

HOME COOKING

Good cooking is essential for the health and well-being of every family. Whoever cooks for their family is building not only a healthy and peaceful home, but a healthy and peaceful world. We encourage all members of the family to study and practice this all-important art. The joy of selecting, preparing, and serving balanced natural foods can be taught to every child. All members of the family can help in the kitchen.

The flavor of foods can be varied. Children need a more naturally sweet taste, such as that of properly cooked grains and vegetables.

Adults and elders may have a variety of tastes, while sick persons tend to dislike strongly flavored dishes, including those with spicy or bitter flavors.

You will want to mind what your children eat and take note of their food preferences. Parents who observe what their children eat, and then see how they behave afterward, can learn much about how to cook for them. It is very important to notice whether your children are happy, sad, crying, fighting, or peaceful, and then remember what it was that they ate to make them this way.

Each child has different needs and wants. If you are sensitive to these differences, you can avoid many problems or sicknesses. Make suggestions to your children about what to eat if they are older and able to understand the importance of food. Point out how the foods they eat affect their behavior. Explain how certain foods cause problems and how other foods are good for their health. However, for children to develop properly, you need to be flexible. Give them time to think about these ideas, and let them make the association between the foods they eat and their physical and emotional health. Rather than imposing rules or using discipline to control their eating habits, let your children experience and discover things for themselves. If parents do not clearly understand the relationship between food and health, their method of handling these matters may become rigid or conceptual.

On the Meaning of Variety

When parents come for advice about foods, I often tell them that they or their children need more variety in their diets. Some misunderstand and think they can now have such items as sweet potatoes, yams, maple syrup, lots of beans, or plenty of fish. "Variety" refers not just to a number of different grains, beans, soups, sea vegetables, pickles, condiments, or desserts, but also to a variety of cooking methods, seasonings, garnishes, and cutting techniques. Do not cook the same way all the time or always use the same ingredients in the same dishes. Continually change your cooking to make it new, interesting, and appealing.

—Aveline Kushi

You need to be sensitive and caring enough to prepare your children's favorite foods for them. If you have several children, you may have to cook several "favorite" foods.

TIPS FOR HEALTHY EATING

Along with selecting and preparing the right foods, families can eat together as often as possible, at least once a day. The following recommendations can help you and your family develop good eating habits.

- *Chew foods thoroughly.* Chewing is essential for good health. We recommend chewing each mouthful until it becomes liquid, as many as fifty times or more. Teach children how to chew properly while they are young. As they grow older, remind them from time to time that chewing is good for them. Parents, be aware that your practice of good chewing, healthful eating, and other positive health habits serves as an ongoing example for your children.

- *Eat only when hungry.* Children and older family members may eat whenever they want to and may enjoy natural wholesome snacks from time to time, but it is better to avoid habitual overeating.

- *Eat in an orderly manner.* Encourage everyone in the family, including children, to treat food with love and care. Eat only when sitting and encourage children to be calm during meals and not to eat while standing, walking, running, or playing, or while involved in other activities such as watching television. Everyone may eat regularly two to three times per day, as much as they want, provided each meal includes the correct proportions of food and each mouthful is chewed thoroughly. Children may eat more frequently when necessary and may enjoy natural snacks from time to time, but again, try to discourage overeating. Habitual snacks can interfere with the eating of more regular and nutritionally complete meals.

- *Leave the table when you feel satisfied—do not wait until you are full.* To prevent wasting food, avoid overloading children's plates. Instead serve the approximate amount of food that they can finish. Additional servings can be given as needed or requested. Adults are also advised to avoid leaving food on their plate.

- *Drink comfortably but not excessively.* Children may drink a slightly larger amount of liquid than adults, but excessive or habitual drinking should generally be discouraged. Do not be inflexible about the quantity that children drink. If they are thirsty, allow them to drink as desired. At the same time, parents should find and eliminate whatever it is that is causing the excessive thirst.

- *For optimum health, it is best for adults to avoid eating three hours before sleeping.* Going to bed shortly after eating causes stagnation in the intestines, sluggish digestion, inefficient absorption, and accumulation of excess throughout the body. Children may eat a little bit closer to bedtime, but for optimum health, it is better for them to avoid eating just before sleeping, except of course for nursing infants.

On Developing Good Habits

It is very important to teach children how to eat properly. And it is easier to teach correct eating habits when children are young. Undesirable habits formed in childhood are difficult for teenagers or adults to break. I remember when I was in college studying Zen. We could make no noise during meals. It was very strict, hard training. Of course, the home environment can be much more relaxed. While it is better to keep the home atmosphere more relaxed and enjoyable, simple table manners will benefit the entire family. Family members should be encouraged to keep a straight but not rigid spine while eating, chew well, and not eat with the fingers. It is naturally easier to catch and correct problems when children are young. If we wait until children become teenagers, it is much more difficult and may result in arguments and disagreements. Giving thanks or appreciation before each meal, or praying to God or nature for your food, is also recommended, as it is important to teach children gratitude. If these simple things—manners, thankfulness, and togetherness—are observed by your family, many problems can be solved or avoided.

Try to have only the best quality food available for your family. Stocking your home with the right foods is the key to health.

—Aveline Kushi

Chapter 2
How Children Develop

T
he splendor of creation can be found in each flower, grain of sand, and individual child. The creative forces that form the largest galaxies, the most delicate flowers, and the tiniest atoms are revealed in a child's daily life.

Endless cycles of birth, growth, development, and maturity are at the root of all things, including human beings. Nowhere are these cycles more apparent than in children. Children change from day to day and moment to moment, transforming themselves before our eyes. Universal order is manifest in the life of every child.

A baby changes dramatically during the first two years. She learns to walk, to use arms, legs, hands, and fingers, to utter simple words, and to take food independently of her mother. She develops a unique personality and a sense of self.

In this chapter, we trace the major landmarks of childhood development until puberty. We also present an overview of human development in general, especially in the realm of consciousness, and see how the changes that take place during childhood fit in with the overall pattern of human development.

By reviewing the stages of child development from the macrobiotic perspective, we hope you will be encouraged to see childhood—and, by extension, all life—in a far larger context than is usually considered. Everything in the universe is constantly changing. Two antagonistic forces—yin and yang—are present in various degrees in all living matter. "Yin" and "yang" are simply terms that we use to represent the most primary forces of nature. Yin represents the primary energy of expansion, and yang, the energy of contraction. These invisible forces create everything in the universe, and manifest on Earth as a downward, contracting force that spirals in from the infinite reaches of space (more yang); and an upward, expanding force generated by the Earth's rotation (more yin). All movement on the Earth, including that of the Earth itself, is created by these dynamic forces. They appear everywhere and in everything. Their opposite yet complementary forces help us to achieve harmony in our bodies and minds.

In this chapter we will categorize stages of development as more yin or more yang. Your child's physical, emotional, and mental growth will reflect, and be in perfect harmony with, the vast order of the universe. We hope that the examples that follow will enable you to begin seeing this order in every area of life. Then, when reference books are consulted for more detailed information on child development, you will be able to understand growth as the expression of the cycles of "nature" in the largest sense of the word.

DEVELOPMENTS BEFORE BIRTH

The most dramatic physical developments actually take place before a child is born. If it were possible to gaze inside the womb, we would witness the growth of a single fertilized cell—too small to be seen with the naked eye—into a new human being with trillions of cells arranged according to a blueprint drawn up over billions of years of evolution.

During the nine months of pregnancy, a human baby passes through an enormous span of evolutionary history, beginning as a single cell, growing in the aqueous environment of the womb, and then emerging into the world like the first amphibians that ventured onto dry land. It took the enormous span of about 2.8 billion years for air-breathing animals to develop on earth, yet human beings accomplish the whole process in only 280 days.

The birth of a baby corresponds to the transition from life in the primordial ocean to life on the surface of the earth, a transition that occurred about 400 million years ago. During each day of pregnancy, the baby passes through the equivalent of roughly 10 million years of biological evolution. The physical, emotional, and spiritual nourishment received by the baby during pregnancy is therefore vitally important. *Tai-kyo,* the approach to prenatal care practiced in Japan and other traditional cultures, is based on the importance of a balanced natural diet, an orderly life, and calm and peaceful thoughts and emotions during pregnancy. (It is covered in detail in our other family health book, *Macrobiotic Pregnancy and Care of the Newborn.*) The baby's fundamental constitution, including the potential for health or sickness, wisdom or foolishness, broad- or narrow-mindedness, and success or failure in life is largely determined by the mother's diet and way of life during pregnancy.

DEVELOPMENTS FOLLOWING BIRTH

Although the speed becomes less rapid, the baby develops very actively following birth. The entire span of evolution, from the first single-celled life to the appearance of Homo sapiens, took about 3.2 billion years to accomplish. Human beings repeat the whole process. At birth, the equivalent of seven eighths of the process is complete; the remaining one eighth—the approximately 400 million years during which life evolved on land—is replicated during the first two years of infancy. This epoch of evolution encompasses the stages of amphibians, reptiles, mammals, monkeys, apes, and, ultimately, man. A newborn passes, step by step, through the equivalent of these stages.

Changes in posture and movement reflect these stages in evolutionary development. The earliest attempts to turn over and to lift the head and crawl correspond to the wriggling movements and belly-down posture of amphibians and reptiles. A baby then starts to crawl in a fashion not unlike that of four-legged mammals, and to half-stand like monkeys and other primates. Finally, an infant stands erect without assistance and takes his or her first tentative steps. The baby is now ready to begin developing in a manner that is uniquely human.

The span between birth and standing corresponds to about 400 million years of evolution, and a baby condenses these developments into approximately 12 to 18 months. That means that the baby passes through the equivalent of about 33 million years of evolutionary development every month, one million years each day, 40,000 years every hour, and more than 600 years every minute. Because development occurs so rapidly during this time, the quality of nourishment that the baby receives is vitally important, as is the type of home environment and the love and care provided by the parents.

THE INFLUENCE OF FOOD ON DEVELOPMENT

Food begins to influence the baby even before conception. It does this by affecting the quality of the parents' reproductive cells and the genetic factors that they contain. The foods eaten by the mother create the quality of her blood, cells, and tissues, and influence the development and maturation of her ova, or egg cells, while the quality of the father's sperm is largely due to the foods that he eats. During pregnancy, the placenta provides nourishment for the baby directly from the mother's blood, the quality and composition of which is determined by the foods that she eats. The nutrients in the mother's blood are very condensed. (In general, foods that originate from animal sources are classified has having a more *yang* or constrictive quality, while vegetable products are classified as more *yin* or expansive.) After being nourished by this type of food for nine months, babies have a more yang quality at birth. They are tiny and wrinkled, and their arms and legs are curled into tightly wound spirals.

The baby's more yang head normally assumes a downward position during delivery, and at birth is larger in relation to the rest of the body than it is later in life. During the first trimester, the head forms about one half of the entire body. It averages about one fourth of the body size at birth. In adults, the head averages about one eighth of the total body size. The comparative size of the brain also decreases as a child grows. At birth, the brain makes up about 10 percent of the body weight, while in adults it makes up only about 2 percent.

After birth, nourishment is naturally provided in the form of colostrum, a clear liquid secreted by the breasts for several days before the mother's milk comes in. It contains antibodies and other factors that convey natural immunity to the baby. Colostrum is thinner, clearer, and more yin than mother's blood, while mother's milk, which is sweet and rich, has a more yin quality than colostrum.

By distilling its nourishment directly from mother's blood, the single fertilized cell is able to develop with incredible speed, so that nearly 3 billion years of evolution are condensed into nine months. Mother's milk, a slightly less concentrated form of nourishment than that received from mother's blood that is secreted externally, also causes the baby to develop rapidly, although at a slower pace than in the womb.

During the time that an infant nurses, his body proportions change greatly. More of the yin components of breast milk—especially certain carbohydrates, fats, and proteins—are attracted to the more yang head. More of the yang components are attracted toward the legs and lower body, both of which are originally more yin than the head. The head, originally in a downward position at birth, gradually assumes a more yin upward position, while the arms, legs, and lower body become more active and well developed and able to support the head and upper body. As these developments occur, the baby gradually changes from a more yang horizontal posture (lying down) to a more yin vertical one (standing).

The more yin quality of breast milk causes the baby to change to a lighter color, while fat cells are deposited below the surface of the skin, smoothing out wrinkles and rounding the contours of the bones and muscles. The baby begins to take on a softer and more well-rounded appearance. The arms and legs are held tightly coiled and close to the body at birth. They gradually relax and unwind as the baby becomes more yin.

The type of food that a baby receives following birth provides the foundation for these developments. When a mother eats a well-balanced diet and breastfeeds her baby, her milk provides the nourishment needed by the baby to accomplish the remaining course of evolution and enjoy a healthy life as a human being.

HOW CONSCIOUSNESS GROWS

The development of human consciousness proceeds in the form of an expanding spiral, beginning with 1) automatic, or reflexive responses, and proceeding through 2) sensory development, 3) emotional responses, 4) intellectual development, 5) social awareness, 6) philosophical development, and 7) universal or cosmic consciousness. Human beings develop naturally through each of these stages when provided with the proper diet and environmental influences. (See Figure 2.1.)

All levels of consciousness function through the intuition that everyone possesses. Intuition can easily be suppressed by an education that is narrow or one-sided, or dulled through improper diet; however, the potential for developing all the levels of consciousness exists in every child. Children intuitively know the purpose of life, which is to play happily on this Earth and freely recognize their dreams together with many other people. Because their physical conditions are normally flexible and unspoiled, children do not feel isolated from the larger currents of life. They have an intuitive faith in life and a seemingly limitless capacity for imagination, freedom, creativity, and adventure. Children are not constrained by time. They instinctively sense that the future is unlimited, and are capable of enjoying every moment as if it were an eternity.

Children can display an inner happiness and contentment that is based on their faith in the order of life and nature and on their ability to freely realize their dreams and become whatever they want to in life.

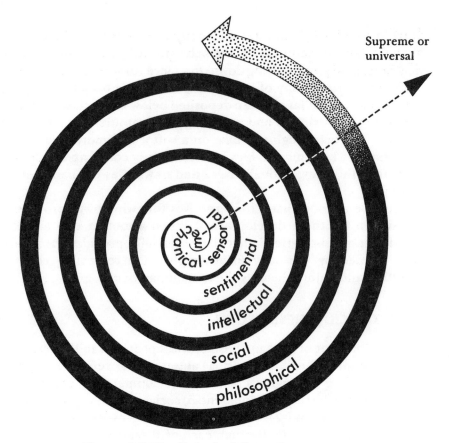

Supreme or
universal

Figure 2.1 The Spiral of Consciousness

Children often say, "When I grow up, I want to become a fireman [or a doctor, etc.]," with full confidence that whatever it is they want to do is possible and achievable. At the same time, when they play, children freely assume a variety of roles that adults would find contradictory—one minute they are cops, the next, robbers; they can shift from being a hero to a villain and back again without any sense of contradiction.

Many spiritual teachers pointed to these and similar attributes as being qualities of a state in which intuition is allowed to function with little artificial interference. In the *Gospel According to Thomas,* for example, Jesus says:

Let him who seeks, not cease seeking until he finds, and when he finds, he will be troubled, and when he has been troubled, he will marvel and he will reign over the All.

Children naturally possess this sense of marvel; they are able to find wonder and delight in a flower, a dog, or an old toy, in themselves, or in the ocean, sky, mountains, fields, and trees.

In another passage of the *Gospel According to Thomas,* we read:

Jesus saw little children who were being suckled. He said to his disciples: 'These children who are being suckled are like those who enter the Kingdom.' They said to him: 'Shall we then, being children, enter the Kingdom?' Jesus said to them: 'When you make the two one, and when you make the inner as the outer and the above as the below, and when you make the male and female into a single one, so that the male will not be male and the female will not be female, when you make eyes in the place of an eye, and a hand in the place of a hand, and a foot in the place of a foot, an image in the place of an image, then shall you enter the Kingdom.'

As we have seen, children have the flexibility to unite seemingly opposite qualities and to shift freely from one role to the next in the course of their play. These are the attributes that Jesus describes.

The level of a child's consciousness continues to expand in scope throughout his life. Sensory perception and physical, or mechanical, coordination are continually refined as a child learns to use tools and develops other motor skills. Meanwhile, emotional responses are refined and expanded during childhood, as the capacity grows to love and be loved, to give and receive, and to develop respect for oneself and for others. At puberty, and through adolescence, children begin to broaden their range of emotions as attraction for the opposite sex awakens and develops. Emotional sensitivity continually deepens and widens throughout life.

Intellectual abilities develop rapidly during childhood. Children learn how to figure things out, to solve problems, to read and write, and to develop and expand their language abilities. They begin to see how things are connected and to develop an awareness of where things come from and how situations develop. They also become aware that certain actions will produce certain results, while opposite actions will produce opposite results. The ability to form concepts, make informed choices, and arrange one's ideas in an orderly sequence develops rapidly during childhood and adolescence. Although the basic foundation of intellectual consciousness is laid during these early formative years, new knowledge, information, and insights are added throughout life. Our conception of the world continually broadens as new dimensions of understanding are added.

As children grow, they become increasingly aware of the world outside their families. They associate with friends and classmates, and start to relate to the larger society both as individuals and as members of various groups. Their basic sense of how to relate to other people comes largely from their early family experiences, even as their scope of social awareness grows to include a concern for humanity and for the world as a whole.

Social consciousness deals with our relationship to other people and, ultimately, to how we relate to the human race as a whole. Philosophical, or spiritual, consciousness encompasses these relationships, and extends beyond them into the realm of our relationship to God, or the universe. The seeds of philosophical understanding can appear during childhood. Children sometimes ask, "Mommy, where did I come from?" "What is God?" "Why do I have five fingers, one nose, one mouth, and two ears?" and "Where do people go after they die?" Like everyone else, children do wonder about the most basic questions of existence. Parents can provide them with proper guidance to pursue their lifelong quest for solutions.

The potential for developing through all of the levels of consciousness, including supreme or universal consciousness, begins during childhood. Whether consciousness matures fully during life depends, to a large degree, on the quality of early care that children receive. (Please refer to another of our books, *The Book of Macrobiotics: The Universal Way of Health, Happiness, and Peace,* for further explanation of the seven levels of consciousness.)

DIET AND THE DEVELOPMENT OF CONSCIOUSNESS

How children are nourished during early life is one of the most important aspects of child care. The full development of consciousness depends on a properly nourished and healthy body, including the proper functioning of the brain and nervous system.

The decision of whether to feed an infant breast milk or a substitute will have a fundamental influence on the entire life of the child. The subject of infant nutrition is crucial not only to the child's physical, mental, and spiritual health, but also to the quality of the relationships that develop within the family.

The following section explains in detail the effects of mother's milk and alternative forms of nourishment on the developing infant. We hope you, the reader, will consider this matter seriously, and investigate further if there are any questions. There are many excellent books available on the topic of breastfeeding.

At least 80 percent of human brain development occurs during pregnancy and the first three years of life. Therefore, how a mother eats throughout pregnancy—especially during the final trimester, when brain development is rapid—is vitally important, as is the quality of food eaten by the child during the first three years. Animal studies have shown that dietary deficiencies adversely affect brain development. Reductions in the size of the brain and in the number of cells that it contains, and disruption in the balance of brain enzymes, were some of the changes noted in animals on deficient diets. Disturbances such as these can impede normal brain function and the proper maturation of consciousness. Research has also linked inadequate diets during infancy and early childhood to developmental problems such as impaired physical control, clumsiness, overexcitability, and a lowered threshold to environmental stimuli. Current evidence points to a decreased intellectual capacity among inadequately nourished children, affecting their physical and mental coordination, language skills, and capacities for social interaction.

When a mother eats a well-balanced diet, however, her milk contains the proper balance of nutrients essential for the normal development of the brain and nervous system. The composition of mother's milk changes as the baby continues nursing so as to meet the rapidly changing needs of the baby, including the rapid growth and development of the brain.

Breast Milk Versus Cow's Milk

No other form of nourishment meets the needs of an infant as efficiently as breast milk. In fact, recent studies show that other forms of nourishment—such as cow's milk formula—may impede normal brain functioning and development. An article published by the La Leche League in 1976, entitled "Biological Specificity of Milk" by W.B. Whitestone, contained a report on studies that have shown that breast-fed children developed better reading and spelling skills than their counterparts who were fed cow's milk formulas.

Human infants are unique in the animal kingdom in that so much of their early nourishment is used for the development and growth of the brain. The human brain is about 23 percent of its adult size at birth, while the brain of a calf is nearly 100 percent developed at birth. A calf gains up to 75 percent of its adult weight during the first six weeks, and needs plenty of protein and minerals for the growth of muscle and bones. Human infants, on the average, gain less than a pound per week during their first six weeks. Their need for protein and minerals is much less than that of a calf, but their need for carbohydrates—which are used in the formation of healthy nerve and brain cells—is much greater. Cow's milk is naturally better suited to the rapid growth and development of the calf's massive bone and body structure; it contains up to three times as much protein and four times as much calcium as human milk. However, cow's milk is not the ideal food for brain development. Human milk, with up to twice as many carbohydrates, is far better suited to the growth and development of the human brain and nervous system.

Since cow's milk is lacking in carbohydrates, some type of sugar—usually in the form of cane sugar, brown sugar, or corn syrup—is generally added to cow's milk formulas to provide enough calories. However, simple sugars such as these destroy B-complex vitamins, including thiamine, or vitamin B_1, which is naturally present in the outer layers of brown rice and other whole cereal grains. Thiamine and other B vitamins are essential for healthy development and functioning of the nervous system, including the capacity for learning. If enough of these vitamins are destroyed, a child can develop difficulty in digesting carbohydrates, and an excess of pyruvic acid can accumulate in the blood, resulting in an oxygen deficiency. Lack of oxygen can easily impair the functioning and development of the brain, which depends on oxygen and glucose for energy.

The intake of refined and other simple sugars disrupts the body's normal levels of blood glucose. The more sugar one consumes, the lower the blood sugar level tends to be. The brain uses about 50 percent of the glucose in the blood, and when the blood glucose level is disrupted, the functioning of the brain is affected. Sugar also contributes to a depletion of the body's mineral reserves, some of which, including zinc, iron, and magnesium, are essential in glucose metabolism. Depletion of minerals contributes to reduction in the chemical energy needed by the brain. Whenever the energy available to the brain is reduced, the area that receives priority is the *limbic system*, the part of the brain that controls the automatic processes necessary to maintain life. The brain centers that control the higher levels of consciousness—including intellectual capacities and social adjustment—are the first to be denied sufficient energy.

The development and functioning of the brain and nervous system are closely related to the condition of the intestines and digestive tract, through which all nutrients are absorbed. The intake of cow's milk formula disrupts the normal functioning of the digestive tract and is associated with ulcerative colitis, diarrheal infections, colic, and other digestive disturbances. Digestive upsets frequently produce behavioral disturbances. Problems such as periodic irritable crying, crankiness, crying during bowel movements, and, in some cases, convulsions, have been noted in children suffering digestive reactions to cow's milk formulas.

Breast milk promotes a healthy acid medium in the intestines that encourages the development of beneficial bacteria, some of which synthesize B-complex vitamins. Cow's milk furthers the development of an alkaline medium in which harmful, putrefactive bacteria more easily flourish. It also lacks the compounds found in breast milk that make the intestinal tract resistant to harmful bacteria. Harmful bacteria interfere with the activities of the beneficial bacteria, including the synthesis of the B-complex vitamins necessary for normal brain functioning.

The Introduction of Solid Foods

The structure of the baby's digestive tract suggests that whole cereal grains and other vegetable products are the ideal baby foods once solids are introduced. Unlike the digestive tract of the carnivore, the human digestive system is long and convoluted. It is better suited to the digestion of whole grains and other plant fibers that do not rapidly decompose and produce toxic bacteria as animal proteins do. The putrefaction of animal proteins in the digestive system also destroys beneficial bacteria, including those that synthesize the B vitamins that are necessary for the proper functioning and development of the brain.

The structure of the teeth and digestive system suggests that Homo sapiens evolved on a mixed diet consisting largely of whole cereal grains, beans, seeds, fresh local vegetables, and other vegetable foods, with animal products comprising a minority of average consumption. Animal quality food—mother's blood—was the only source of nourishment during the period of life in the womb. More yin quality animal food—mother's milk—is the most natural source during the period of nursing. Once the baby stands and teeth come in, the milk-drinking stage comes to an end. From then on, it is preferable for nourishment to come primarily from cooked vegetable foods.

The more yang quality of animal food eaten in the womb promotes the development of mechanical and rudimentary sensory consciousness. Mother's milk, a more yin form of animal food, promotes refinement of the baby's mechanical and sensory abilities and causes emotional consciousness to awaken and grow.

The development and refinement of consciousness beyond the milk-drinking stage depends on the introduction of properly prepared vegetable foods. If some animal foods are eaten, it is recommended that they comprise only a small portion of the child's diet. The consumption of a large volume of animal food tends to limit the development of consciousness to the sensory and mechanical levels. The higher and more refined stages depend more upon the intake of vegetable foods. The intake of milk or other dairy products beyond the normal milk-drinking period often limits the development of consciousness to the emotional or sentimental levels. The remaining levels of consciousness may fail to develop properly as a result.

Aside from having a fundamental influence on the development of consciousness, childhood diet is a primary factor in future health and well-being. Two health problems that are medically linked to a poor diet—obesity and heart disease—begin with eating habits acquired during infancy and childhood. Dr. Anthony Gotto, president of the American Heart Association, stated, "The important thing is to get kids eating the right foods as early as possible. If they develop good eating habits when they are young, they are more likely to eat healthily when they are older."

A naturally balanced diet—a diet that lowers or eliminates the risk of obesity, heart disease, cancer, and a host of physically and mentally debilitating disorders—is a fundamental aspect of macrobiotic child care. Starting children on the road to lifelong health and well-being is one of the most essential tasks of parenthood. Ideally, proper diet should begin even before birth in the way a mother and father eat prior to and during pregnancy. When parents eat a balanced natural foods diet, they provide their children with the foundation for future health and the development of the highest level of consciousness. With good health and clear judgment, children will be well equipped to deal with life's struggles and may realize their dreams and experience much happiness throughout their lives.

HOW BABIES DEVELOP (FROM NEWBORNS TO TWO)

In the period following birth, a baby learns how to coordinate basic mechanical and sensory functions and to use the body in new ways. The large muscles of the body are controlled by more yang, contracting energy while the smaller muscles are governed by more yin, expanding force. Thus, gross motor developments involving the movement and control of the large muscles are classified as more yang while fine motor developments, which include more delicate muscle control and especially the coordination between eye and hand, is more yin. Of course, all muscle movements involve expansion and contraction, or yin and yang, but in varying degrees.

Speed of Development

No two children develop at the same rate. Although the general pattern of development is similar from baby to baby, the speed at which physical, emotional, and mental development takes place is unique for each child.

The large variation in the speed of development is due to differences in the foods children are given. It is better if children are not given foods that will cause them to mature too quickly. A diet containing dairy foods, for example, will make children grow faster physically, but it is difficult for mental growth to keep up with the abnormally stimulated physical growth. A baby whose teeth erupt very early or who shows signs of maturing extremely early is suffering from an unbalanced diet, usually containing a high percentage of animal protein. Protein is an essential factor for growth, but taken in excess it speeds up development beyond a healthy, natural rate. In temperate climates it is better for animal foods to comprise at most about one eighth, or 15 percent, of the human diet. In most cases, babies do not need any animal foods at all; they can obtain all the protein they need from their mother's milk and from vegetable foods. Low-fat, white-meat fish can be added to an older child's diet, if desired.

On the other hand, some children develop very slowly. Babies who are not walking by the time they are almost two could be suffering from excess salt in their diet or not enough fresh vegetables. Because of its constrictive, or more yang, physiological influence, too much salt prevents a baby from expanding and growing normally. Fresh vegetables, on the other hand, are essential because of their expansive, or more yin, physiological effects. It is recommended that babies be fed primarily lightly cooked rather than raw vegetables, however, since cooking makes the tough vegetable fibers more easily digestible. In the case of children who eat foods containing sugar or chemicals or who consume large amounts of fruit or fruit juice (such as daily orange juice), slow development could indicate another type of weakness: mental retardation caused by the harmful effects of these foods on the nervous system.

Early Senses

As the baby's senses develop and become more refined, mechanical abilities gradually come under sensory control. Earlier, unconscious responses to sensory stimulation, such as the various newborn reflexes, are referred to as *sensorimotor behavior,* while actions that are controlled consciously are referred to as *psychomotor behavior.*

The senses develop from those dealing with the "more yang" immediate environment to those dealing with vibrations coming from greater distances. The immediate environment is classified as more yang because it is more contracted in relation to the larger, more expanded environment of the earth and the universe. The more immediate senses—touch, taste, and smell—mature more rapidly than do hearing and sight—the senses that deal with more yin forms of vibration.

In the past, it was believed that a newborn's behavior was entirely reflexive and mechanical. It was felt that the senses developed over time. However, researchers have recently found that newborns have the capability to see, hear, smell, and respond to touch. Infants only hours old seem to have the ability to focus on objects that are placed in front of them. Whether a newborn sees or hears in the same manner as an adult or an older child, however, is still an open scientific question.

Infants can see and hear, but in a manner that is qualitatively different than the way adults or older children do. Being small, compact, red in color, very active, and thus very yang, infants are better able to sense general vibrations, rather than isolating specific concrete physical objects or sounds. When a newborn looks at his mother's face, for example, he is "seeing" her vibrational quality and general physical characteristics and does not focus on her specific features. As the baby becomes more yin—larger and more expanded—the ability to focus sharply on more specific objects and sounds—that is, yang ones—develops. It is therefore better not to force a newborn to focus on specific objects or sounds but to let these abilities unfold naturally as the baby grows.

Development of Physical Coordination

Babies begin moving their arms and legs while in the womb and continue to do so after birth. A baby's posture and movements reflect a more yang condition, resulting from the intake of condensed animal food in the womb. Newborns move their arms and legs in a stiff and jerky manner, while keeping them more tightly curled and close to the body. The intake of mother's milk and other more yin forms of nourishment causes their movements and posture to become more graceful and relaxed as time passes.

The intake of a more yin quality of food also gradually causes the head to become more yin and gravitate toward an upward position. A baby begins lifting the head while lying on the stomach. The neck muscles gradually become strong enough to support the head in an upright position. When newborns are first held upright, the head has a tendency to fall forward and then move backward. Because the head tends to flip-flop, anyone who holds the baby must be careful to support the head properly. A baby gradually gains the ability to hold the head steady, although it still tilts slightly forward. Ultimately, the baby is able to hold the head steadily in a completely upright position and turn it to the left and right.

Babies use the ability to control the head to graduate to the next level of large muscle control: learning to roll over. They first roll over from front to back by using the weight of the head to pull the body over. Then comes rolling over from back to front. When a baby can roll over, parents need to be aware that he or she can roll off a bed, table, or sofa and must watch the baby carefully.

From the third to the sixth month, a baby gains the ability to sit when placed in an upright position without being supported. During the next three months, a baby learns to sit up without help. The more vertical posture of sitting increases a baby's range of perception and opens the possibility of new dimensions of consciousness. The rapidly developing brain can now receive electromagnetic energy directly from the heavens via the spiral on top of the head.

Crawling represents the next major step in the baby's development. The age at which babies start to crawl varies widely, usually occurring between the sixth and twelfth months. However, not all babies crawl; some go directly from sitting to standing.

Standing is one of the most recent developments in biological evolution. It usually occurs between the ninth and twelfth months, though some babies stand earlier. Standing opens possibilities for the growth and expansion of consciousness into unique human dimensions. Walking gives the baby independence and freedom of motion, which increase the opportunities for learning and growth. Once a baby learns to stand, the next step is walking. This normally occurs between the tenth and sixteenth months, although earlier and later walking are not uncommon.

When a baby begins to crawl and walk, he explores the world with a seemingly limitless curiosity. Parents often need to adjust their living arrangements to meet the baby's newfound abilities. For example, preventive measures must be taken to keep the baby from getting into things that could be harmful, like household cleaners and poisonous plants. The infant must be kept away from stairs and open windows, and must be continually monitored both inside and outside the home during waking hours.

Soon, a baby learns to stoop, pick things up, and carry them. Around the middle of the second year, babies learn how to climb stairs one step at a time with assistance and how to descend them in the same manner. It takes a while longer for children to manage stairs by themselves. Running is the next skill to be acquired, usually around eighteen months to two years. It is during this time that babies begin actively climbing up stairs and onto furniture by themselves, and need careful watching by the parents to avoid accidents.

At the same time that mental development is proceeding, children are also developing physically. Mental development follows physical development, and it is important for children to be active in both play and learning. It is better to minimize interference with a child's physical development. For example, if parents are overprotective or frequently pick up a child who is just learning to crawl or walk, development of independent abilities can be impaired. As we saw earlier, during the embryonic period a baby develops the equivalent of about 10 million years of biological evolution each day. Developments in the womb equal roughly 2.8 billion years of water evolution. About a year and a half after birth, babies can stand up straight, eat their own food, walk, and talk. This period of development corresponds to the remaining period of land evolution, totaling about 400 million years. This means that a baby passes through the equivalent of 600–800 years of biological evolution every minute during roughly the first one-and-a-half years. Interrupting a baby's natural crawling or walking interferes with the child's independent development during this period.

Crawling is very important to a baby, because it develops and strengthens the muscles and joints. Accompanying the child's advancing motor skills is the development of her brain and powers of consciousness. Only after babies have become proficient at one stage can they develop normally to the next stage of physical and mental development. Therefore it is important for a child to be active and to develop naturally at his own pace. She should not be interrupted or forced to develop according to an artificial schedule.

Eye-Hand Coordination

While a baby is learning to walk, she also develops a variety of movements that require coordination between the eyes and hands. As babies gradually focus on objects, they begin to follow them from one side to the other and up and down. Babies also hold their hands in front of their faces, and enjoy looking at them, and eventually can move their hands to their mouths whenever they want.

The automatic grasp reflex gradually diminishes, and the baby learns how to reach out and consciously grasp things that she sees. Being very yang, babies usually pull things toward themselves and put them into their mouths. This normally occurs between three and six months, although it may occur sooner. By the sixth month, most babies have enough coordination to be able to pass objects from hand to hand and to rake small things in with their fingers. They also develop the ability to bang objects that they are holding, and to grab things with both hands.

An important milestone is reached when a baby begins to grasp things by managing the complementary/antagonistic relationship between the thumb and index finger. Soon the baby develops the ability to pick up small objects, and then progresses from the simple grasping or moving of objects to the use of objects—such as a spoon or a cup—to accomplish a task. Early in the second year, children learn how to hold a cup with two hands and to use a spoon, although they frequently spill food. They also learn how to let go of and drop things and eventually to throw objects—such as cups, bowls, or toys—across short distances. Children often make a game out of these newly acquired skills.

During the second year, a baby learns to place blocks on top of each other and to drink from a cup. Soon the child will learn to use a variety of objects such as crayons and pencils. Before the end of the second year, the baby may enjoy playing with simple toys and, by the age of two, is usually able to open doors and to make simple marks on a piece of paper with a crayon or pencil.

Emotional Development

Birth is an emotional experience for both mother and baby. While the baby in the womb was totally dependent upon her mother, she is separated physically from her at birth. Interaction with her mother lies at the root of emotional development and is most complete when the baby is fed naturally at the breast. Feeding a baby artificially can interfere with emotional development by depriving the baby of immediate natural contact and stimulation. Nursing allows the baby to reconnect periodically with her mother. The baby naturally enjoys the stimulation provided by the breast and begins to recognize and enjoy the sound of her mother's voice and her energy as a whole. As she begins to focus on more concrete objects, she starts to recognize the details of her mother's face. Gradually, the baby begins interacting directly with her surrounding environment, eventually including other people. She soon recognizes her father, other members of the family, and other close people, and distinguishes familiar from unfamiliar people.

During the first year, a baby gradually adjusts both to physical separation from her mother and to her new environment. However, babies use their connection with their mothers as the base from which to explore their new surroundings. As they assume an increasingly vertical posture, their capacity for remembering the past and anticipating the future starts to develop. Soon, the baby internalizes familiar people and places. Babies often cry when their mothers leave them alone or when they are placed in an unknown setting without any familiar people around. Babies also begin to anticipate the future. For example, a baby learns from experience that her mother or father, or another familiar person, will return after separation and that her crying will bring food or comfort from her mother.

The emotional climate of the family produces deep and lasting effects on a baby's developing character. This is especially true of the mother's thoughts and emotions. More positive, happy, and peaceful thoughts and emotions have more positive effects on the baby, while unhappy, disturbed, frightful, or depressed thoughts produce negative effects. The influence of thoughts and emotions on a baby's development is especially profound during pregnancy and the period of nursing. If the mother, father, and other members of the family are happy, positive, peaceful, and emotionally well-balanced, then the baby will tend to develop similar characteristics. On the other hand, parents who are negative, argumentative, or emotionally tense or restless often convey a similar emotional makeup to their children, especially when the children are given an unbalanced diet.

Teething

The twenty baby teeth normally come in during the first two-and-a-half years, although there is considerable variation in the age at which the teeth first appear. The teeth emerge as the baby changes from a horizontal to a vertical posture and indicate that the process of land evolution has been accomplished. When teeth appear, a baby can begin to eat whole cereal grains, local vegetables, beans, and other whole natural foods. The baby's digestive tract is now ready to begin processing foods taken from the vegetable kingdom.

The first teeth usually come in around the age of six months, although they may appear as early as three months. The two lower front incisors are normally the first to come in, followed by four upper incisors several months later. At a year old, the two lower lateral incisors usually come in, as do the first four molars. The canine teeth then appear, usually at sixteen to eighteen months, normally followed by the remaining four molars between the twentieth and twenty-fourth months.

Some children experience discomfort as the teeth come in, including inflammation and swelling of the gums as well as pain. Some experience discomfort during the entire period that teeth are constantly coming in. Fever and diarrhea sometimes accompany teething and are sometimes evident up to four months before a tooth actually appears.

Teething problems are the result of imbalances in the baby's diet. Foods eaten by the nursing mother and those fed to the baby must be chosen carefully to avoid problems with the teeth. More yin foods such as sugar, soft drinks, tropical fruits, highly acidic vegetables, spices, refined flour products, honey, and too much oil can interfere with the smooth development of the teeth and produce tooth malformation. They can also cause inflammation of the gums and discomfort in the teething child, as excessive factors in the bloodstream tend to gather around the emerging tooth so as to be discharged from the body. Cow's or goat's milk can also weaken the teeth and produce discomfort, as can too much salt or too many animal products in the diet of the nursing mother. Animal foods and salt can cause the baby's developing jaw to contract and can reduce the amount of space needed for the teeth to come in properly. Breastfeeding beyond the normal length of time can also have a harmful effect on the development of teeth.

Bowel and Bladder Control

An infant's awareness of and control over her bowel functions proceeds together with developments in her mouth, which is at the opposite end of the digestive tract. Newborns possess well-developed sucking and swallowing reflexes that allow them to eat and drink without thought or conscious effort. Similarly, a newborn's bowel movements and urination occur without conscious participation. As babies begin to focus on eating, they start to become aware of the sensations associated with elimination. From the twelfth to the eighteenth months, babies become increasingly conscious of bowel movements, and this corresponds to the appearance of the first molars and the ability to begin chewing foods. During the second half of the second year, at approximately the time when the remaining baby teeth come in, children become ready to learn to control their bowel movements.

Voluntary control of the sphincter muscles normally becomes possible between the ages of twelve and eighteen months, although it takes many children longer to learn to control their bowel movements. A baby begins to gain voluntary control over bowel movements and urination as liquid and solid nourishment become more distinct. Initially, liquids and solids are combined in one food—mother's milk. As a baby takes less mother's milk and more semi-solid foods, the distinction between solids and liquids becomes more pronounced. Consumption of semi-solid or solid foods results in a more solid bowel movement, and chewing stimulates the muscles of the entire digestive tract and helps make it possible to consciously contract the sphincter muscles. More yang, solid wastes are easier to retain and then release in a controlled manner than are more yin, liquid wastes, and as bowel movements become more solid, they tend to occur less often and with more regularity.

Bowel control tends to occur anywhere from one to one-and-a-half years before a child gains control over urination, although in some cases they occur simultaneously. The age at which control over urination is achieved usually ranges from eighteen months to three years. Control over urination during sleep is usually the last step in gaining control over elimination. Night control is usually established after daytime control, although both may occur at the same time.

Learning to Talk

Babies begin talking in a very natural way, by making their own sounds and creating their own words. If they were not taught a language, they would probably invent their own, naming objects in the way that Adam did. By allowing your infants frequent use of "baby talk," you foster their creative abilities. Babies left to their own speech fabrications will fashion sound according to their original perception of the world.

You need not teach any definite words to babies until they are about three or four months old. Then you can gradually introduce adult words, repeating them very slowly. Adults normally speak more rapidly than infants because adults' brain waves are shorter than children's. Therefore, when talking to children, you need to speak more slowly so that children can understand easily and learn words more quickly. If you speak too rapidly, they will have a more difficult time understanding. When you read to your children, you should use the same principle. If you read a story slowly, after one or two times they not only will understand it but may even begin to memorize it.

The language of babies is a highly symbolic one. A baby condenses many meanings into one word. Children have a full range of concepts but cannot formulate them in precise detail. The scope of babies' concepts is actually as broad as adults', but their concepts are not expressed in such analytical detail. The adult mentality gives clarity and precision to each part of that generalized understanding. An adult may use about ten thousand words to express concepts for which a child uses only about twenty. During the early period of mental development, if children are deluged with adult concepts, it will be more difficult for them to develop innate, intuitive understanding. It is better to let children talk—to themselves, to dogs, to flowers, to anything—in their own language. Then gradually more detailed adult expressions will emerge.

Babies begin making sounds as soon as they are born and begin to enjoy this new activity during their first three months. They become increasingly sociable and responsive during the second three months, smiling and giggling when someone talks to them. Children often begin imitating simple words after babbling in their own language for several months, usually during the nine- to twelve-month period. They often begin by saying "mama" or "dada," and recognizing the sound of their name. After their first birthday, babies often begin pointing at and naming things in their own intuitive language. As children approach the middle of their second year, they usually have about ten words in their vocabulary and begin stringing words together into simple phrases. By the age of two, children usually have more than three hundred words in their vocabularies and are able to make short sentences. They can understand simple sentences and enjoy listening to stories, looking at pictures in books, and making simple marks on a piece of paper with a crayon and pencil.

During the third year, a child's intellectual growth flourishes; her vocabulary normally expands to over a thousand words. The average two-and-a-half-year-old learns new words every day and begins to speak in more complicated sentences.

EARLY CHILDHOOD (FROM TWO TO SIX)

The years from two to six are often referred to as early childhood. It is during these years that a child's spiral of growth widens considerably, with new physical, emotional, intellectual, and social developments taking place simultaneously. On the whole, children become increasingly conscious of themselves as individuals, and begin forming their own unique personality and sense of self. It is during this time that children start to become active outside the home and receive a great deal of influence from teachers, peers, and other people. The following sections discuss the major developments during early childhood.

Development of Greater Physical Coordination

Children use their vertical posture and increased mobility to develop a variety of skills. They learn to balance left and right, forward and backward, up and down, movement and rest, and tension and relaxation. They start to do things like climb stairs; run; jump; sit in a chair; hop and skip; ride on a kiddy car, tricycle, or bicycle; throw or catch a ball or beanbag; and walk in a straight line. Their movements gradually become more skillful and graceful and more like those of grown-ups. Children learn to control the forces of heaven and earth within their bodies. Movements such as walking or running forward, jumping, throwing, standing up, and rolling or twirling toward the right require them to use more of the Earth's expanding force. Walking backward, sitting down, catching a ball, or rolling or twirling toward the left require the use of heaven's downward force.

All movements occur because the various spirals of the human body are either contracted or rotated inward, or expanded or rotated outward. The arms, hands, and fingers can be curled either toward or away from the body, or rotated to the right or left. The legs and feet also move in a similar pattern, as does the head, neck, spine, and torso. Running involves contracting each leg spiral toward the body and then thrusting it down and away from the body. It also involves coordination between the right side of the body, which conducts more of earth's force, and the left side of the body, which conducts more of heaven's force, as well as coordination between the legs and lower body and arms and upper body. Walking and skipping, twisting the torso, throwing, catching, jumping, and other activities involve coordinating the body's various spiral structures with the forces of heaven and earth, or contraction and expansion. (The universal spiral form is found throughout nature.) Children's bodily flexibility and conductivity to environmental energies allow them to explore the possibilities of movement with seemingly boundless energy, enthusiasm, and joy.

Development of More Refined Sensory Perception and Motor Control

As mental and physical coordination become more refined, children gain the ability to perform a variety of more delicate and controlled tasks. During the third year, they learn how to turn a doorknob, hold a crayon or pencil, unscrew lids from jars, stack blocks on top of one another, and draw vertical lines. They also learn how to distinguish small objects at a distance and can often discriminate between small printed letters.

Children learn to control their fingers with greater skill during their fourth year, and can pick up small objects, handle scissors, and use a pencil in a more controlled way. During their fifth and sixth years, increasing muscle control enables them to do things like use scissors to cut on a straight line, draw a simple stick figure of the human body—sometimes with simple details such as eyes, a nose, a mouth, and hair—and copy simple block letters. The ability to hold a brush, pencil, or crayon continues to improve, so that as intellectual and language abilities develop, they become able to write letters, words, and numbers to make increasingly expressive and complicated drawings. Increasingly fine sensory abilities also make it possible for them to learn how to read.

Development of a Wider Range of Emotional Responses

Early childhood is a time of rapidly changing and seemingly contrasting emotions. Children alternate between feelings of independence and dependence; between self-importance and the sense of being a small part of a larger group; and between self-assertive or insistent behavior and easy-going and more flexible behavior. In general, however, children develop a greater sense of identity and individuality during these years, and become increasingly sensitive to the wishes of parents and other people. The important thing to remember is that children are flexible and that their behavior changes from one moment to the next. If children are eating well, their emotions are generally smooth and steady, without the extreme tendencies produced by an unbalanced diet. Always remember that behavior and emotions are fluid and change in response to the child's environment and day-to-day diet.

One of the most noticeable aspects of childhood behavior is the alternation between more yang, *focal*, or concentrated activity, and more yin, *peripheral*, or diffuse activity. When children are going through a more focal stage, their energy is directed more inwardly. For example, they may not wish to go outside as much as usual, they may stick more closely to their mothers, and they may become less eager to get involved in new situations. During a more peripheral stage, children may have difficulty staying inside, sitting still, or focusing on one particular thing. They are often eager to explore new territory, meet new people, and try new things.

These and other complementary characteristics are influenced by the quality of food that a child receives and by the alternating rhythms of the environment. A diet based around more centrally balanced foods—whole cereal grains, beans, seasonal vegetables, and other supplementary items—promotes an even balance of both tendencies. Children who are nourished in a more balanced fashion tend to behave more evenly without becoming one-sided or extreme. They tend to be energetic yet peaceful; physically active and mentally bright; and very individualistic yet socially cooperative. In Figure 2.2 the foods that are located in the center of the spectrum are balanced. Items such as sugar and fruits, which are furthest from the center, are extremely yin foods. Eggs and poultry, on the other hand, are extremely yang items. Note that most foods located near the center are those emphasized in the macrobiotic diet.

A diet based on extremes—for example, more yang items such as salt (especially in processed foods), meat, eggs, poultry, and other animal products; and more extreme yin items such as simple sugars, fruits, chemical additives, raw vegetables, and spices—promotes more excessive behavior. Children who are fed such a diet often swing back and forth between extremes. They may become depressed or withdrawn, with sudden outbursts of anger or crying; they may seem brashly self-confident

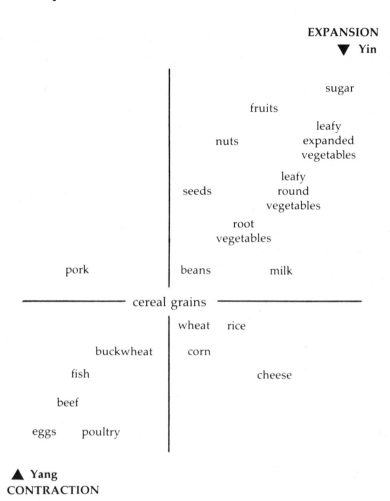

Figure 2.2   General Yin (▼) and Yang (▲) Categorizations of Foods

and demanding and then suddenly become insecure and fearful; or they may become unpredictable, stubborn, or difficult to manage.

Behavior is also influenced by cyclic changes in the environment. Children are especially sensitive to these changes. Environmental energy continually changes from season to season, from full to new moon, from morning to evening, and from day to night. During the autumn and winter, environmental energy becomes more subtle and quiet. Behavior tends to become more focal and inward, and home activities like reading, listening to music, or playing with blocks or toys are more appealing at these times. During the spring and summer, nature erupts with expansive force. Outdoor play, physical activity, and more diffuse behavior naturally occur in these seasons.

As we approach the full moon, the energy in the atmosphere becomes more expansive. Children tend to be more active during this half of the lunar cycle. Conversely, the new moon is a time of more quiet energy, and behavior tends to become more focal and inward as it approaches.

In the morning, most children spring from their beds and actively begin their day. School children wash, dress, eat breakfast, and then leave home. Morning is a time of active, rising energy and more outgoing, energetic, and peripheral behavior. Conversely, downward energy predominates during the late afternoon, evening, and nighttime. Children are naturally more quiet and reflective during these times, eventually returning to their beds to sleep.

Understanding how behavior changes in response to environmental and dietary factors is invaluable in helping parents discover why their children act the way they do.

Development of Language and Other Intellectual Abilities

Children use their greater mechanical, sensory, and emotional powers to acquire language. The acquisition of language occurs as the result of the interplay between yang and yin, or input and outflow. Language skills develop through the alternating sequence of listening and speaking and reading and writing. As the range of input that a child receives widens—for example, to include words and letters as well as actual objects and feelings—so does the ability to respond with language. The acquisition of language occurs in the form of a spiral that becomes continually wider and more complex throughout life. The average rates at which new words are learned during early childhood are presented in Table 2.1. As with all childhood development tables, including size and weight charts, these rates are simply estimates. A wide range of variation exists between one child and another.

Language itself has a variety of complementary functions, such as that existing between the more yang, self-directed function, and the more yin, outward-directed social function. When a child uses the self-directed function, she speaks to herself as a form of play, with little or no concern over whether someone else is listening. A child also uses language to communicate with others. At this time the social function

Table 2.1 Acquisition of Language

Age	Average Number of Words
12 months	3
18 months	22
2 years	272
3 years	896
4 years	1,540
5 years	2,072
6 years	2,562

From *Early Childhood Years* by Theresa and Frank Caplan, Perigee, 1983.

of language becomes more important. As a child grows, self-directed speech becomes internalized in the form of thinking. Children shift flexibly back and forth between both aspects.

As children develop, they learn to manage both the more yang sound vibrations of language and the more yin visual images of writing. When children learn to read, they do so by associating visual symbols, or letters, with both the corresponding sound vibration and with their image of the thing represented. It is better not to try to teach children to read before they show interest and are able to understand and speak to some extent—in other words, not until they have familiarized themselves with the vibrational aspect of spoken language.

Children learn about things through direct contact with them. After seeing the brightness of the sun and experiencing the warmth of its rays, a youngster develops an image and concept of the sun. The concept of water is established after children play in the bathtub or have a drink of cool clear water on a hot summer day. Ideas develop from a child's experiences.

Children learn to think abstractly by playing with actual objects, that is, by touching them, lifting them, putting them in their mouths, and comparing them with other things. By playing with things they are learning to discern complementary, or yin and yang, tendencies such as large or small (size), more compact or more expanded (shape), brighter or darker (color), beginning, middle, and ending (sequence), hard or soft (texture), wet or dry (humidity), and hot or cold (temperature).

Yin and yang also provide the framework for understanding space and distance. Children begin to play with spatial relationships soon after birth, as they become aware of basic distinctions such as self and object, near and far, up and down, and left and right. Children initially use the more yang sense of touch to measure space, but as time passes, they start to rely on their more yin visual perceptions.

Studies on how children learn show a fairly uniform sequence of development. Learning abilities develop one after the other in stages. The same principle applies to the development of consciousness in general. Children must fully develop through a particular level before the next one can be mastered. They cannot skip levels of consciousness nor can they be forced to learn certain concepts before they are ready.

Development of Social Awareness

Social relations also develop in the form of an expanding spiral. Most of a child's social interaction takes place within the family. The dreams, values, and perspectives of parents and other close family members are a primary influence in the development of a child's social outlook. Parents who are hardworking and humble, and who actively pursue a dream for the benefit of others, convey these values to their children. A warm, cooperative, and loving atmosphere at home helps a child to become a warm and loving adult.

Children use their developing motor, sensory, and language abilities to become increasingly active in social relationships. Around the age of two, children tend to engage in what is known as *parallel play*. When placed with other toddlers, they tend to watch each other and engage in small activities, but are playing more alongside rather than with their friends. By the age of three, however, they begin interacting more with others. They play together with their friends and begin to talk about what they are doing. They sometimes assume a variety of roles and begin to pretend. By the age of six, children usually engage in group play that involves a variety of more complex interrelationships.

Development of Food Awareness

Newborns eat in an instinctual and automatic manner. The sucking and swallowing reflexes are especially well developed at birth, and infants are strongly attracted to the sweetness of mother's milk. As the senses become further developed, babies begin to appreciate the taste and texture of foods and begin to recognize them by sight and smell. They derive pleasure from eating. When children are provided with a wide range of wholesome, natural foods, they learn to distinguish foods that are healthful and natural from those that are not. Children who do not eat meat or other fatty animal foods, for example, often find them repulsive and have no desire to eat them. As their range of social contact widens, children who eat a naturally balanced diet may find it difficult to understand why people eat foods that are unhealthful and, to them, unappealing. The preference for more balanced foods suggests that the instinct for maintaining health exists in children. When provided with the appropriate choices, children tend to select the foods that are the most wholesome and natural, although they may temporarily experiment with other foods as well.

Development of an Understanding of Nature

When provided with the proper environment, including a well-balanced diet, children develop a love and appreciation for nature. The alternating cycles of heaven and earth—day and night, waking and sleeping, movement and rest, and the progression of the seasons—provide the background for all learning and development. The recurrent pattern of nature causes children to develop an intuitive faith in the order of the universe. This basic understanding lies at the root of common sense and the ability to achieve health and happiness in life.

OLDER CHILDREN (FROM SEVEN TO SIXTEEN)

In traditional countries, the order of the universe helped men and women to comprehend the cycles of human life. In one cycle, girls were understood to begin a new phase every seven years and boys every eight years. The differences in time span are based on the physiological differences between the sexes. Women, for example, have fewer red blood cells than men (about 4.5 million per cubic millimeter compared with about 5 million per cubic millimeter), a smaller average body size, and a heart rate that averages about seven beats per minute faster. Women change more rapidly than men. Puberty, for example, begins about two years earlier in girls than in boys.

The age of seven in girls and eight in boys marks the beginning of a new cycle of development. It lasts until fourteen in girls and sixteen in boys and includes the onset of puberty. In the past, it was normal for puberty to start later than it does today. For girls to begin puberty at fourteen and boys at sixteen was not unusual. Today, however, it typically begins at age ten in girls and twelve in boys. Some children begin even younger. The increasing consumption of animal foods in the twentieth century is the most prevalent factor contributing to the drop in the age of puberty. In Eastern countries, however, it was believed that early puberty was not necessarily advantageous. Later maturity was traditionally considered to be more favorable for health and well-being. In the sections that follow, we discuss some of the changes that occur during the latter part of childhood.

Permanent Teeth

The appearance of permanent teeth indicates that a child's organs and bodily systems are becoming increasingly like those of adults. Permanent teeth begin to appear around the age of six, when the first molars appear behind the baby molars. They continue to come in until the third molars or wisdom teeth appear, usually between the ages of seventeen and twenty-one. Children lose their twenty baby teeth during this time and acquire thirty-two adult teeth. The adult teeth are usually completed by the age of twelve to fourteen, with the exception of the four wisdom teeth.

The adult teeth correspond to the vertebrae in the spine and also to all of the major organs and glands. When a permanent tooth appears, it shows that the organ it corresponds to has achieved a greater level of maturity. Table 2.2 shows the order in which the permanent teeth normally appear.

When a child has trouble with permanent teeth, it is generally due to imbalances in the diet during the time that they are coming in. Food is a primary factor influencing the size, shape, quality, spacing, and angle of the teeth, including their resistance or susceptibility to decay. A balanced natural foods diet furthers the growth and maintenance of strong and healthy teeth. The modern diet—rich in simple sugars, refined flour, and dairy and other animal products—contributes to a wide range of tooth and gum disorders. Problems with the teeth are related to the quality and functioning of the organs and systems to which they correspond. (For a discussion of what the teeth reveal about one's internal condition, you may wish to refer to one of our other books, *How to See Your Health: The Book of Oriental Diagnosis.*)

Growth Patterns

Physical growth tends to slow down during the latter part of childhood. The rate of growth becomes logarithmically slower from birth until puberty. The most rapid increase occurs before birth, when the rate of

Table 2.2   Estimated Time Schedule for Permanent Teeth

Age	Tooth	Location	Corresponding Organs and Functions
6–7	First molars or "six-year" molars (4)	Behind baby teeth	Lower digestive vessel, especially ascending colon
7–9	Incisors (8)	In place of first incisors (8)	Respiratory and circulatory organs and glands
8–10	Premolars (8)	In place of first molars (8)	Upper intestinal region; excretory system
10–13	Canines (4)	In place of first canines (4)	Liver, gallbladder, spleen, pancreas, stomach
	Second molars or "twelve-year" molars (4)	Behind first molars	Lower digestive vessel, especially transverse colon
17–21	Third molars or "wisdom teeth" (4)	Behind second molars	Lower digestive vessel, especially descending colon

growth in inches per year is about twenty. During the baby's first year, growth slows to about half the prenatal rate, to about ten inches; then during the second year the rate slows to half that of the previous year, to about five inches. Growth continues to slow down during the third and fourth years, reaching about half that of the baby's second year, or between two and three inches per year, at age five. This slower rate of growth continues until puberty, at which time growth accelerates. This acceleration in growth is known as the *adolescent growth spurt,* and today it most often occurs between ages nine and twelve in girls and between ages eleven and fourteen in boys. Growth during the years of seven to ten, just before puberty, is generally the slowest of any time during childhood.

A child's rate of growth does not remain constant throughout the year but varies from season to season. Children tend to grow taller in the spring and fatter in the fall. Diets tend to become lighter or more expansive in the spring, and this results in more vertical growth. In the autumn and winter, the diet generally becomes more yang or contractive, and also includes more proteins and fats. This causes more horizontal growth.

Boys and girls generally grow at about the same rates until around the ages of seven and eight. It is at this time that differences between the sexes become increasingly pronounced. Girls are more yang at birth and tend to be attracted to more yin proteins, liquids, fats, and carbohydrates during childhood. As a result, they tend to gain more fat during their adolescent period. Boys are more yin at birth and tend to be attracted to more yang minerals, proteins, and carbohydrates during childhood and thus experience a greater degree of muscle and bone growth during adolescence. The more yin components in a girl's diet tend to be attracted to the lower abdomen, buttocks and thighs, producing the characteristic triangle of the female form (▲). The more yang components in a boy's diet tend to be attracted toward the shoulders, causing the upper body to become more well-developed. This produces the characteristic inverted triangle of the male form (▼).

Emotional, Intellectual, and Social Development

As physical growth slows down just before puberty, a child's mental development accelerates. Children associate with teachers, playmates, and friends, and their scope of interaction continues to widen. They become interested in the outside world and their relationship to it, and are more keenly aware of male and female differences. Toddlers and young children often have playmates of both sexes, but during the latter part of childhood, they usually make more friends of the same sex.

The latter part of childhood is ideal for learning, study, and the development of intellectual and artistic abilities, as well as for the development of physical strength and coordination. Children can become actively involved in reading, writing, mathematics, cooking, music, art, sports, and other activities that challenge them mentally and physically.

In many traditional cultures, boys and girls were educated separately. The separation of sexes was often continued through primary and secondary school, and in many colleges. Many traditional educators felt that the separation made it easier for young people to concentrate on their studies and to develop a strong sense of identity.

Children in the middle years are in a stage of transition from toddlers to teenagers. They change from being completely dependent upon their parents to being more independent. They develop a longer span of concentration, more fluent speech, greater physical agility and control, the ability to reflect about themselves and their actions, and to regulate their emotions and behavior. Their thinking becomes deeper, involving larger areas of the brain than in early childhood, and they begin seeking explanations for many of the things they see around them. As children begin school and leave the home on a regular basis, they are exposed to many outside influences and begin comparing them with the attitudes, dreams, and patterns of daily life that they have observed at home. They become increasingly sensitive to the way in which others see them.

Children also develop the ability to take responsibility for small chores around the house, such as keeping their rooms clean, helping in the kitchen or in the garden or yard, and helping out with younger brothers and sisters. They also do not seek or require the more constant care and attention they did at a younger age, and begin taking initiative in expanding their horizons. They want to demonstrate—to themselves as well as others—greater independence by doing things like walking to school by themselves, riding their bicycles without supervision, crossing the street, and playing outside with their friends.

Even though children act more independently as they grow older, however, they still look to parents for approval and guidance. What they learn at home forms the basis of how they evaluate society. Parents, brothers and sisters, and other family members can help them to understand the many things they encounter in society and to cope with and overcome any failures, disappointments, and rejections that they experience. Some children may begin to question the values or practices that they learned at home as a result of being exposed to new ideas and ways of doing things. It is important for you to be sensitive to the many questions that your children have and to address them with love and understanding.

In the chapters that follow, we discuss some of the practical aspects of child care, starting with the foundation of a proper diet and daily care for health and well-being, and including tips on how to develop a healthy, loving, and supportive home environment.

Chapter 3
Introducing Children to Macrobiotics

I n Chapter 1, the importance of including the right amounts of balanced foods in your diet was discussed. A diet based on whole grains, vegetables, beans and sea vegetables, and soups was emphasized for optimum health.

Your child's nutritional requirements and tastes are different from yours and those of other family members. This chapter will help you meet the ever-changing needs of your growing youngster. Use the suggestions in this chapter as a guide in determining the best time to introduce new foods to your child, and to modify your family's dishes for your child to meet his preference for softer, less seasoned foods. Ways to vary your meals and satisfy your child's tastes are also included, as are warning signs that you can use to detect conditions caused by dietary imbalances. Please remember that these are general guidelines only; you must be flexible and adapt them to each child's changing needs.

If your child experiences an eating problem or if his body is not in balance, consult an experienced macrobiotic counselor and your pediatrician or other health care provider.

FEEDING YOUR CHILD

When babies reach the age of six to eight months, their first teeth begin to appear. Weaning can be begun at this time by gradually introducing solid foods. Some babies may show an interest in eating solid foods before this time, but as a general rule most are not so interested. Since babies are very yang and grow rapidly, it is important that their foods be very light and softly cooked. Use a larger proportion of water than for adult foods, and do not include salt in the beginning. After baby foods have been cooked over a low flame until soft, they can be placed in a suribachi or a hand baby food mill and puréed. Cereals can be made a little more yin by adding a very small amount of grain sweetener, such as good quality barley malt or rice syrup, on occasion.

Until the age of six to eight months, when the baby's teeth first appear, babies may be fed breast milk only. When the teeth begin to come in, decrease the amount of breast milk very slowly while increasing the volume of softly cooked solid foods as shown in Figure 3.1.

Introducing Solid Foods

The first foods that we introduce to the baby are whole cereal grains, beginning with rice, which is cooked very softly, mildly seasoned with the sweeteners mentioned, and puréed to a very thin creamy consistency. Introduce other grains one at a time. Let the baby get used to each for about a week before introducing another grain. Gradually add different grains over several weeks, to make a wide variety for the baby. If we introduce too many foods at once, babies may become confused and refuse to eat any solid foods, and may return only to breast milk.

Gradually introduce vegetables like broccoli, carrots, squash, cabbage, onions, and kale, and very tiny amounts of sea vegetables, such as kombu and wakame. These can be cooked and mashed together with the grains. It is recommended that softly cooked whole cereal grains of different varieties comprise at least half of the baby's intake.

Many times we are not careful enough in weaning babies properly and gradually. All children are different and must be weaned according to their individual needs and preferences. Most babies can be fully weaned by the age of one to one-and-a-half. Weaning a baby too soon may cause emotional as well as digestive problems.

As your child becomes older, the volume of water used in cooking can gradually be reduced. Slowly begin to give your child foods that have a consistency similar to adult foods, but that are still slightly softer and very mildly seasoned. By the time your child is about four years old, he can generally eat most of the foods you eat but more mildly seasoned. By the time children are about eight years old, they usually can eat whatever is served for adults. However, if some adult dishes are very strong or salty, it may be best to prepare a small volume for children with less salt. Until your child becomes an adult, it is wise to be very careful of strong or salty-tasting dishes.

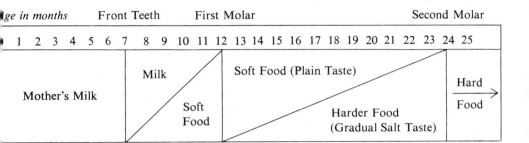

Figure 3.1 General Guidelines for Feeding Children

You will want to observe what your children eat daily throughout childhood and notice how they react to various foods. This will enable you to learn how to cook for your children, what their likes and dislikes are, how to handle any imbalances or sickness, and how to create happy and healthy children.

General suggestions for introducing solid foods are discussed in the following sections. Generally speaking, foods are listed in the order in which they are introduced. These are general guidelines only, not inflexible rules. Please modify and adapt them to your baby's changing needs and condition. Flexibility and sensitivity to your baby's needs are the key to implementing a healthful natural diet.

Whole Cereal Grains

Brown rice is usually the first cereal grain that is given to babies. It is very easy to digest, and babies generally like its taste. Rice is also the most balanced whole grain in terms of nutrients.

Cereals can be introduced around the age of six to eight months. You may give your baby cereal that is cooked with about five to seven times more water than grain. No salt should be added to the grain until around the age of one to one-and-a-half years. Instead of sea salt add a very tiny piece of kombu to the grains while cooking. Remember, kombu and other sea vegetables spread out while soaking, so use a very small piece of dried sea vegetables, less than a half inch square.

The main grains for babies are brown rice, barley, and sweet brown rice. Millet can be used from time to time also. Older children may be able to eat a small amount of buckwheat in the form of occasional soba noodles or kasha, but may become tight and contracted if they eat too much of it. Buckwheat, a very contracting food, is best not given to babies. Wheat, rye, and flint corn are more difficult to digest and are not usually recommended. Corn on the cob may be given in the summer, or fresh corn may be mixed with rice. All grains should be soaked prior to cooking to help make them softer and more digestible.

Cook your baby's cereals in their whole form. Do not grind them into flour before cooking, as your child needs the whole energy of the grain in order to digest it properly. After cooking grains in their whole form, you can place them in a suribachi or baby food mill and purée them to make them easy to swallow and more digestible.

Slowly begin reducing the amount of water used in making your child's grains over a period of two to three years. When preparing cereals for a baby six to ten months old, use five to seven times more water than grain. For a one year old, use three to four times more water than grain. By the time children are four years old, their whole grain dishes are just slightly softer than those of adults. As you reduce the volume of water used, also reduce the amount of grinding and puréeing in preparing the food. Eventually, mashing the food with a fork to make it soft should be enough, rather than milling or puréeing it.

If you continue to feed your child very soft or watery foods longer than necessary without giving enough finger foods or foods of firmer consistency, your child's intestines may become weak. If the intestines do not function properly, your child may not obtain enough nutrients from daily foods. By the time children are one-and-a-half to two years old, they can eat primarily softly cooked but unpuréed foods or finger foods such as soft cooked vegetables, sushi, small rice balls, or an occasional unsalted rice cake. Noodles and fu can be introduced around the age of ten months. Oatmeal, whole corn grits, and other minimally processed whole grain cereal products may also be introduced for occasional use.

Vegetables

Vegetables can be introduced approximately one month after the baby has been eating whole cereal grains and has adjusted smoothly to them. It is best to begin by introducing the sweeter vegetables such as squash, carrots, cabbage, onions, daikon, Chinese cabbage, and broccoli. Cabbage and cauliflower can be introduced slowly and withdrawn temporarily if gassiness results. Children do not particularly care to eat foods that have a bitter, sour, or hot taste. Sweet-tasting round, ground, or root vegetables are best. Babies often have difficulties chewing and digesting hard fibrous leafy greens, so it is better to use those which are softer and less tough, such as broccoli, cabbage, Chinese cabbage, or kale. Many times children do not enjoy eating leafy greens, so a special effort must be made to ensure that they do eat some. Greens may have to be mixed in with a child's grain or soup.

Soups

Soups or vegetable broths may be introduced after your child is six to seven months. They may include vegetables cooked with a tiny amount of either wakame or kombu sea vegetables. Soups can be cooked until the ingredients are very soft, and then puréed for a creamy consistency. Sea salt and tamari are best not added until children are about one to one-and-a-half. Mildly seasoned soups, including light miso soup, can be given after the age of two.

Beans

Beans can be introduced after one to one-and-a-half years, but many babies do not care for them until they are about two. It is very important not to give too many beans as they can be difficult for your baby's young intestines to digest, and may create digestive problems if eaten too often. Give them to your child in very small quantities only. Chickpeas, azuki beans, and lentils can be introduced for more regular use than other high-fat beans, along with kidney, navy, and other suitable beans for occasional use. Beans can be cooked with a very tiny amount of kombu to help soften their hard shells and to make them more digestible. Beans can be cooked well and thoroughly mashed before being served to babies.

Tofu and dried tofu can be included in the diet when your child is about ten months to one year old. Tempeh can be served after one-and-a-half to two years. Tempeh makes children very energetic, and for this reason, it is recommended that it be very mildly seasoned and cooked slowly over a low flame until it is very soft and easily digestible.

Sea Vegetables

Wakame and kombu are usually the first sea vegetables to be introduced in the child's diet. When cooking whole grain dishes, you can add a tiny amount of kombu instead of salt. Kombu can be cooked with root vegetables or nishime dishes. A tiny amount can also be cooked with beans. It is much easier for a baby to eat sea vegetables if they are cooked with other foods.

Sea vegetables such as arame and hijiki are usually not included in grain and bean dishes, but can be cooked with vegetables such as carrots, squash, onions, or dried daikon. Sea vegetable side dishes are mashed and served in very small quantities. Arame and hijiki can be introduced after a child is one to one-and-a-half years old. Because roasted nori is soft and easy to eat, children often like to snack on it. Nori can be introduced when the child is around one, but be careful not to overdo it. Sea vegetables are naturally salty and contain many minerals. Children can become too yang if they eat too large a volume.

Fruits and Sweets

Locally grown, temperate-climate fruits can be cooked, mashed, and given to children over the age of one to one-and-a-half. Young children can have a small serving an average of three or four times a week. It is ideal to give babies good-quality grain sweeteners more often than fruit sweets. Offer children grain puddings or warm amazaké, or add a little grain sweetener to their cereal from time to time. A few raisins can be sprinkled on top of their breakfast cereal on occasion. Some mothers think that babies should be given fruits from the beginning, but this is actually unnecessary. It is best not to force children to eat fruits or to give them to children too soon. Sweet-tasting vegetable and grain dishes are preferable.

On Snacks

Kanten is a very nice dessert for children. It is better for children to eat kanten at room temperature rather than icy cold. Warm or room temperature amazaké is also better than chilled amazaké. Always remember that rice balls, mochi, noodles, and raw carrots or celery are enjoyable as snacks. These snacks do not cause problems with children's health. It is important for children not to eat desserts before they go to bed. It is better for children to have them during the day or early in the evening.

—Aveline Kushi

Fish

Fish may be enjoyed occasionally by older children. A small portion of white-meat, non-fatty fish may be given from time to time, on an average of once a week. If you notice that fish makes your child very aggressive or irritable, it may be better to avoid it or serve it only on rare occasions such as holidays. Some children will not eat fish until the age of two or three, while others may refuse to eat it until they are older.

Pickled and Pressed Vegetables

Light pickles or mild pressed salads may be introduced after a child is two to three years old. Pressing is a form of marinating in which sliced vegetables are placed in a small pickle press and layered with sea salt. They should be very lightly salted and preferably have a sweet taste. They are best given in only very small quantities.

Beverages

During the time that babies are taking only breast milk, it is usually unnecessary to give them anything else to drink. When weaning begins, a baby may be given very mild, weak bancha or grain teas. Do not force babies to drink if they are not thirsty. Children over a year old can occasionally have a little warm apple juice or amazaké that has been diluted in water, or a combination of apple juice and bancha or grain tea.

Bubbly or carbonated waters can be enjoyed by older children on occasion. Be careful, though, not to give them to children too often. It is better to let children drink the fresh spring or well water that we use in daily cooking. They can also enjoy apple or carrot juice from time to time, but watch their condition closely to see how the juice affects them.

Oil

Oil is difficult to digest unless it is cooked with salt. As babies or small children should have only tiny amounts of salt, it is better not to give them too much oil. Natural oils can be obtained from grains, beans, and bean products, as well as from breast milk. Be very careful when introducing oil. When used excessively, it can cause a rash on the face or even a fever. It can also be a primary cause of diarrhea or green-colored stool. When you do begin to introduce oil, it is a good idea to serve a small amount of boiled red radish or boiled dried daikon at the same meal. These will help your child to digest the oil, and can be cooked together with grains or other vegetables or used in soups.

Seasonings

Sea salt can be introduced after a child is one to one-and-a-half. Only one or two grains of salt should be added to grain or vegetable dishes. Gradually increase the amount of salt in your child's diet over a period of several years. An eight- to ten-year-old can usually take the normal adult foods, but some dishes may need to be seasoned more mildly. A very small amount of tamari can be introduced in cooking after a child is one-and-a-half to two years old, while very light and mild miso soups can be introduced after two years of age. Tamari should be used in cooking and not as a condiment by children (or adults).

Children are usually able to eat the standard macrobiotic diet by the age of four or five, with a moderate use of salt, condiments, pickles, and oil. It is generally better to avoid giving items such as ginger, scallions, raw daikon, or other strong-tasting foods to babies or infants. A mild, naturally sweet taste as in grains and vegetables is used most frequently in preparing baby foods.

Condiments

Condiments that contain sea salt may be introduced after the age of one to one-and-a-half; however, they are best used only occasionally rather than on a daily basis, and in very tiny amounts. They can gradually be used more often and in slightly larger amounts as children grow. As with seasonings, adult-strength condiments can generally be used by children at the age of ten, but the use of salt is something that parents must continually monitor to prevent excess. It is better not to give young children stronger condiments like tekka, shio-kombu, very strong pickles, salt sauerkraut, and umeboshi paste. Some children may develop a taste for tamari soy sauce, and may want to use it on noodles or in other dishes. Parents need to watch this very carefully. It is better if children do not get into the habit of using tamari as a condiment, especially on rice or other cereals. If they occasionally use a few drops on noodles, fu, or mochi, it is recommended that parents be sure they use only a very tiny amount.

Snacks

Children can have difficulty digesting too much oil. It is therefore best if they are reasonable in their intake of oily snacks such as corn and other chips. Ideally, children eat items such as these on rare occasions only. Crackers and cookies can be eaten once in a while but not often. Dry, baked flour products need a lot of chewing, which is difficult for children. Also, the intake of dry baked goods tends to make children thirsty and causes them to drink more than usual. Rice cakes are better than hard, dry crackers or cookies, and can be enjoyed with a little apple butter on them from time to time. Be careful not to give children too much nut butter or tahini. Seeds and nuts are difficult to digest without thorough chewing, and are best eaten only on occasion. Children can enjoy a few raisins once in a while, or for a special treat, try cooking them with a little kuzu (a starch made from a wild vine) or kuzu and fruit and serving them as a dessert. Occasionally raisins can be cooked in cereals.

Snack foods that may be eaten regularly include rice, vegetable, or noodle sushi, carrot and celery sticks, noodles or noodle salads, rice cakes, any other whole grain or vegetable items. Other snacks are best used only occasionally.

WARNING SIGNS OF DIETARY PROBLEMS

There are several symptoms that may indicate an excessive intake of salt or an overly constricted condition. These signs are very important and require immediate attention if they occur at any time during childhood. Parents should suspect an overly yang condition if children display any of the following signs:

- Constant hunger or desire to eat.
- Screaming. When a child screams, it is often a sign of an overly yang condition. Whining, on the other hand, usually means that a child is too yin.
- Tightness, lack of flexibility, or lack of motion.
- Loss of the ability to crawl or walk.
- The development of bowed legs, as in rickets.
- Failure to grow. If a child is small at birth, for example five or six pounds, it is not necessarily a cause for concern. Smaller babies often have more vitality and capacity for growth than oversized babies.

After birth, however, children normally grow very rapidly. Too much salt can inhibit growth and cause children to remain small and contracted.

- Poor circulation. Salt can cause the peripheral capillaries to contract and inhibit blood flow. Cold hands or feet or a pale color may indicate this problem.

- Abnormal weight. There is no fixed rate at which children gain weight. The standard height and weight charts that are commonly used today are often unreliable. The growth rates on these charts tend to reflect averages among formula-fed children. Normal ranges for breast-fed children, or for children who follow a macrobiotic diet, have not yet been developed. Some children gain weight more rapidly, others more slowly. Babies who are smaller at birth tend to gain more rapidly, while larger infants tend to gain more slowly. As children get older, their rate of physical growth tends to slow down before adolescence.

  As long as children have good appetites, parents need not be overly concerned about their weight. If children become abnormally thin or fat, however, it may be a sign of too much salt or a sign of some other imbalance in the daily diet. An excessive intake of salt can cause a child to contract and become tight and skinny. In some cases, it can cause a child to retain water, fat, and other more yin substances and to become overweight.

- Dry or rough skin. Children normally have soft and smooth skin.

- A change in bowel movement toward dark or hard stools. The bowel movement is one of the most important things to check when trying to determine whether your child's condition is too yin, too yang, or in balance. Color and consistency, as presented in Figure 3.2, are the two main factors to consider. A soft, yellow bowel movement is best for nursing infants. As children get older, the bowel movement normally becomes more yellowish-brown and firmer in consistency. If children have frequent green and watery stools, their condition is chronically out of balance. A child who eats macrobiotically normally has one bowel movement per day. The stools of macrobiotic children do not have an unpleasant odor.

- In rare cases, a high fever. Fevers caused by too much salt are not as common as the other symptoms presented here. Please refer to Chapter 5 for a discussion of the other dietary imbalances that cause fever.

- Irregular appetite. As already stated, salt can cause children to eat

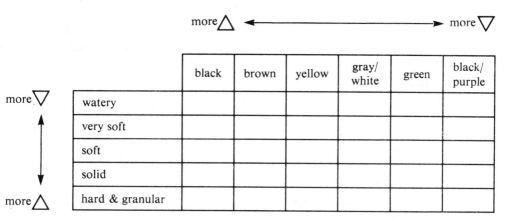

Figure 3.2   Classifying Bowel Movements by Color and Consistency

excessive amounts of food. Conversely, it can also cause the appetite to diminish because of its constrictive effect on the digestive organs.

MODIFYING YOUR CHILD'S DIET

The preceding symptoms can also result from the overintake of baked flour products or from a lack of variety—including fresh, leafy greens—in the diet. When such symptoms occur, or if you suspect an overly contracted condition in your child, your child's diet needs adjusting. In addition to eating a modified diet, your child may enjoy daily warm baths. Bathing helps the body discharge excess salt and minerals.

The first step toward creating a more natural balance is to limit your child's intake of excessively yang foods. Try limiting or temporarily avoiding the use of salt in cooking for your youngster. Nonsalty condiments can be used in place of salty ones. Grains such as sweet rice or oats—which are fattier than brown rice, barley, or millet—can be included more often. If necessary, the child's grain dishes can be prepared with a little more water than usual, so as to create a softer and creamier consistency. On occasion, a small amount of barley malt, rice syrup, amazaké, or raisins can be added to soft breakfast cereals. Puffed whole grain cereals can also be eaten with amazaké from time to time. Vegetables that become sweet when cooked—carrots, squash, cabbage, daikon, and onions—can be served to your child daily, together with lightly steamed greens, and pressed or boiled salads. A small amount of umeboshi or brown rice vinegar can be used as a seasoning when desired. Shiitake mushrooms can also be cooked with root vegetables or frequently used in soups. The special shiitake tea mentioned in the discussion of fever in Chapter 5 can also be given on occasion, perhaps several times per week for a month or so.

It is better to use lightly cooked vegetable dishes to restore your child to balance rather than a large amount of fruit, liquids, or concentrated sweeteners. In this way, the child can return to a more balanced condition without swinging to the opposite extreme. A small amount of cooked apple, pear or other fruit sauce, apple juice, fruit kanten or compote, or a small piece of fresh northern fruit may be eaten on occasion. It is better to keep the intake moderate.

Gomashio, umeboshi, and sweet nori condiments are good for certain conditions.

- *Gomashio* is normally a very good condiment for older children. Made from whole sesame seeds and sea salt, gomashio can be added to the diet of those with iron or calcium deficiency. When you make it at home, you can freely adjust the proportion of seeds to salt to suit any age or condition. When making children's gomashio, grind the seeds a little more finely than you would for an adult. More finely crushed seeds are easier to digest. Put the toasted seeds into a suribachi and grind them until they are about 75 percent crushed. The ratio of salt to seeds can be about one to twenty-five. As children get older, gradually adjust the proportion of salt to seeds. It can be about one to twenty by the age of ten. Condiments can also be made without salt. Plain toasted sesame or sunflower seeds are fine for children. A condiment can also be prepared with roasted sesame seeds and a small amount of roasted wakame sea vegetable. Roast the ingredients and then crush them in a suribachi as done when making gomashio.

- *Umeboshi* can be used medicinally for children with stomach trouble or other digestive upset. A very small piece can be put in their soft cereal. Children also enjoy rubbing a little umeboshi plum on their corn on the cob. Be careful about the amount of umeboshi that children eat. Even when they are five or six, it is better to limit their intake to an occasional half plum. As with other condiments, umeboshi should not be given to a child who is becoming too tight. Stop giving umeboshi to your child until his condition returns to normal.

  If children eat something a little bit salty, such as a piece of pickle, once in a while, there is usually no need to worry. But watch their condition to see how it affects them.

- *Sweet nori condiment* is very mild and can be given to children on occasion. Nori condiment can be sweetened by adding a little barley malt while it is being prepared.
- *Sauerkraut* tastes milder and less salty when cooked. Milder sauerkraut is usually better for children.
- *Ginger* and condiments with a spicy flavor are generally too strong for children.

Eating Habits

Your children's food should be tasty and attractive. If your children are not hungry, do not force them to eat. If you do, they will usually end up playing with their food. It is best to serve children only small quantities of food at a time so that they do not waste any. If they want more, give them small portions so that they finish what is on their plates. Remember that children do not require the same amount of food that adults do. Encourage children to give thanks before and after each meal. It is important for them to learn to have an appreciation for food and for the natural world that provides it.

DEALING WITH EATING PROBLEMS

Many children experience eating problems; however, with a few variations in approach, a little innovation, and some insight, you may persuade your child to eat healthfully and to develop good eating habits.

When Babies Refuse to Wean

A mother can begin to wean her baby when he is between the ages of one and one-and-a-half. Some children are very easy to wean, while others do not want to stop nursing. Each baby is different. If your baby refuses to be weaned, try to be patient and to rely upon your common sense. You may need to be firm when offering solid foods instead of breast milk. Remember, however, that weaning must be done gradually, until eventually your child is breastfeeding just once a day, at bedtime. If you can reduce the number of nursing periods to just one a day, it will make it easier for you to wean the baby entirely. Weaning a baby without a gradual reduction in the number of feedings may result in his refusal to eat solid foods. If the baby foods that you prepare taste delicious and look appetizing, the weaning process will go more smoothly.

When Children Refuse to Eat by Themselves

When a baby first begins to eat solid foods, his mother will, of course, have to feed him. Most children quickly become interested in using a spoon and feeding themselves. Mothers can teach their babies to do this properly without making too much of a mess. Some children may refuse to feed themselves because they feel insecure or neglected and want more attention. Try to figure out why your child is refusing to feed himself, and then correct the problem. In most cases, children are naturally curious and want to eat by themselves.

Overeating

As mentioned earlier in this chapter, a common cause of overeating is the overuse of salt or the consumption of too many dry, baked flour products such as cookies, bread, or crackers. When this occurs, reduce your child's intake of these items and include more fresh and lightly cooked dishes.

Undereating

Undereating is often caused by a lack of variety in the diet. Many children like to eat greens. However, it may sometimes be difficult to get them to eat enough greens or other vegetables. Find out which vegetables your children like and let them have as much as they want. Then gradually increase their variety. Sometimes, you may have to disguise vegetables by cooking them in soups or grain dishes. Put vegetables in sushi or cut them in interesting shapes with a cookie cutter or a knife. Practices such as these will arouse your children's interest and make it easier for them to begin to eat a variety of vegetables.

A child who eats too many snack foods may refuse to eat a well-balanced meal of grains, vegetables, sea vegetables, beans, and other dishes. You as parents will want to make sure that your children do not snack to the point of interfering with their regular diet.

School Lunches

Ideally, the school of the future will serve balanced, natural food lunches prepared daily according to macrobiotic principles. Chefs will be selected from among persons who have studied macrobiotic cooking, and will work with parents in determining daily meal plans. Parents will then not have to worry about children eating junk foods or high-fat, high-sugar items while in school.

At present, however, parents cannot depend on the quality of foods offered in school lunch programs. In certain areas, some parents have interested schools in including more natural items, but the public schools have generally been slow in adapting a more natural nutritional approach.

A more sensible plan is for children to avoid unhealthful foods at school by bringing a lunch from home. If necessary, you can meet with your child's teacher or principal and explain why you wish to prepare your child's lunch. If schoolchildren enjoy a hearty breakfast, then they can usually get by with a lighter lunch. Then, when they return from school in the afternoon, they can enjoy a light snack of noodles, sushi, leftovers, fried rice, or some other dish.

Sushi and rice balls are ideal foods for lunch boxes as are sandwiches made with whole grain breads. Carrot or celery sticks, lightly boiled or raw salads, mochi, an occasional raw apple or piece of naturally sweetened pie, and other simple dishes can also be included. Many of these items can be made to look like the foods that other children take for lunch. Wholesome, natural dishes can be made to resemble practically any food so that children who bring a macrobiotic lunch from home do not have to appear especially "different." Remember that a growing number of families eat a more natural diet and many children bring specially prepared lunches to school. Specific suggestions for preparing a variety of school lunches—including recipes and menus—are presented in *Macrobiotic Family Favorites* (see the Recommended Reading List).

TEACHING HOW FOODS AFFECT BEHAVIOR

The foods that parents prepare and serve to their children daily are the most important factors in determining how the children interact with other children and adults. The actions and behavior of parents and other adults also influence children, but the key factor is daily food. Children who eat well generally develop a good-natured, peaceful disposition and enjoy interacting with other children and adults. Watch what your children eat and observe how different foods affect their behavior. Through careful observation, you will learn how to adjust your cooking to help them. It is a good idea not to make a habit of telling your children how they should and should not behave. When they eat something and do not feel well, or if they do not get along with others, do not scold them or make them feel bad. Talk with them and try to get them to see how certain foods affect them. Show children how they can change. Teach them at an early age to notice how food affects their behavior and health.

Try to teach, encourage, and inspire children rather than dominate or control them. In this way, they will be happy.

Chapter 4
Daily Care

There is a proverb in the Orient: "The soul of three years lasts a hundred years." This traditional belief reflects the idea that whatever children learn in their first three years will influence them throughout life. The parents' character and lifestyle have a tremendous impact on their children. If the father and mother are happy, loving, and positive about life, their children will probably assume a similar attitude. If they quarrel or have a negative outlook, their children can easily grow into quarrelsome or negative adults.

Children are often mirror images of their parents. If parents spend their evenings watching television, for example, their children will probably grow to imitate them. Similarly, adults who behave in an offensive way may find their children copying their manner. A baby watches her parents very carefully. They are crucial models for her development. When children behave in an unacceptable way, parents must recognize their influence and responsibility.

If profanity is used at home, parents should not be surprised if children start to use the same words. When adults use elegant and respectful language, children tend to develop a similar way of speaking. People who are spiritual do not use profanity. They prefer more refined and respectful language. Setting the right example begins as soon as your child is born.

WELCOMING A NEW BABY

When a child is born, she naturally becomes the center of the family. If the parents are eating well and in good health, they should have very little difficulty adjusting to the new baby. It will happen quite naturally. Of course, with the birth of a child, parents do need to make some changes in their daily lives. If a mother is eating well, the quality of her breast milk will most likely cause her baby to be very peaceful, a good sleeper, and, in general, healthy and content. When this is the case, parents have the freedom to go out socially with their new baby and have their privacy as well. Of course, once the baby arrives, the parents will most likely limit their social activities to those that they can easily handle with the baby present and those that are most peaceful for the baby as well. If a mother is not eating a balanced diet—eating too many sweets or too much salt, for example—problems may develop with her breast milk and her baby may not enjoy a balanced physical condition. It is very important for a mother to eat well during the time that she breastfeeds, both for the health of her child and to make her adjustment to parenthood as well as her husband's as smooth as possible.

HELPING OTHER CHILDREN ADJUST TO A NEW BABY

Before a new baby arrives, it is best to prepare older children by talking with them about the baby. You can invite them to go shopping for baby clothing and accessories. Be careful not to talk too much about the coming baby, however, because your other children may become jealous. When the baby arrives, try not to focus attention exclusively on the baby when your older children are present. Sometimes, older children may think that their parents like the baby more than them if their parents are always talking about the new baby. Try to give the older children a little more attention to reassure them that they are still loved. Involve your older children in bathing the baby, changing diapers, and other simple routines. The arrival of a new baby can be difficult, especially for children under five. Parents need to be understanding, patient, and loving at this time.

CREATING THE BEST HOME ENVIRONMENT

Education begins at home. Guiding children to become healthy, loving, and happy adults is one of the joys and responsibilities of parenthood. Home education is a joyful, loving process. Ideally, parents should create a home environment that does the following: encourages their child's natural curiosity, her dreams, and her ambitions; instills through example the values of honesty and modesty; allows their child to be responsible for household chores; and establishes good family relations and family togetherness.

Encourage Natural Curiosity

Children are always seeking to learn, to know, and to understand. Encourage this natural curiosity. It is easy to misunderstand a child's questioning. When a child asks, "Mommy, how did I come here?" a mother may blush and say, "Ask Daddy." When she asks her father, he may say, "You're too young to know about these things. When you start school, ask your teacher." Later, if she asks the teacher, the teacher may say, "Your parents will discuss the facts of life with you when you're old enough. Better get busy with your math and reading."

In this case, the parents may think that the child is asking about sex, but what she really wants to know is how she came to be born on this Earth. She may be seeking answers to very large questions. If you respond to this curiosity, you can help your child develop insight, a rich imagination, and a large view of life. Try to use simple, clear, and poetic language when explaining things to children. The simpler and clearer, the better.

"How" and "why" are two things that children always want to know. However, these questions are usually not answered in school. If, for example, a child questions why one and one equals two, she would probably be thought strange. Or if a child were to ask a science teacher, "Why does gravity exist?" the teacher would probably answer, "Simply because it does."

Children are required to memorize a great deal of information in school, but are rarely encouraged to ask "how" or "why." Since these questions are usually ignored, the natural curiosity that children possess is usually extinguished by the time they finish school. As a result, adults often do not know the answers to the most fundamental questions of life or how to solve such basic problems as what to eat to keep their health.

When children come to us with questions, we should encourage them to think and discover solutions for themselves. We should use our understanding of the order of the universe and nature to point our children in a direction. Parents can judge their own understanding by the way that children react to their explanations. If our expression is dry and conceptual, children will let us know by rapidly losing interest. If our expression is clear and dynamic, children will become attentive listeners.

Encourage Dreams and Ambitions

Whatever your children hope to do, you as parents should encourage them to follow through with their ambitions. If they want to play the piano, garden, learn to cook, study physics, or whatever, support them totally. Nourish their aspirations and grow with them.

When Michio came to America, he did a variety of odd jobs, such as washing dishes and working as a bellboy. He wrote often to his parents in Japan. They had trouble understanding why he was doing such things after having graduated from Tokyo University, which is the top university in their country. They expected him to be more like his classmates who were climbing the corporate ladder or making places for themselves in the fields of education and government. Both of his parents were educators, and they wondered why he was not pursuing a similar career.

More than fifteen years after Michio had left Japan, his parents came to America with the hope of convincing him to return. They worried about him. They believed that had he remained in Japan, he would have become far more successful. They stayed in our home in Cambridge, Massachusetts, where we gave evening classes for a small group of students. When class finished, Michio would go down to the basement to pack brown rice, azuki beans, miso, and other macrobiotic staples for sale to a small group of students and friends. This small business eventually grew into Erewhon, one of the largest distributors of natural foods in the world.

For two weeks, his parents observed our actions without comment. Finally, one morning, they said, "Michio, we would like to talk to you this evening." We expected them to ask us to return to Japan. We knew they were acting out of love and could not think of a way of refusing them, even though we had committed ourselves to continuing our macrobiotic activities in America.

That night, they attended the class. They sat in their usual places at the back of the room and kept silent. When the class had finished, they waited until everyone left and then closed the door. Michio steadied himself. Suddenly, to his complete surprise, his parents knelt in front of him and bowed. Then, his mother said, "Michio, we want to become your students," and added, "I don't know much about macrobiotics yet, or about what you are teaching. But if you ever need someone to test whether or not what you are saying is true, let me be that person. I don't mind giving my life for your dream. Your father and I support you completely."

When we visited Japan almost ten years later, other family members had a similar reaction to our macrobiotic pursuits. We went to the Kushi family temple described in the Introduction and met with a large group of relatives, many of them elderly, including several in their nineties. We spoke for close to three hours. The following morning, several relatives came to our room and said, "Everyone who listened to you yesterday has decided to begin macrobiotics. We would like to become your students."

We experienced a joy similar to the one we felt when Michio's parents had recognized our activities many years before. We felt very thankful to be part of such a wonderful family. Our parents and relatives have inspired us to return our happiness unconditionally to others.

As these stories show, the love and encouragement of parents and other elders are so important for a child's happiness. Nourishing the dreams and ambitions of children can be far more important than giving them money or possessions. Encourage children to pursue their hopes and ambitions.

Instill Honesty

During the Russo-Japanese War, Japan's naval forces were led by a man named Admiral Tōgō. Even though it was relatively unsophisticated, the Japanese Navy overcame tremendous odds and managed to destroy the Russian Navy in the seas around Japan.

Admiral Tōgō never sought fame or personal glory. He was a traditional samurai. He often told stories, including one about lying. When he was a boy, his mother would occasionally give him a piece of rice candy as a treat. She kept the candy in a jar on a high shelf in the closet. One day, he asked her for a piece of the candy, and she told him there wasn't any. That afternoon, when she left the house, he went straight to the closet and piled up cushions so he could reach the jar. He found several pieces of candy there and climbed down and ate them. On the following day, his mother went to the closet to get him a piece of candy and discovered the empty jar. She asked if he had stolen the candy, and he replied, "No, I didn't. There wasn't any candy left. You told me so." His mother was quiet for a moment. Then she knelt down in front of him. She bowed and said, "I was wrong. I'm sorry that I lied to you. It was my fault, and I'll never lie to you again." At that moment, he understood how wrong it was to lie. He also saw what a wonderful spirit his mother had. The experience created a deep love and respect for his mother and taught him a lesson that influenced his adult life.

If, instead of self-reflecting, she had tried to conceal her mistake or had attacked or reprimanded her son, his attitude would have been very different. Her approach had a deep and long-lasting effect; Admiral Tōgō was known throughout his life as an extremely honest man.

Parents are encouraged to keep their promises to children. If we tell children that we will take them to a museum or buy them a new toy, we should be sure to do what we say. If we break our word, children will learn to distrust us. Breaking promises is a form of lying. Therefore, be careful not to make promises that cannot be kept.

Choose a Modest Lifestyle

Modesty is very important. It is better to keep food, clothing, and everyday items as simple and natural as possible. An abundance of rich foods or material goods, or an overly protective environment can make a child weak. Children who are spoiled often cannot cope with difficulties and problems later in life.

Many great people grew up in humble surroundings where they learned to be moderate. Many leaders were taught from childhood to be modest. In Japan, for example, the shogun received a very strict education. As a child, he would accompany samurai and other adults on hunting trips. In the evening, the adults would sit around a camp fire and eat the wild game caught during the day. The mood was festive, with plenty of eating and drinking. However, the future shogun was not allowed to participate. Instead of enjoying the wild game, he had to eat more humble fare, such as roasted brown rice and pickles.

The members of the Imperial Family received similar training. The crown prince was not permitted to sit in a chair or on cushions if anyone in his party had to stand. He could not eat white rice, sugar, or other refined foods. Because of this custom, the diet of the Imperial Family has remained simple. Even today, members of the emperor's family eat brown rice, fresh garden vegetables, miso soup, pickles, and sea vegetables.

After World War II, some people began to feel it was unfair that the emperor could not enjoy meat, cheese, sugar, and other luxury items. It was even suggested that he stop eating brown rice and, like most Japanese, begin to eat white rice. The emperor understood their feelings but very politely told them that he preferred to continue to eat brown rice. Someone then suggested that brown rice did not taste as good as white rice and was more difficult to chew. Even though he disagreed, the emperor finally compromised by eating a mixture of partially polished rice and barley in order to please his people. He felt it improper to eat completely polished rice, regardless of public opinion. The diet of the Imperial Family is now more humble than that of the average Japanese family.

Let Children Help Around the House

Children are often eager to help with household chores. They enjoy working with their parents, brothers and sisters, and other people in the home. When children express the desire to participate, let them do so. They can help with cooking, cleaning, taking out the trash, and other chores that are suitable for their ages. Encourage children to take part in your daily routines.

Establish Order in Family Relations

It is important to treat younger members of the family with love and care. Grown-ups need to view children with patience and understanding, although their behavior may at times seem disorderly or immature. We should also show respect and love for the elders in our family even if, at times, we disagree with their opinions. When parents receive older guests in their home with politeness and respect, children learn to extend similar courtesy to teachers and elders in society. Children observe how their parents relate to others and imitate what they see.

Age distinctions are often blurred by language. The pronouns "you" and "I," for example, are used in English regardless of a person's age. We address a three-year-old child as "you," and do the same with a seventy-year-old grandmother. A second-grader refers to himself as "I," as does a retired grandfather. Parents address their children as "you," and children do likewise when addressing their parents. Some people even address their parents by their first names. However, other languages often utilize a variety of pronouns for different occasions. In Japanese and French, for example, more polite forms are used when addressing an older person, and informal words are used when speaking to peers or juniors. Ideally, language should acknowledge differences in age; it is better if we relate to children in a way that is a little different from the way we relate to our parents and elders.

Encourage Family Activities and Togetherness

In the past, families shared or discussed their experiences regularly; today, however, this practice is less common. People today tend to pursue their own interests, and often do not involve their parents, children, or other family members in what they do. Traditional families, on the other hand, would usually gather together for the main meal and frequently pray or attend religious services together. Holidays were also times when kinfolk would gather to give thanks and enjoy festive dishes.

As we have said, it is important for families to eat together at least once a day. But besides sharing mealtimes, it is important to do a variety of other things together. Holidays and birthdays are wonderful occasions for family gatherings. Grandparents, brothers and sisters, and other relatives not living at home can be invited to these events. A variety of special party foods can be enjoyed by everyone.

Picnics, outings to the beach or countryside, concerts, movies, and visits to museums are only a few possible family activities. Reading stories to children in the evening is also very enjoyable. If someone in your family plays a musical instrument, your whole family can enjoy an informal concert or group sing-along.

Events that involve the whole family bolster confidence and increase cooperation and harmony. Such activities help members realize that they are supported by a larger group.

OUR CHILDREN ARE OUR FUTURE

Creating a family is a marvelous thing. We could have been born on one of millions of other planets in the universe, or we could have been born a thousand years ago or a million years from now. But we as individuals—our spouses, parents, children, and brothers and sisters— chose this planet at this time. Our relationship to the people in our family and to our friends is truly precious.

The possibility of developing unconditional love is present within every family. Families are microcosms of the order of the universe in which the laws of love and harmony continually work. The members of a family share blood and spirit, yet each member is unique. The complementarity that exists between husband and wife, parents and children, brothers and sisters, and seniors and juniors broadens and deepens the underlying harmony. A family is like a stream that flows through time and space. Growth, learning, sharing, and loving are all part of the stream. Joy and sadness, difficulty and happiness, and youth and old age are waves that come and go. Yet the stream continually flows on and becomes a mighty river.

To guide children toward health and happiness is to do the work of God. It is far more important than building an empire or acquiring a billion dollars. Even if you conquer the world, you have not fully developed if you are unable to create a happy and healthy family. The health and happiness of your family is a barometer of your spiritual development. Titles such as king, emperor, scientist, president, or professor are only human creations, whereas a happy and healthy family is the creation of the universe itself.

Making your family healthy and happy is a direct contribution to world health and world peace. What we do for our families is our contribution to the world. There is really no difference between the health and well-being of your family and that of your community, the nation, and the world. Educating children to become healthy, productive, and fulfilled adults will benefit humanity now and in the future. Our children are our future. How this future unfolds is up to us.

RECOMMENDATIONS FOR DAILY LIVING

Along with selecting and preparing the right foods, the health and well-being of every family member are also enhanced by keeping a clean, orderly, and natural environment in the home. The way we orient our daily lives—from the type of activity we engage in to the materials we choose for clothing, toys, and home furnishings—has a strong influence on all family members. The following recommendations can help the whole family enjoy a more natural, healthful, and satisfying way of life:

- *Wash as needed, but avoid long hot baths or showers.* It is better for children not to take very hot baths or remain in the tub or shower until their skin becomes wrinkled, as this drains minerals from the body.

- *Every morning and/or night, scrub and massage the entire body with a hot damp towel until the skin becomes red.* If you do not have time to scrub your whole body, at least do the hands and feet, making sure to do each finger and toe. Scrubbing activates circulation and the flow of energy throughout the body. Parents can do this for their children and encourage them, when they become old enough, to do it themselves as a daily health habit. A hot towel rub makes one feel refreshed and renewed.

- *Encourage family members to wear only cotton clothing next to the skin, and especially cotton undergarments.* Cotton allows the skin to breathe and exchange energy with the environment. It is better to avoid wearing synthetic, woolen, or silk clothing directly on the skin. Many shops and mail-order houses sell high-quality baby and children's clothing made of cotton. It is better for adults to avoid wearing excessive metallic jewelry or accessories on the fingers, wrists, or neck, and to keep such ornaments simple, graceful, and as natural as possible.

- *Go to bed before midnight and get up early in the morning for the most restful sleep.* It is also best for children to go to bed and get up at regular times, as this establishes a more harmonious natural rhythm.

- *Encourage every member of the family to be as active as possible in daily life and to participate in home activities* such as cooking, scrubbing floors, cleaning windows, and washing clothes. Children can participate in simple household chores such as cleaning, sweeping, cooking, doing dishes, raking leaves, shoveling snow, and taking out the trash. Systematic exercise programs such as yoga, Do-In (a form of self massage) and sports are also healthy and enjoyable, and are things that the entire family can do together. It is important to encourage children to develop physical strength, flexibility, and endurance so that they may enjoy a healthy and productive life. Children can also be invited to assist with cooking or, with proper supervision, to try cooking by themselves from time to time.

- *Encourage all family members, if their conditions permit, to go outdoors often and in simple clothing.* Walking barefoot on the beach, grass, or soil, whenever possible, is recommended. It is important for children to play outside in the sunshine whenever possible, preferably once a day, regardless of the season. Frequent family outings to the beach, mountains, parks, or other outdoor recreation areas are also recommended. Encourage children to have regular contact with nature as a means of developing a sense of wonder, marvel, and appreciation.

- *Keep the home clean and orderly.* Pay particular attention to the areas where food is prepared and served. Involve children as much as possible in daily clean-up activities. Keep children's sleeping and play areas clean and orderly, and encourage them to take responsibility for keeping these areas neat and clean.

- *Use natural materials in the home.* Sheets, futons (Japanese-style sleeping cushions), towels, and pillowcases made of cotton, incandescent lighting, natural wood furnishings, and cotton or wool carpets all contribute to a softer and more natural home environment. Try to keep children's toys and playthings as "natural" as possible—the energy of wooden toys, for example, is preferable to that of toys made from plastic or metal or the energy of electronic devices.

- *Use a gas or wood stove for cooking, if possible, rather than electric or microwave cooking devices.* Microwave ovens and electric stoves disturb the natural energy of food. Microwaves cook food from the inside out, causing individual molecules to "explode," a phenomenon that resembles the uncontrolled proliferation of cells in cancer. Microwave ovens generate radiation and electromagnetic waves. A background paper issued in 1989 by the Congressional Office of Technology Assessment stated, "It is now clear that low frequency electromagnetic fields can interact with individual cells and organs to produce biological changes." Laboratory experiments suggest that electromagnetic fields can interfere with DNA and stimulate chemicals that are linked to cancer in cells.

- *Avoid or minimize the use of electric objects close to the body,* including electric shavers, hair dryers, stereo headsets, blankets, heating pads, toothbrushes, and toys.

- *Keep large green plants in the home* to freshen and enrich the air. Plants can also be placed in children's play areas. Make sure they are nonpoisonous in case of accidental ingestion. Keep the leaves of plants out of the reach of small children. Open windows daily to permit fresh air to circulate, even for a short time in the cold weather.

- *Use earthenware, cast iron, or stainless steel cookware in the kitchen,* rather than aluminum- or teflon-coated pots.

- *Encourage family members who watch television to do so at a distance and to sit at an angle to the set in order to minimize exposure to radiation.* Color television is best minimized or avoided for maximum health, as is watching television during mealtimes. It is better to encourage children to develop creativity and imagination through study, reading, art, music, sports, daily chores, hobbies, and play outside than to allow their natural capacities to wane as a result of an overdependence upon television, video games, and other forms of prepackaged entertainment.

On Family Entertainment

Families do not sing together as they often did in the past. Children should sing at home and at school. When my children were small, we would often sing together, but since we did not know many English songs, we usually sang Japanese ones.

It is not a good idea to let children watch television for many hours at a time. Children should be encouraged not to watch programs that show violence, or wild, strange, or sexual behavior, or use vulgar language. Such shows are best avoided, as they disturb a child's natural perception and can blind children to many things around them. Select movies, television shows, and music that is most suitable for children. Encourage them to play outside whenever possible, and take them often to parks or outdoor play areas. Ask them to help clean the house or to be active in sports rather than watch television. If children are watching too much television, parents can spend more time doing other activities with them. Visit the country, which offers children a natural environment and the opportunity to observe nature and the changing of seasons more clearly than they can in the city.

—Aveline Kushi.

According to recent surveys, the average American household watches television for four to five hours each day. In a survey conducted by the American Academy of Pediatrics, children between the ages of two and twelve were found to spend an average of twenty-five hours a week in front of the television. Many were found to spend more time watching television than attending school. The American Academy of Pediatrics also found that television viewing promoted the eating of poor-quality foods as well as obesity. Many of the commercials on television feature high-fat and highly sugared foods. Children often eat while watching television and are much less physically active. The so-called "video revolution" of the 1990s, in which cable television, VCRs, and video games have proliferated, has increased the potential for excessive viewing on the part of children and other members of the family.

Encourage children to participate in life through direct experience and not to content themselves with the role of spectators.

Encourage them to continually challenge themselves physically, intellectually, and creatively.

- *Avoid cosmetics and body-care products that have chemicals in them.* Use natural soaps for laundry and washing, and natural toothpaste, sea salt, dentie tooth powder, or clay for tooth care.

ACTIVITIES OF DAILY LIVING

You should take an active role in the various aspects of your child's life—from helping her to sleep soundly and comfortably to instilling good cleaning and grooming habits.

Sleeping

You are encouraged to observe each of your children to find out what each child's sleeping cycle is. Some may want to go to sleep early and wake up early, while others may want to stay up later and sleep later. Try not to force them to sleep earlier than they are generally used to as this may cause them to wake up very early in the morning. It can be very tiring for the parents when a child wakes up too early. When children are very young, they naturally want to go to bed early, but as they grow older, their sleeping times need adjusting. At a young age, they usually go to sleep around seven or eight o'clock and wake up around six or seven. Older children may go to bed between eight and nine and sleep until seven or eight. Once they are in school, some children may not want to go to bed early, but it is important that they go to bed at a reasonable hour so that they will be alert and able to concentrate on their studies. Try different approaches to help them relax and go to sleep at an appropriate hour on school days. Giving them a warm bath, reading a book, and telling them a story, or encouraging them to listen to relaxing music may calm children enough so that they feel sleepy.

• Napping

When children are very young (under a year old), they usually take a nap in the morning and one later in the afternoon. As they grow older, they may take only an afternoon nap. After the age of two or two-and-a-half, most children are no longer interested in taking a regular nap. Do not force your child to nap if she does not want to sleep. When children are tired or need sleep, if their surroundings are made more calm and relaxing, they will go to sleep. After the age of three, most children will nap only occasionally.

• Sleeping Materials

We recommend that futons, mattresses, sheets, blankets, quilts, pillow-cases, and other sleeping materials be made of high-quality cotton. If your child still wets the bed at night, you can place a plastic or rubber sheet on top of the mattress, but always place a heavy cotton sheet over it so that the cotton is against your child's skin. Stop using the plastic sheet when the child stops bed-wetting.

Sleepwear can also be made of high-quality cotton material. Cotton is warm and comfortable while you are sleeping. It is better to wear loose-fitting pajamas. Pajamas with attached socks or foot extensions are not recommended as they interfere with the circulation and often make children uncomfortable and unable to sleep properly. Some children feel confined when they wear pajamas of this type. Instead of wearing socks or pajamas with feet, the child can be covered with an extra blanket if necessary.

• Sleeping Position

In some parts of the world, children sleep on their stomachs. How-ever, we have observed that children sleep better and more soundly on their backs. If children are sick or not feeling comfortable for some reason, they will often sleep on their stomachs. But if they eat high-quality food prepared properly, they will sleep very well on their backs.

• Effects of Food on Sleep

Dinner is a very important meal for children. What is served for their evening meal can determine the time they go to sleep, how often they wake during the night, and what time they get up the next morning. For the evening meal, it is better to serve foods that are easily digested. If a mother wishes to give her children snacks or desserts, it is better if she serves them at lunch or sometime before dinner. If desserts are eaten too late in the evening, they may not be easily digested and may cause problems with sleep.

If children eat fruit or drink juices in the evening, it may cause them to wet the bed. Try not to give children salty or oily foods at night, as these can cause them to crave liquids. Drinking too much can then cause bed-wetting. It is better to give children foods that have the type of energy that will help them to hold in liquid while they sleep. Mochi or sweet vegetables are often good for this purpose.

• *Effects of Books and Media on Sleep*

Books, television, and movies also affect how children sleep. You must carefully select the books, television programs, and movies that your children see or read. In fact, it can be worthwhile for you to see a movie first before taking your children to see it. The shows and cartoons on television are often violent or disturbing for youngsters. If children are allowed to watch such programs, they may be afraid to go to sleep or may have nightmares. Books with ghosts, monsters, or other upsetting subjects in them are not recommended, especially not at night. You should be as careful in selecting your children's entertainment and reading material as you are in selecting their food. Children will be much happier as a result.

Waking Up

Some children wake up with a smile, some cry, and some are irritable. A child's mood may also vary from day to day. Children have different reactions to the foods they eat, the events of the previous day, and other factors in their environment. Try to see the connection between these factors and your child's condition when she wakes in the morning. You need to be happy, smiling, and pleasant when you wake your children in the morning or after a nap. If you are annoyed that your child got up too early or if your greeting is not pleasant, your child may be upset the entire day or until you reassure him that you are not upset or annoyed. Some children are very hungry when they wake up, and if their breakfast is not prepared quickly, they become upset and irritable. If you do not always get up before or when your children do, you can occasionally make small rice balls or sushi for them to eat before breakfast is ready.

If your child wakes up many times during the night, try to discover the reason. The problem may be due to something that was eaten at dinner, such as bread, fruit, beans, or other foods that are difficult to digest. The same is true with dreams or nightmares. You need to understand how different foods create different effects on your child's mind and thinking. In this way, you can come to understand how foods produce dreams. Some foods can cause children to have happy dreams while others produce unhappy ones.

Grooming Habits

Washing, bathing, and cleaning the teeth can be fun and enjoyable. If you request your children to do these things in a demanding or unrelaxed way, they may develop a dislike or disinterest in these activities. Nagging never accomplishes anything except frustration and upset. Teaching good habits to older children is much more difficult so encourage grooming habits at an early age. It is important to begin regular grooming habits when children are young so that they will continue them as they grow older. When your children are young, you can play games with them to heighten their enjoyment of these activities. Singing songs or counting fingers and toes while trimming nails can help focus your child's interest and make him feel more relaxed. Washing and combing young children's hair has to be done gently and peacefully. Children may develop a dislike or even a fear of shampooing or combing the hair if they get soap in their eyes or if their hair is pulled when it is combed. If you and your spouse have regular bathing and cleaning habits, your child will tend to imitate and develop these habits also.

• *Bathing and Washing*

We recommend that children be given a mild warm bath every day. The best time for children to bathe is in the evening just before bedtime, but not immediately after the evening meal. A bath directly following dinner may interfere with digestion. A bath just before bed can help the child relax and have a deep and peaceful sleep. If your family eats later in the evening, you can give your children a bath before dinner is served. If daily bathing is done routinely and is a happy time for children, they will tend to develop regular bathing habits as they get older. Most children prefer to have a parent in the bathroom with them while they are bathing, to help them wash and enjoy their bath. A parent can supervise bathing until children are about five to six years old. Of course, children under three need constant adult supervision. Older children enjoy bathing by themselves, especially when they reach the age of nine or so. If an older child wishes to bathe without anyone present, including younger brothers or sisters, it is better to respect her wishes.

When babies and young children wake up in the morning, parents can make it a practice of quickly washing their faces and hands. If this habit is established early on, children will usually continue it throughout life. Washing up before meals is also very important and can be taught to children at an early age.

• *Cleaning the Teeth*

Cleaning the teeth can begin as early as one-and-a-half to two. You can begin teaching your children about cleaning their teeth even before that by letting them observe family members doing it. It is a good idea to purchase a small children's toothbrush and keep it on hand for the younger child to use as soon as she begins to show interest. You can show children the proper way to brush their teeth and encourage them to do so regularly so that by the age of five or six, they enjoy doing it by themselves every day.

• *Dressing and Undressing*

As we have mentioned, the best children's clothing is made of high-quality cotton fabric. Cotton keeps a child cool in the summer and warm in the winter. It is the ideal natural fabric for clothing. Cotton is also easy to clean and lasts longer than synthetic fabrics. It is also very smooth and comfortable to wear. In the winter, woolen jackets, sweaters, mittens, and hats can be worn on top of cotton clothing.

It is better if your child's clothing is loose-fitting and comfortable, and allows him freedom of movement. It is more difficult for children to relax and play in tight, restrictive clothing. Tight clothing can make a child uncomfortable and irritable.

The quality of your child's shoes is also very important. Soft cotton or canvas sneakers are comfortable and practical. Children's feet grow very quickly. You need to pay careful attention to this, making sure that as your child's feet grow, her shoes are comfortable. It is very difficult for children to relax if their shoes do not fit properly. Shoes that are too big can also cause problems, as a child may trip and fall easily, and may not be able to run, jump, and play with total freedom.

On Rice Straw Sandals

When I was a young girl living in the countryside of Japan, I wore rice straw sandals. They were very comfortable and inexpensive. Sometimes, my friends and I would go for long walks or picnics wearing one pair of these sandals and carrying another in a knapsack with our rice balls. If we were running and playing and one of our sandals broke, we would leave the pair on the ground to decay and return to the soil, and would wear the extra pair in our knapsack to go back home. If both pairs broke, we could always buy another pair for just a few cents, as many farm houses had these sandals hanging up outside to sell to people walking by. It was so convenient and comfortable, and we never had to worry about shoes.

—Aveline Kushi

As we have already said, high-quality cotton pajamas are best. Synthetics often hold too much body heat and make children uncomfortable. Pajamas with feet attached also tend to keep the body too warm during sleep. Some children feel confined when they wear pajamas of this type. Pajamas with attached feet often have plastic soles, which are not recommended. If a child's cotton pajamas have attached feet, simply cut the feet off to make them more comfortable for your child to sleep in. When pajamas are comfortable and loose-fitting, a child can enjoy freedom of motion and can sleep soundly. In the morning, children can remove their underwear and pajamas and put on fresh, clean underwear and clothing.

If children always have clean and neat clothing when they are young, and if parents teach the importance of dressing properly, children will tend to develop orderly habits of dress. If the proper care of clothing is neglected, it is much more difficult to encourage older children to dress well and to take proper care of their clothes.

CHILDREN'S ACTIVITIES

In order to cultivate your children's creativity and offer them many opportunities to find enjoyment and happiness, it is important for them to be physically and mentally active. Encourage children to participate in a broad spectrum of activities. Sports, gymnastics, dancing, painting, drawing, playing piano or other instruments, and pottery and other artistic classes are only a few of the activities children can participate in. Encourage them to have a wide variety of friends to broaden their social experience. Children are usually much happier if they are busily involved with many activities and social experiences.

Playing and Creating

As children gain increasing fine-muscle control, they naturally become interested in using crayons, pencils, pens, and paint brushes. You can guide your children in how to hold these objects so they can draw or paint, or how to make the appropriate lines or strokes when they learn to write. Leave the creation of drawings and paintings to your child's imagination. If your child requests help or asks you to make a drawing, there is no harm in complying, but it is better not to interfere with what the child is creating. Let children initiate and create their own style.

After your child finishes a drawing, discuss what it is that she has drawn and what the drawing means. It is best for adults not to tell children what they think a drawing represents. Rather, you should try to encourage them to offer their own explanations.

The materials that your child uses for drawing, painting, or play should be safe, nontoxic, and made of natural substances. Provide your children with clay, paper, paints, and crayons to play with rather than plastic or synthetic materials. Children can be encouraged to use crayons as they are safe. Pencils and pens can be given to older children or to younger children if properly supervised. Cutting out paper drawings with safe children's scissors is also a very good activity. Try to encourage your children to play and develop their creativity rather than pursue more passive activities like watching television. Television has a strong influence on how children behave so when they do watch it, make sure that the program is suitable.

Encourage your children to invent their own play and games. If your children have too many toys, they may become frustrated and confused. They may not play with their toys or may have difficulty deciding how to go about playing with them. Having fewer toys can make things simpler for a child. When your children are very young, even when they start to crawl, let them help pick up and put away their toys. If they are taught how to do this at an early age, most children will develop orderly habits and will clean up after themselves when they play. If children do not learn this when they are young, it may be difficult for them to change later.

• *Selecting Children's Toys*

It is better to select high-quality handcrafted toys or toys made from more natural materials rather than mass-produced or electric toys. If a child's first toys are of a more natural quality, she will often enjoy and be satisfied with them; however, if plastic or electric toys are bought first, there may be some difficulty switching an older child over to more simple wooden toys. Children can be much more creative with simple, natural toys that require energy and imagination. The vibration of wooden toys is peaceful and not upsetting. Electric or battery-operated toys can sometimes be frustrating for children to play with. Plastic toys tend to break easily, causing a child to become upset, whereas wooden toys are usually stronger and last for many years. Sturdier wooden toys can be handed down from child to child. In the long run, they are more economical and certainly more ecological than disposable plastic items.

Playing Outside

Playing outside in all seasons is very important for a child's physical and mental health and well-being. Children who spend a great deal of time outdoors are usually happier, and eat and sleep better than children who spend much time indoors. Children need open spaces in which to run, jump, play, and enjoy freedom with little adult interference. You can, of course, accompany your children on outings to look after their safety. You can also join in the play when your children request it, or to help them get started. It is much easier for children to play outside if their homes are in the country. For children who live in cities, parents may have to devote a little more time with them at the park or playground. It is helpful for children's social development if they can go to a park or playground every day to play with other children.

It is important to take your children to a variety of places such as the beach, the zoo, parks, farms, and the forest, instead of visiting the same place day after day. Taking children to many different places will stimulate their creativity, imagination, and desire to learn. They will have the opportunity to observe many types of people and social situations.

It is also important for parents on an outing with their children to stop periodically to point out different flowers and trees, and marvel out loud at the beauty of our natural world. Look up at the sky and ask your children if they find it wonderful and beautiful to look at. Point out different clouds, birds, and animals. Try to instill in your children a deep wonder about and appreciation for nature. If your children develop love and respect for nature, they will treat it with care and respect when they become adults.

Developing physical strength is very important for a child's health and confidence. Encourage children to participate in as many sports and game activities as possible. Children who are physically strong are often happier, healthier, and more confident. If a child is physically weak, encouraging him to participate in sports activities can help him overcome this problem.

Social Play

It is very important for children to be socially active even at an early age. You can encourage sociability by taking children to parks and other places to meet and play with other children. Open up your home to your children's friends. Encourage your children to invite their friends home to play and encourage your children to visit their friends' homes as well. This can help your children learn how other people live, how to cooperate and play happily in an orderly manner, and how to share with friends. It is very good for children to have a wide variety of friends so that they can learn to communicate with a variety of people and be flexible under many different circumstances.

Parties, social events, play groups, sports, school activities, and after-school programs are also recommended to help children develop social awareness.

Balancing Play and Study

In planning your child's day, allow time for active play and for more quiet activities, such as looking at picture books, drawing, or studying. Parents can set aside time each day for toddlers to learn how to make things or to read or study together. If children develop these habits when they are young, they will usually continue into adulthood. When children start school, it is important that they have time to sit quietly and read or do their homework. School children need a clean, quiet, and orderly space for studying and doing homework. It is better for them to finish their homework before watching television. If they stay up late watching television—promising to do their homework afterward—they may become too tired to do it.

If children are not interested in studying or in doing homework, or are too active to sit quietly, simple dietary changes can usually help them calm down. A warm bath will often help a child to relax.

You can stimulate your child's interest in study by making it fun and interesting. Usually, if you participate actively in encouraging and occasionally helping your children with their studies, they will take much more interest and pride in what they do. Also, if children frequently observe their parents studying and reading, they will usually try to imitate them. It is better not to nag your children about doing homework. Help them set up a quiet time each day for their studies. When necessary, you can adjust your schedule to spend time with your child to help with homework. It is better if children do their homework in a relaxed, enjoyable atmosphere. If there are younger children in the family, see to it that they are in bed or occupied in some way so as not to disturb the older child while she is studying.

Participating in Household Chores

When children are eleven to twelve years old, or even younger, parents can begin teaching them how to sew, knit, wash clothes, iron, wash dishes, and fold and put away clothing. They can also be involved in doing chores around the yard and in helping with younger children by reading and playing with them.

Teaching children to cook when they are young is very valuable training; however, it is better to wait until they are older before teaching them how to cut vegetables, as their coordination is usually not well enough developed to handle a knife properly. Once children are taught how to use a knife, they will often try to do it without supervision and this can be dangerous. Put knives out of the reach of younger children. It is difficult to provide constant supervision for one child when trying to cook and care for other children. It is better to wait until children are eight or nine before teaching them to cut vegetables. Younger children can learn how to make things that are safer and easier and do not require using a sharp knife. Children around the age of two can also be shown how to wash their dishes after meals.

HELPING YOUR CHILD TO REACH MILESTONES

Parents often want to know what they can do when their child seems to be slow in walking, clumsy with kitchen utensils, or having problems with teething or toilet training. Sometimes, the best course of action is no action. Consult the following sections for tips on making your child's learning experiences the most pleasurable and rewarding. As always, contact your pediatrician if you have any serious concerns.

Walking

It is best if children learn to walk without much parental involvement. Do not attempt to force them to walk before they are ready. Children should really try to do this themselves. Parental involvement should be limited to making sure children are safe and not in danger of hurting themselves. Just be there to supervise and guide them when they need it. Some children walk very early, as young as ten to eleven months old, while others do not walk until they are two. Do not worry if another child is walking before yours. Each child is unique, and her rate of growth and development should be respected. Wait until your child is stronger, more confident, and interested in walking. If a child is being fed high-quality food every day, do not worry; she will walk when she is ready. Occasionally, children can be placed in a walker or a bouncer to help them strengthen their leg muscles. Be careful, however, not to leave children in these devices for extended periods as they may become very tired, and it may hurt the child's back to sit or stand for too long a time. Do not take drastic measures to force a child to walk. Using daily foods to make a child strong enough to begin walking is the best method.

Bowed legs or knock-knees are caused by imbalances in the diet. Bowed legs are often caused by overeating. Too much salt in the diet can increase a child's appetite and result in overeating. If a child has this condition, extraordinary measures are usually unnecessary. Simply make the adjustments in the child's food and in how it is prepared, and the condition will tend to correct itself. If a child's feet point inward, the cause is usually too much yin food. If they point outward, the cause is too much animal food. Simple changes in diet can help these conditions return to normal.

Using Eating Utensils

Parents can actively teach children to use spoons properly when eating. Gently try to discourage them from eating with their fingers by showing them how to use a spoon. It is better for young children not to use a fork as it can be dangerous. Children using forks need careful parental supervision. Do not leave a child unattended while she is using chopsticks. Do not allow children to walk or run holding any pointed object. If they fall, they could seriously injure themselves. It is the responsibility of parents to teach children to eat properly and safely. If children are left to themselves, they will frequently eat with their fingers, often wasting food, creating a mess, and developing habits that will be difficult to break later on. Children who eat with their fingers may continue to do so even when they are older. This can be embarrassing and frustrating for both parents and child.

Teething and Other Teeth-Related Problems

Some children get their first teeth at four months, but as a general rule, the first teeth come in at about six to eight months. Some babies may not get teeth until later. Do not worry about this. All babies are different and develop at different rates. If you are eating well and feeding your baby quality foods, she will probably not have much trouble when her teeth do come in. It is only when the diet is out of balance—creating an overly yin or yang condition in the baby—that teething problems arise.

If the baby wants something to chew on, she can be given a large piece or section of raw carrot. Make sure that it is big enough to hold on to and too large to choke on. When you give your baby a piece of raw carrot, be certain to supervise closely to make sure that none of it is bitten off. You can also purchase high-quality wooden rattles for babies to chew on. In addition, you can make hard teething biscuits with whole wheat pastry flour. Shape the dough into thick cookies with interesting shapes. Bake them in a slow oven until they are very hard and do not break. Do not use salt or oil when making them. You can also massage your baby's gums occasionally with your finger or let her chew on your finger.

When the permanent teeth begin to come in, be very careful to offer children a well-balanced diet to help them keep their teeth in good condition. Cavities can be caused by overconsumption of extreme foods: sweets such as grain candy, cookies, juice, and concentrated sweeteners, which are excessive yin, or salty foods or condiments, which are excessive yang. Be careful not to give children too many of these items.

When teeth protrude outward, the cause is too much yin (fruit, juice, concentrated sweeteners, etc.), while teeth that point inward are caused by more yang types of foods, especially fish and salty dishes or condiments. Gray spots on the teeth are caused by too much salt. Discolored teeth can be caused by either extreme. Soft teeth are often caused by a lack of minerals or by the intake of too much yin food.

It is much easier to prevent problems with the teeth by giving children a naturally balanced diet than it is to correct the problems once they have developed.

Toilet Training

Toilet training takes time and patience on the part of parents. Several weeks of concentrated effort may be required. The earlier toilet training is started, the better, because children who are trained earlier usually require less time to learn to go to the toilet by themselves. Children will usually not train themselves, although there are some exceptions. You really need to make an effort to guide them properly. Early training can be done more easily if you set up a regular time to place the child on the potty seat. Also, younger children often give signals when they are ready to have a bowel movement. Babies often prepare for a bowel movement by puckering their lips tightly and making their expression look more serious. They may also make certain noises that you can come to recognize. When children are about to urinate, they sometimes make little noises or become a little fussy. If you have the time to begin training your baby at a young age, it will be much easier for both you and the child.

When babies are still in diapers and have not yet been trained, it is important to check their diapers periodically to make sure they are clean. Leaving your child in soiled or wet diapers will make her very uncomfortable and irritable. Babies may develop a rash if their diapers are not changed regularly or if they are not properly cleaned after each changing. These practices are very important in helping children learn good bathroom and cleanliness habits.

OTHER PARENTAL CONCERNS

Single Parents

As we saw in the Introduction, the number of single-parent families is increasing. Some families consist of only one parent from the beginning. Other single-parent families may result from divorce, separation, or the death of one of the partners. At present, it is estimated that one in three American families are single parent families. (In Great Britain, the rate is approximately one in four; in Australia, one in six.) In about 90 percent of these cases, the father is the absent parent.

It is difficult for the single parent to play the role of both parents. One way to help compensate for the missing parent is to make opportunities for the child to associate with others: visit parks and playgrounds and attend parties and other social events. Visiting with friends and their families will also help a child adjust to having one parent. If children are socially active and do things together with their parents, they will be happier and adjust more smoothly.

Avoiding Accidents

A balanced natural diet, strong, clear cooking, and a little common sense are primary in preventing accidents. When your child's food is balanced, her coordination, intuition, and judgment function more efficiently. Accidents are much less likely when the child has a more balanced condition. Parents need to observe their children's diet and condition continually so as to correct any imbalances.

Common-sense precautions in regard to potential hazards are, of course, necessary. When babies gain the ability to roll over, they must be watched continually and not left unsupervised on tables or other high places from which they could fall. When children start to crawl or walk, you need to safeguard potential problem areas such as stairs, electrical outlets, and kitchen cabinets. Children like to climb on furniture so you must discourage this hazardous activity. Potentially hazardous objects, including kitchen utensils and matches, and potentially dangerous substances like household cleaners, need to be kept safely away from children. It is best never to leave young children without proper adult supervision. They also require careful attention when playing outside.

Your health, judgment, and good sense are, obviously, essential in maintaining the health and well-being of your children. Young children depend entirely upon the good judgment of their parents for their health and safety. Proper eating, an orderly, natural lifestyle, and a loving concern for the welfare of your children can help in preventing most problems. You must also teach children about safety, including how to cross streets and how to relate to strangers, as soon as they begin to explore the world around them.

When your children reach the age at which they start to go outside by themselves, you can establish the routine of having them always tell you where they are going and what they will be doing. You can ask your children to call when they arrive at their destination, and to let you know when and how they plan to return home. It is important to be aware of what your children are doing and where they are going. When your children return home, ask them what they were doing and if they enjoyed themselves. Always keep the lines of communication open and friendly.

Parental Guidance Suggested

Approaches to the question of parental guidance can be divided into two general categories. The more yang approach is *authoritarian*. It often involves rigid rules or attitudes that parents wish to impose upon their children. It frequently employs punishment if children break these rules or fail to do what parents expect. In extreme cases, parents may believe that their children are inherently bad and must be re-formed, with physical punishment if necessary.

The more yin approach to discipline can be referred to as permissiveness. In recent times, it has developed largely as a counterbalance to the perceived harshness of the authoritarian approach. In extreme instances, parents allow children to do almost anything they wish in their belief that any type of restraint may be harmful to the child's development.

It is important to remember that each child is a manifestation of the infinite universe, or God. Children are by nature no more "bad" than the sun, the stars, or any other natural phenomenon. On the contrary, if their natural tendencies and instincts are allowed to mature fully, all human beings seek universal love and harmony. The characteristics usually thought of as negative aspects of human nature represent the incomplete development of humanity's natural tendencies. It is important, therefore, to love all children unconditionally and to respect their integrity as a manifestation of God.

In the Introduction, we saw how imbalances in daily diet and environment can lead to the abnormal psychological conditions that produce child abuse. Striking or punishing a child out of anger, devising some form of calculated punishment, or ignoring a child's safety are indications of physical and mental imbalance. An overly rigid or authoritarian approach to children often develops when the consumption of meat, eggs, fish, poultry, or other yang foods—including salt and minerals—becomes excessive. An overly permissive approach develops more easily when refined or chemicalized foods, tropical fruits, sugar, chocolate, milk, ice cream, and other more yin items are overemphasized in the diet.

For example, hitting children is usually the result of anger or frustration on the part of the parents. Psychologists have discovered that children who are hit usually do not remember what they were punished for and do not change their behavior as a result. Children who are hit rarely feel sorry for their actions, and striking children tends to establish a pattern of physical abuse in the household. Children who are hit, often begin to hit their younger brothers and sisters, and grow up with the belief that violence toward other human beings is an acceptable method for solving problems.

It is up to the parents to educate and guide their children toward a proper way of life. When children behave in an unhealthy or abnormal way, parents should realize that they themselves are the major cause, either through providing children with excessive or unbalanced food or through the example of their own daily behavior.

In a more balanced approach, harmony is the underlying principle of relations between husband and wife and parents and children. Harmony is either maintained or disrupted primarily by the quality of food prepared daily. The question of how children behave cannot be separated from the overall health and way of living of the family as a whole. A more balanced approach is neither authoritarian nor permissive to the extent that no constructive guidance is provided. It is based on a keen observation of how children are behaving and an understanding of the underlying causes of their behavior. When behavior becomes out of balance or one-sided, parents can lovingly help their children reestablish equilibrium.

When children develop a behavioral problem, discuss it with them and try to find out the cause. It may be something they are eating, or it may be due to inattention from you, the parents. When talking with your children, let them see how their behavior may not be in their best interests or in the interest of family harmony. If children consistently repeat their mistakes without learning from them, a more firm approach may be necessary; however, always remember that food and the home environment are the underlying cause of most problems, and that behavior itself is basically the reflection of the quality of these factors.

Teaching Children to Care for Their Health

When your children are very small, you will want to begin to teach them how to take care of their health. Show them how to chew properly. If they have a stomachache, explain to them that instead of eating heavy foods at that time, a simpler meal will make them feel much better. Make sure to check their bowel movements every day when they are very young. When your children are older, you can ask them to let you know whenever they have a problem with their bowel movement. For example, tell them to notify you if their stools are too dark, or if they develop diarrhea or constipation. There is no need to discuss their bowel condition every day, but if it becomes abnormal, it is important for your children to tell you right away. If you explain to them why this is important, they will not feel embarrassed to discuss it. If older children wet the bed often, it is also a sign that their condition is somewhat out of balance. It is important to discuss problems such as these and to cooperate with children in making the appropriate changes in their diet so as to correct imbalances before they become serious.

Teaching children how to create harmony and attain balance gives them an essential tool for their future health and happiness. Begin by explaining foods in terms of yin and yang. Tell them, for example, that animal products, such as meat, poultry, and eggs, are very yang. Explain that sugar, honey, tropical fruits, spices, soft drinks, chocolate, and candy are very yin. Tell them that these foods are generally too extreme for use in maintaining health, and that more centrally balanced foods like whole grains, beans, and fresh local vegetables are best for maintaining a healthy condition.

If children develop some type of symptom such as a runny nose or sneezing, ask them what they ate in order to help them see the connection between their eating and day-to-day condition. You can also explain their condition in terms of yin and yang by telling them, for example, that a runny nose or sneezing is often caused by excess yin foods and drinks.

When explaining things in yin and yang terms, it is better to avoid using words like "good" and "bad." Yin and yang are simply complementary yet antagonistic tendencies that are found throughout nature. Thinking in terms of "right" and "wrong" can lead to a one-sided view of life.

Parents can show their children how yin and yang apply to all areas of life. Adults should try to express themselves simply and poetically in language that children can understand. Yin and yang can also be taught by pointing out the spiral pattern in nature. Draw children's attention to the many spirals that exist in nature, from galaxies to the spiral on top of the head. (Please refer to Aveline Kushi's book for children, *Lessons of Night and Day,* for ideas on how to express yin and yang in a simple, colorful, poetic manner.)

Using Home Health Care

In the following chapter, we discuss the macrobiotic approach to common childhood illnesses. In some cases, we recommend simple home care applications, including light massage, compresses, and palm healing. The following are general comments on home care for children.

For generations, traditional families employed a variety of simple methods for home health care. Basic shiatsu, or finger pressure massage, simple compresses made from items used every day in the kitchen, and special dishes and beverages were used commonly in the home. Mild shiatsu, for example, can be given to children (or adults, including senior citizens) to help relax and harmonize their overall condition. In traditional families, husbands and wives would frequently exchange shiatsu massage, and would periodically offer a simple treatment to their children or elderly parents as well. We recommend that all members of the family learn basic healing arts as a part of home health care.

Palm healing is usually not a problem for children because it makes them calm and relaxed. Just be careful to apply your hands very lightly, and make sure that your child is kept properly covered and warm during an application. If your child falls asleep during palm healing, the application may be continued until it is complete. Simply tuck the child in after you are finished.

When compresses and other home applications are used, make sure that they are very mild in comparison to those used by adults. Adjust the application to fit each child's needs. This may seem like a minor point, but it is very important. If parents are inexperienced in using macrobiotic applications, it is best not to do anything drastic or strong. It is also a good idea to call a macrobiotic center. When children have fever, it is usually better to give them milder applications, such as putting green cabbage leaves on the forehead. Stronger applications may cause a reaction and increase the recovery time needed by the

A Word to Grandparents

It is important for grandparents to cooperate with their children when it comes to grandchildren. It often happens that grandparents and parents have different ideas on child-raising. If so, the issues should be discussed openly in order to reach a suitable agreement and to avoid arguments or misunderstandings. In this way, parents and grandparents relate to the children in a similar manner. This is also much better for the children. It is less confusing and makes for better communication between children, parents, and grandparents. Grandparents need to respect their children's ideas on how to raise their children. Remember that the parents are the ones who are responsible for their children twenty-four hours a day, whereas grandparents can enjoy a much easier and relaxed relationship with their grandchildren. At the same time, grandparents possess a wealth of experience in child rearing. Parents are fortunate if they can turn to their own parents for advice and suggestions.

child. Examine the child's bowel movement every day; if he is constipated, a simple enema can be given after two or three days. Many simple problems start in the intestines.

It is not necessary to give extreme or unusual tasting medicinal foods or drinks to children. For instance, if a child has a fever, we usually recommend warm apple juice or mildly roasted grain tea, but for an adult, we usually recommend fresh grated daikon tea. Daikon tea is too strong for young children, and they usually do not like the taste. Sweeter or more mild tasting drinks are more appropriate for children. When children are sick, it is often necessary to adjust their surroundings to keep them comfortable. You may, for example, wish to turn up the thermostat to make sure their room is warm or use a humidifier to keep the air moist. The atmosphere in the home is very important at all times, and especially when a child is not feeling well.

It is important for parents to remain calm and positive when children become sick. Children are very sensitive to their parents' emotions, and may become frightened or upset if the parents are tense.

Many books recommend placing a child in a cold bath when a fever develops; however, this may cause an extreme reaction, such as a seizure. In the past, parents would keep children with fevers warm and not let their skin get cold. When children are kept warm, they naturally perspire, and this cools the body. If parents place children in a cool bath, apply cold towels, or give a cold water sponge bath, the surface of their skin will contract and become tight. When this happens, the discharge of a fever goes deeper into the body instead of coming out. This can be especially dangerous in cases of measles.

If problems arise, watch your child's diet and find out what she has been eating. This will help you decide what steps to take. If a child's diet is balanced, and if her mother ate well while she was pregnant and breastfeeding, the problems that arise are usually less extreme and easier to correct. Children who eat well sometimes intuitively know what they need to correct a problem and may refuse remedies that are too extreme. Parents should observe and learn from their children's responses.

Chapter 5
Keeping Children Healthy

Children come to this Earth from the infinite universe, and childhood is a stage in their return journey to infinity. Health and peace, joy and adventure, and wonder and marvel are all natural states for children. They exist when children live in harmony with the laws of nature. But what is health?

Health is much more than freedom from illness. It includes continual growth, flexible change, and joyful adaptation to the ever-changing world. It is the natural outcome of a way of life in harmony with the cycles of nature. When children are healthy, they enjoy the following attributes:

- *Boundless energy, creativity, and enthusiasm.* Healthy children play from morning to evening without growing bored or exhausted. Little ones may, of course, require a nap from time to time, but when they are awake, they are active and full of energy; so much so, in fact, that parents often have trouble keeping up with them. A good way to evaluate our own health is to consider how well we keep pace with our children.

    A healthy child will approach life with a spirit of adventure. The energetic pursuit of dreams and ambitions—including the capability to play, make believe, fantasize, and daydream—is a sign of good health and sound development. These capacities foster children's development, and help them realize their dreams throughout life.

- *A good appetite.* Children normally have healthy appetites, and not simply for food. A good appetite includes the desire for love, friendship, adventure, knowledge, and new experiences.

Children are born with an unlimited curiosity. This is reflected, as they grow, by their love of riddles, games, puzzles, and things that need to be figured out. They are always asking questions, and have a tremendous desire to participate in life.

Children also seek love and friendship. They have no trouble making friends with children of their own age, with adults, or even with younger children or babies. Through their rich imaginations, they can also become friends with toys, animals, trees, rocks, and almost anything else they come into contact with. The ability to make friends easily is a sign that a child is healthy and well adjusted.

Too much rich food or too many luxuries can spoil a child's appetite. For example, children are naturally attracted to sweet-tasting foods. If they indulge in sugary snacks, soda, candy, ice cream, or other poor-quality foods, however, they will spoil their health. It is important for parents to use good judgment when selecting their children's snacks and sweets. At the same time, children need opportunities to solve problems and confront challenges. This helps them to develop endurance, vitality, and patience. They will then be better equipped to deal with the challenges that arise during their lives.

It is an expression of parental love to encourage moderation. When your children are old enough, explain to them that overindulgence can lead to dullness, stagnation, and weakness. Help them to understand that moderation actually strengthens and enhances their ability to participate in life. Moderation is not punishment; it is a means to further one's growth and development.

- *Deep, sound sleep.* When children are healthy, they enjoy good, sound, sleep. Energetic physical and mental activity produces deep and restful sleep. When a healthy child sleeps, he is not bothered by nightmares or rootless, disturbing dreams. These come from imbalances in the brain and nervous system that result from excesses in the daily diet and environment. Television, movies, and other types of mental stimulation can also interact with a poor-quality diet to produce disturbing and frightening dreams.

- *Good memory and imagination.* Good memory is a sign of health. Memory provides the basis for all learning. Learning to walk, to control bowel movements and urination, and to speak, read, write, and do arithmetic all rest on the foundation of memory. Children learn to remember letters, numbers, and words, and to recreate scenery, people, and events, as well as emotions and feelings. They also have an intuitive memory of their spiritual origins. Imagination, creativity, ambition, and future plans or dreams are all based on memory. Memory is the foundation of health and happiness.

The ease with which children make friends is a result of their universal memory. Children intuitively remember their origin in the infinite universe, and realize instinctively that all people and things share the same origin. More relative or artificial distinctions such as race, occupation, nationality, or religious belief are usually not important to children and do not interfere with the desire to make friends. Children are naturally citizens of the world.

- *Freedom from anger, fear, and other negative emotions.* As we saw in the Introduction, negative emotions correlate to physical disorders. In Oriental countries, for example, anger was described as "pain in the liver." Stagnation and other liver troubles frequently result from eating too many animal foods, baked or overly cooked dishes, and mineral salts. Foods such as these can interfere with the natural flow of Earth's energy up the right side of the body. In this case, energy becomes stagnant and accumulates in the liver. Then, like a volcano, this stagnated energy periodically explodes in an outburst that we call anger. Children who are naturally healthy do not have this stagnation and thus rarely experience anger.

Fear is related to an imbalance in the kidneys, often as a result of the overintake of fluids, saturated fats, sugar, animal proteins, and mineral salts. The kidneys stabilize the flow of energy in the body by harmonizing the energy that flows up through the right and down the left side of the body. When this balancing function is disturbed, a person loses confidence and stability.

The tendency toward fear is, of course, reinforced when parents strike or punish children, or when children experience artificial or painful procedures such as injections, operations, x-rays, and so on. Teachers or other adults can instill fear when they assume an overly authoritarian or disciplinarian posture. Fear of nuclear war and of failure to measure up to expectations, as well as fear of the future in general, are becoming common among children today. Underlying imbalances in the diet promote fear rather than a positive confidence in the future based on the desire to meet and overcome these challenges.

Abnormal mental or emotional conditions relate directly to imbalances in diet and upbringing. These imbalances distort the normal patterns of energy flow through the major organs and the body as a whole. As a result, these disruptions can prevent more healthy emotional and intellectual responses.

The perception that physical health affects the emotions is not new. Traditional societies around the world have recognized the link between an individual's physical health and his emotional expression. Various cultures, in fact, have discussed this connection in a highly detailed way.

Today, researchers are finding that there indeed appears to be a relationship between mind and body. In the future, we can expect growing scientific recognition of this fact, and the application of this relationship to solve a wide variety of problems.

In Table 5.1, we present common psychological problems and correlate them with the major organs of the body. The dietary and psychological imbalances that promote these tendencies are also presented.

The underlying physical conditions that are associated with these psychological disturbances are preventable through proper diet. A centrally balanced diet—with an ample variety of wholesome foods and styles of cooking—can help the body maintain the proper flow of energy. The organs and systems then function smoothly and efficiently, creating physical and emotional well-being. In cases where problems already exist, a balanced diet can help in the recovery of more harmonious psychological and emotional states.

At the same time, changing the psychological factors that contribute to the particular problem will accelerate recovery. For example, a child who is continually put under pressure to behave properly or to perform according to certain expectations can easily become frustrated or angry, especially when he eats plenty of animal protein and fat. Parents can help change this situation by treating the child in a more relaxed and supporting manner while, of course, adjusting the child's diet. Parents may also begin to show more of an interest in the things the child is doing, and actively support whatever he is engaged in.

Children who frequently become overexcited, nervous, or hysterical often improve when provided with situations that challenge their abilities to a reasonable degree. Solving problems and overcoming difficulties helps them to become stronger and more self-controlled. Spoiling children who manifest this problem only serves to reinforce their behavior. Encouraging self-discipline can help the child recover a healthy equilibrium. Keeping a calm and relaxed atmosphere at home will, of course, help the child become more peaceful.

Doubt and suspicion can be offset by providing children with a stable and dependable environment. Keeping promises and estab-

Table 5.1 Effects of Psychological and Dietary Factors on Emotions and Health

Psychological Symptoms	Related Organ Dysfunction	Contributing Psychological Factors	Contributing Dietary Imbalances
Anger Argumentative, explosive, or abusive behavior; frequent complaining; hitting or punishing others; bullying.	Liver and gallbladder	Too much external control or pressure; lack of recognition, appreciation, or encouragement.	The overconsumption of extreme yang foods including meat, eggs, poultry, and cheese; too many baked flour products or salt; and a lack of freshness in the diet. (These foods interfere with the smooth upward flow of energy.)
Excitement Nervousness; frequently changing one's mind; overly emotional behavior.	Heart and small intestine	Lack of discipline; parents spoil children; overly sentimental parental care.	Excessive yin and yang combined, including animal foods, sugar, hot spicy foods and tropical fruits; too many raw foods.
Doubt Suspicion; lack of warmth; an overly critical attitude.	Spleen, pancreas, and stomach	An undependable environment.	Excessive yin foods and beverages, including milk, ice cream, butter, soft drinks, sugar, tropical fruits, and spices.
Mental Rigidity Stubbornness, narrow- or closed-mindedness; rejection of others' advice or opinions.	Lungs and large intestine	Loneliness; lack of warmth; a cold, uncaring environment.	Heavy, fatty foods; foods with a sticky quality; baked foods; salt.
Fear Insecurity; anxiety; overprotectiveness.	Kidneys and bladder	An overly protective environment; parents often critical of others.	Excessive yin and yang combined, especially saltier or more heavily cooked dishes; extreme yin including drugs.

lishing dependable routines in daily life contribute to the establishment of faith and trust.

The tendency toward mental rigidity, stubbornness, or narrow-mindedness can be offset by providing a warm, loving, and supportive home environment. Mental rigidity and stubbornness can cause an individual to become isolated from others. Therefore, it is important for parents to get involved in their children's activities and offer them frequent companionship in order to offset loneliness and isolation.

Fear or anxiety can be offset by reassuring children about their bright future and allowing them freedom to experience things for themselves. Being overly protective can often increase anxiety, especially later when children are alone and must confront difficulties by themselves. Parents can also minimize this tendency by not speaking negatively about others and by frequently showing praise and admiration for others in front of their children.

- *A joyful response to the environment.* Healthy children respond joyfully to the changing world around them. They are able to respond in an original and flexible way, without more set or predictable patterns of thought and behavior.

  Open-mindedness is also a characteristic of healthy children. They can entertain new ideas and situations without prejudice or preconceived notions. Children are usually much more adaptable than adults—who tend to be more set in their ways. Children are also very resilient; they are able to spring back from illness, failure, or difficulty and resume their play and activities with rapid speed.

- *Wonder, marvel, and appreciation.* Children find wonder everywhere. They intuitively sense a oneness with all things, and are grateful for their lives as human beings on this Earth. Their appreciation is often expressed simply in their joy of living, or in simple expressions of love and tenderness toward parents, brothers and sisters, and friends.

UNDERSTANDING SICKNESS

The majority of illnesses that affect normally healthy children are of the adjustment variety. *Adjustment sicknesses* arise when a normally healthy child eats some type of extreme or unbalanced food that sets off a discharge that may take the form of fever, coughing, runny nose, sore throat, or vomiting. Adjustments usually come on suddenly and pass as soon as the excess is discharged and the child returns to a more balanced condition.

Aside from simple adjustments in diet and home care, it is preferable not to interfere with the natural process of discharge unless the symptoms become severe. If a child eats well while the adjustment is going on, he can quickly return to normal and experience a strengthening of natural immunity and self-healing power.

Children also adjust to their environment by discharging factors that were taken in during the embryonic period. Measles, for example, represents the discharge of more yang factors taken in during the time in the womb. The discharge of these factors furthers normal growth and development.

Another type of discharge can occur from imbalances in the mother's diet during the nursing period. These may take the form of rashes, eye discharges, or a runny nose. As with other simple adjustments, the symptoms normally subside once the mother's intake of extreme foods is stopped and a more balanced diet adopted.

In some cases, however, a baby will discharge even when the nursing mother is eating well. These discharges can be the result of an overly yin or yang diet during pregnancy.

Degenerative sicknesses are more serious. They result from the chronic deterioration of the body's organs and functions, and are more infrequent among children and young people than they are among adults and older people. These illnesses normally take longer to develop, and result from chronic imbalances in the daily diet and way of life. The degenerative process may not produce noticeable symptoms until many years have passed. However, even though they may not reach a critical stage until years later, degenerative processes frequently begin in childhood. Many children and young people have elevated cholesterol levels and hardening of the arteries, both of which lead to heart disease. Children also suffer from degenerative conditions such as epilepsy, asthma, cystic fibrosis, multiple sclerosis, diabetes, muscular dystrophy, and mental disturbances, as well as cancer and AIDS. Cancer is now the second leading cause of death among children aged five to fourteen.

Another category of disorders occurs when an acute, severe adjustment leads to a rapid deterioration in the quality of the blood, cells, and organs. These *adjustment/degenerative* disorders occur when a chronically unbalanced diet creates an abnormal condition in the blood and body fluids, cells, and tissues. With this underlying condition as a base, adjustments can escalate into a more serious degenerative condition. Examples include meningitis resulting from improper handling of the measles, as well as pneumonia, polio, rheumatic fever, smallpox, and sudden infant death syndrome (SIDS). An extreme or unbalanced diet weakens natural immunity and increases susceptibility to infectious disorders. Children with more healthy autoimmune systems enjoy natural immunity from many of the common infectious conditions encountered during childhood.

In general, simple adjustments involve a child's daily *condition*, especially blood quality, which is always changing in response to diet and environment. Degenerative sicknesses are much deeper. They affect the *constitution*, including the structure and quality of the organs and tissues. The constitution begins forming in the womb, and degenerative disorders frequently originate with the foods eaten by the mother during this period or even prior to conception when foods affect the parents' reproductive cells. The wide range of birth defects, for example, results from extremes in the diet or environment during pregnancy or before conception.

An extreme diet during pregnancy can create constitutional weakness. These deficiencies are often the basis for the development of many degenerative conditions that appear in childhood or later in life. The macrobiotic diet and way of life, however, strengthen the constitution and can prevent the development of many degenerative conditions. The constitution is not completely formed until maturity. It is influenced by the quality of foods eaten in childhood and during the period of growth. Many children who have started macrobiotics have experienced improvement in a variety of chronic conditions and an overall strengthening of their physical and mental vitality. Children who are macrobiotic from conception, or prior to conception, are often born with strong constitutions. If they continue to eat well, they can enjoy good health throughout their lives and remain free of more serious illnesses.

CHILDHOOD DISORDERS

In the following sections, we present the macrobiotic approach to common childhood problems. It is important to remember that these recommendations are for educational purposes and do not represent medical advice. They should not be used in place of qualified medical care. Emergency cases require prompt medical attention. At the same time, we suggest that you contact a qualified macrobiotic center or instructor when making changes in your child's diet or way of life, or when using home therapies. Appropriate resources are now available throughout the world, and we advise all parents to make use of them. Thousands of parents have used simple methods such as those that follow, and have found them safe and effective in keeping their children healthy. Eating appropriate foods is one of the methods for improving health. Therefore, the recommendations in this chapter often include the names of particular foods. When these names are *italicized*, recipes can be found in Chapter 6. Directions for preparing externally applied treatments (i.e., washes and massages) appear in Chapter 7. The names of these treatments appear in SMALL UPPER CASE letters in this chapter.

The recommendations for home care provided in each section are safe, simple to use, and very effective. However, it is far better to avoid imbalances on a day-to-day basis, or to deal with them as they develop, rather than try to make adjustments after imbalances begin to cause troublesome symptoms.

Study, discussion of health problems with friends, and experience will enable parents to develop good judgment and be sensitive to the conditions of their children and other family members. Remember that a balanced diet and way of life are the factors that determine our physical and emotional well-being.

Adenoiditis

See Sore Throats and Tonsillitis.

Attention Deficit Syndrome

See Hyperactivity.

Bed-Wetting and Sleeping Difficulties

There are many varieties of bed-wetting, the medical term for which is enuresis. In one variety, a child does not develop nighttime bladder control. In another, a child develops control but lapses into periods of wetting the bed.

It is commonly thought that bed-wetting is caused largely by emotional or psychological problems. Although these certainly play a role in many cases, dietary imbalances are often the more direct, underlying cause.

The two main types of bed-wetting have opposite dietary causes.

Accidents, Emergencies, and First Aid

Accidents are a major source of injury and suffering for children today. Like physical and mental disorders, they often have their root in daily diet and way of life. Alcohol abuse, for example, is a leading cause of automobile accidents, including those among young people.

As a fundamental way of preventing accidents, you can provide your children with a balanced, natural foods diet and an orderly, yet flexible, way of life. Being continually aware of your children's day-to-day condition and eating habits is also important in accident prevention.

Parents naturally possess an intuitive sense in regard to their children's health and well-being. A mother will often know instinctively whether her children are safe or in danger, or whether they are healthy or sick, even when apart from them.

Parents' intuitive awareness of their children's condition is strengthened by a balanced natural diet. Many animals have an instinctive awareness of danger and are thus able to avoid it. Animals live with the rhythms of nature and eat natural unprocessed foods.

The modern highly processed diet dulls the capacity for natural intuition. Items such as sugar, alcohol, and drugs and medications weaken the nervous system. When this happens, our ability to avoid potential hazards, or to respond quickly and appropriately should an emergency arise, becomes diminished. Foods such as meat, cheese, milk, and other fatty items also dull the nervous system. Excess in the organs, tissues, and glands diminishes our receptability to the environment and makes it more difficult to respond appropriately. Many people today have a layer of hard fat just below the skin. (This condition is common in thin people as well as in the overweight.) Not only does this condition interfere with the body's ability to discharge toxic excess, but it also reduces sensitivity to the social and physical environment. A person with this condition is often insensitive to potential hazards and may become overly confident or careless.

We recommend that you eat well and encourage your children to do so as well in order to avoid accidents. You also need to learn the basics of first aid in case an emergency does arise. You can familiarize yourself with basic fundamentals such as:

- *How to deal with wounds, including first aid for severe bleeding and methods to prevent infection.*
- *How to deal with specific injuries, including those involving the head, eyes, back, chest, and so on.*
- *How to recognize and treat shock.*
- *How to deal with breathing emergencies, including artificial respiration. Water and boating safety are also important.*
- *How to deal with choking and swallowed objects.*
- *What to do in case of accidental poisoning.*
- *How to classify and treat burns.*
- *How to deal with frostbite and exposure to cold.*
- *What to do in the case of heatstroke, heat exhaustion, and heat cramps.*
- *How to respond to sudden illness such as fainting, convulsion, or febrile seizures.*
- *How to prepare dressings and bandages, and how to make an appropriate first aid kit.*
- *How to respond to bone and joint injuries, including sprains, fractures, and dislocations.*
- *What to do for foreign objects in the ears, eyes, and nose.*
- *How to respond in an emergency: how to administer appropriate first aid, enlist help from bystanders, contact the appropriate emergency medical services (EMS) personnel, and be of help to the medical staff at the hospital emergency room.*
- *How to adjust your child's daily diet during recovery from accident or injury.*

There are many good books that deal with the basics of first aid and emergency care. We recommend that all parents consult texts such as Standard First Aid and Personal Safety *published by the American Red Cross. The macrobiotic approach to first aid and emergency care is outlined in* Macrobiotic Home Remedies *(see Recommended Reading List). You may refer to this text for more specific guidance and advice. Once an emergency situation has been stabilized with the appropriate medical assistance, we recommend contacting a qualified macrobiotic advisor or educational center for additional suggestions and guidance.*

Some children consistently release urine early in the evening, soon after going to sleep. Others wet the bed later at night or early in the morning.

BED-WETTING IN THE EARLY EVENING

In the early evening, atmospheric energy is becoming more still or quiet. We may say that it is settling down. If your child eats too many yin foods, he will be more likely to wet the bed early in the evening, when atmospheric energy is more contractive. An overly expanded bladder releases urine so as to contract along with the energy of the environment.

An overemphasis on yin foods or beverages in the diet can also interfere with sound sleep during the early evening. When a child has difficulty going to sleep, or tends to wake up soon after going to bed, the cause is often too high an intake of excessive yin items. An overly yin condition prevents the child from "settling down" into a deep and restful sleep.

BED-WETTING IN THE EARLY MORNING

The Earth's atmosphere begins to "awaken" in the early morning. Energy begins to move in an upward direction. The bladder normally expands and relaxes at this time, as urine accumulates in it. When children wet their beds in the early morning—say, from 2 A.M. to 7 A.M.—the cause is often a preference for salt or other excessive yang items. These can cause the bladder to become chronically tight and constricted, and limit its capacity to hold urine. Excess can then easily spill over in the form of bed-wetting.

A more yang imbalance can cause your child to have difficulty sleeping during the early morning hours. Your child can easily become restless and unsettled during this time if the diet contains too many excessive yang factors.

DIETARY CHANGES

When the bladder is overly expanded, the intake of excessive yin foods and beverages can be reduced or avoided. Fruits and fruit juices, sugar and concentrated sweeteners, too many salads or raw vegetables, spices, or too much fluid can contribute to this condition. However, do not overcompensate by trying to give your child too many salty foods. The use of salt should at all times be appropriate for your child's age and condition. A balanced macrobiotic diet with appropriate variety would be most beneficial. Simply be careful about your child's intake of fruits, concentrated sweeteners, salads, and fluids.

For an overly contracted condition, reduce or avoid the intake of excessive yang items. Meats, eggs, and poultry are best avoided, and white-meat fish is recommended only for occasional consumption. Within the appropriate macrobiotic diet, be careful about your child's intake of salt and baked flour products, and be sure that your child enjoys plenty of lightly steamed or boiled vegetables. High-quality yin items, such as hot apple cider, baked apples, or cooked northern fruits, can often help relax the bladder when consumed on occasion. (Recipes are in Chapter 6.)

These recommendations may also be applied when children have trouble sleeping, depending upon whether the child wakes up earlier or later in the evening.

Behavioral Problems

See Hyperactivity.

Chicken Pox

Chicken pox is a common childhood illness, although many macrobiotic children never experience it. When a child's intake includes many fatty or oily items, including milk, chicken, eggs, pizza, fried foods, and chips, or too many simple sugars, including those in fruits, refined sugar, and concentrated sweeteners, the excessive factors contained in these foods may erupt in a skin discharge. The discharge is thought to be triggered by a virus; however, not everyone who is exposed to the virus develops chicken pox. Some exposed children develop a very mild form of the illness with only a few blisters, while others develop a rash and blisters over the entire body. These differences in susceptibility are due to differences in diet, physical constitution, and environment.

The main symptoms of chicken pox include low-grade fever, aches and pains, and a loss of appetite. As the blisters turn to scabs, the child with chicken pox often experiences itching. The scabs usually peel off within ten days or so.

DIETARY CHANGES

Children with chicken pox may eat according to the standard macrobiotic diet, with appropriate adjustments for their age and condition.

During the time when the chicken pox is developing, it is better not to serve animal foods to your child; however, a small piece of broiled white-meat fish may be eaten on occasion if craved, together with a garnish of one or two tablespoons of grated raw daikon and one or two drops of tamari. It is better for the child with chicken pox to avoid buckwheat groats, soba noodles, and buckwheat flour. Salad, raw fruits, and fruit juices are best minimized or avoided until the condition clears up. It is also better to reduce or avoid bread, muffins, cookies, pancakes, and other flour products; however, whole wheat noodles or unleavened sourdough bread may be eaten occasionally. Your child's intake of sweets is best limited to occasional cooked fruit desserts, while the use of oil nuts and nut butters is best minimized or avoided. Your child can enjoy lightly toasted sesame seeds sprinkled on various dishes, and other roasted seeds can be eaten as snacks.

Your child can return to the standard macrobiotic diet appropriate for his age and condition once the chicken pox clears up.

Special Dishes and Preparations

For aches and pains, a mild *Ume-Sho-Kuzu Drink* may be given once a day for several days. The drink should be mildly seasoned—much more mildly than for adults—and children who have not yet begun to include salt should not be given this drink. This beverage is also helpful for headaches.

For lack of appetite, children can take one or two bowls of *Special Rice Cream* each day for several days, in addition to their other grains and normal dishes. A small volume of macrobiotic condiments may be used when appropriate.

RECOMMENDATIONS

Children with chicken pox can rest at home as they recover. The condition can spread to other susceptible children until the blisters have all dried and formed scabs. Children can be kept at home during this period.

A warm daily RICE BRAN (nuka) BATH can help relieve itching. Your child can soak in hot nuka water for several minutes daily, or a towel or face cloth can be dipped in warm nuka water and used to pat the affected area. A skin wash can also be made with dried daikon or turnip leaves.

Itching often becomes worse when wool or synthetic fibers are used for clothing or sheets, pillowcases, or blankets. Cotton pajamas, underwear, bathrobes, and bedding are preferable to synthetics to minimize itching. Soaps and shampoos made from natural vegetable materials are also preferable to those containing chemicals.

PALM HEALING can be used to ease the discomfort of headaches, fever, or other symptoms.

Colds and Flu

The average child today has as many as eight colds a year, an indication that our modern diet and lifestyle have become increasingly unnatural. Children between the ages of three and six usually have more colds than older or younger children.

Colds are much less frequent among children who eat a balanced, natural foods diet. Colds represent the discharge of excess in the diet. The accumulation and discharge of excess often provides fertile ground for one of the more than one hundred cold viruses that have been identified so far.

The symptoms of a cold are usually nasal discharge as well as sneezing, coughing, and fever that usually does not exceed 102°F. Some children develop pink, watery eyes and a slight whitish-yellow discharge from the eye. Irregular bowel movements and sometimes diarrhea can accompany colds.

Influenza, or the "flu," includes many of these symptoms, along with body aches, vomiting, diarrhea, headache, and flushing of the neck, face, and chest.

Colds primarily involve the upper respiratory organs—the throat, sinuses, and nasal passages. The flu also affects these areas, but usually produces more generalized symptoms throughout the body. In some cases, it involves the digestive organs, a condition commonly known as "intestinal flu."

THE COLD CYCLE

Colds and flu typically follow a natural course. They represent a movement of excessive energy within the body. The typical cold cycle begins with a more yin, expansive, and outward phase, and finishes with a more yang, inward, or consolidated phase. The more yin phase is commonly called the acute or early stage of a cold. It generally lasts for three or four days, during which time excess begins to accumulate and is discharged through the upper respiratory tract. At first, the discharge is usually watery and loose, and the cold virus takes root in and spreads throughout the mucous membranes of the nose and throat. Fever begins during this stage, and the child may start to discharge through coughing.

Once the initial stage has been completed, the cold cycle enters a phase of consolidation and resolution. This is commonly known as the late stage of a cold. The thin, watery discharge usually becomes thicker and yellowish in color. The immune system begins to resist further spread of the virus, and appetite and energy start to return. Swollen, inflamed mucous membranes gradually return to a more contracted, normal state. Coughing usually continues through this stage, and may be worse in the evening during the time when energy in the lungs and large intestine is normally more active.

Ultimately, more normal discharge processes take over the elimination of the remaining excess. Discharge is then accomplished through the kidneys, skin, lungs, and intestines. At this time, the cold resolves itself and the child returns to a normal condition.

THE FLU CYCLE

The flu normally follows a cycle similar to that of a cold, lasting from three days to a week. In some cases, however, one cycle is not enough to discharge accumulated excess, and several flu cycles may occur one after the other. Symptoms sometimes disappear after several days and then return unexpectedly.

These cycles can be subdivided into the five general stages shown in Figure 5.1. The stages of onset and acute symptoms represent more yin, or expansive phases, while gathering, consolidation, and resolution are more yang phases.

DIETARY CAUSES

When the discharge of a cold involves the upper body—the nasal passages, head, and throat, for example—the primary cause is excessive yin items in the diet. These can include simple sugars, concentrated sweeteners, fruits and fruit juices, spices, tomatoes, potatoes, and other highly acidic vegetables, soft drinks, and ice cream, as well as consump-

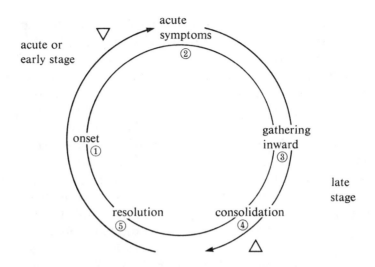

Figure 5.1 The Cycle of the Common Cold

tion of too much liquid. When the discharge affects the lungs and middle section of the body, including the stomach, the primary cause is the overconsumption of the excess yin items mentioned above plus fats and oils, including those in dairy products, poultry, and other animal foods. Discharges that affect the small and large intestines are caused by too high an intake of more heavy animal fats in addition to the items already mentioned.

Colds tend to be prevalent during the autumn and winter, and there are good reasons why this is so. The diets of many people today do not reflect natural seasonal variations; dietary adaptations can help people adjust to changing weather conditions. In addition, during the colder months, the air in many homes becomes unnaturally warm and dry. This creates a considerable difference between the indoor and outdoor environment. The unusually hot and dry condition inside the home causes many children (and adults) to consume a large amount of extreme yin items, including ice cream, cold soft drinks, tropical fruits, sugar, and fruit juices. These foods cause the person's condition to become disharmonious with the outside environment. One result is a lowered resistance to the colder outside temperatures and to the numerous viruses and bacteria that exist naturally in the environment.

Some children experience continual colds and flu during the winter, while others are rarely affected. Yet both groups are frequently exposed to the same general pool of viruses in the environment. Why is it that some children are greatly affected while others are affected only slightly or not at all? The differences in resistance must be due to a deeper underlying factor, such as one's daily dietary practice. The daily diet either strengthens or weakens natural resistance, and raises or lowers the threshold of infection. The key to preventing colds is found more in avoiding extreme foods that lead to recurring discharges and lowered resistance than it is in isolating ourselves from viruses and bacteria. Strengthening the natural powers of resistance through a balanced diet is the most direct way to prevent these common conditions.

Colds tend to occur with greater frequency among children than adults. Children are generally more sensitive to the effects of food and the environment. Their conditions change rapidly from day to day and moment to moment. Excess tends to discharge more quickly. Adults usually have many more years of excessive diet behind them. Their ability to discharge is often less efficient. Rather than discharging, excess tends to accumulate in the internal organs and throughout the body, leading eventually to a degenerative disorder of some kind.

When children have a chronically unbalanced blood condition, the bacteria normally found in the mucous membranes may spread rapidly during a cold. A secondary infection may also develop, with possible additional complications such as ear infection, sinusitis, sore throat, laryngitis, and, in rare instances, pneumonia (see these sections for further information).

These complications originate with a chronically unbalanced condition in the blood and body fluids that results from an extreme diet. Children who eat macrobiotically generally have fewer colds. Because their overall condition is generally healthy and well-balanced, these children experience minor colds without complication. They normally improve with the help of just slight changes in diet and with simple home remedies and therapies.

DIETARY CHANGES

Children often want to eat less when they have a cold, especially during the first several days. Instead of trying to force them to eat, it is better to have a variety of simply prepared dishes available for when they feel hungry. Children with colds can generally follow the standard dietary guidelines that are appropriate for their age and condition.

Grains may be more appealing when they are soft-cooked or are served in soups. Soft-cooked rice (rice kayu) or millet is often preferred, as is soup with rice, millet, or barley and vegetables. It is generally advisable to limit or avoid the intake of flour products, including bread, muffins, cookies, and creamy, floury cereals. However, whole grain noodles or a slice or two of unyeasted sourdough bread may be served occasionally. *Light Miso Soup* and tamari broth soups may also be eaten if desired.

It is better to avoid the intake of raw salad as well as oil during the recovery period. Vegetables can be lightly steamed, boiled, cooked nishime style, water sautéed, or served in soups and stews. Sweet-tasting vegetables, including squash, cabbage, onions, daikon, and carrots, are especially recommended, although other varieties can also be included.

Bean and sea vegetable dishes may be served as usual. Fish is best avoided during recovery, although a small amount of low-fat, white-meat fish may be eaten if desired. Raw fruits and fruit juices are best avoided. Sweet-tasting desserts can be made with cooked apples and other seasonal fruits. Rice or amazaké pudding may also be served. It is better to avoid the use of concentrated sweeteners during a cold.

Children may enjoy the usual macrobiotic snacks, although nuts and nut butters are best avoided for the duration of the cold. It is also better to avoid juices, sparkling waters, and other more yin beverages during a cold. Bancha twig and cereal grain tea are preferable. Cold or iced foods or beverages are also best avoided. Everything should be hot, warm, or room temperature (more yang). An occasional small cup of hot apple juice may be included.

As the cold begins to run its course, your child can begin to resume his normal way of eating. However, it is better to stay within the above guidelines until the symptoms disappear and your child returns to a completely normal condition.

Special Dishes and Preparations

It is important to remember that the measles begins with symptoms that resemble colds and flu: red, watery eyes, loss of appetite, fatigue, fever, and a hard, dry cough. Therefore, if your child has not had the measles, we recommend waiting to see whether a rash develops before preparing special dishes or external applications, especially those which aid in fever control. If it turns out that your child is developing a case of measles, refer to the section on measles later in this chapter for advice about how to proceed.

If your child has had the measles, the following special dishes and beverages can be used in easing the discomfort of colds and flu.

Easing Coughing and Nasal Discharge

Try *Lotus Root Tea*. Tea made from grated fresh lotus root can be helpful in easing respiratory congestion. Small children can receive one-third to one-half cup; older children can drink a full cup. Lotus Root Tea can be given once a day for several days or during the time that your child is coughing.

Easing Digestive Discomfort, Fatigue, and Aches and Pains

Try *Ume-Sho-Kuzu Drink*. This powdered kuzu root drink can be used to restore vitality and ease digestive upset, including diarrhea. The drink can be given for one to three days. Small children can have one-quarter to one-third of a cup, older children one-half to one cup. (Children who have not yet started to use shalt should not be given this preparation.) The drink should be milder than for adults. *Ume-Sho-Kuzu* can also help restore the appetite.

Reducing Fever

The following teas can help reduce fever:

- *Dried Daikon Tea*
- *Dried Daikon and Shiitake Tea*
- *Grated Daikon Tea*
- *Shiitake Tea*

Remember, if your child has not had measles, wait until it can be determined that the cold is not actually the onset of measles before preparing the special drinks and dishes.

RECOMMENDATIONS

Children can rest at home during the first three to four days of a cold. It may not be necessary for children to stay in bed during this time, although if they want to do so, let them. If the weather is mild, a child with a cold can go outside for brief periods if he feels strong enough and is properly dressed; however, it is better to wait until the fever disappears before permitting your child to go outside.

If your child's cough makes him uncomfortable, the air in the room can be kept slightly moist by placing a pot or two of steaming water in a corner. An electric hot plate can be used to heat a pot of water. Electric steam vaporizers or humidifiers can also be used.

PALM HEALING can be helpful in relieving the discharge symptoms of a cold. Refer to Chapter Seven for additional techniques used to alleviate fever, headache, and stomach or intestinal discomfort.

Treatment of Accompanying Symptoms

Colds and flus are often accompanied by symptoms such as chills, body aches, and headaches. The following is a listing of symptoms and traditional treatments.

Fever

When your child's cold or flu is accompanied by fever that exceeds 103°F, you may wish to use natural external applications such as GREEN VEGETABLE PLASTER, TOFU AND GREEN VEGETABLE PLASTER, and TOFU PLASTER. These plasters do not weaken or interfere with the process of discharge. If you are unfamiliar with these applications, contact a macrobiotic center or instructor before using them.

As mentioned previously, it is better not to apply plasters if a child has not yet had the measles. After a child has had the measles, however, external applications can be used when a simple fever becomes uncomfortably high.

You may also with to apply a WARM ROASTED SALT PACK to the abdomen.

Headaches

The compresses and massage described in the discussion of headaches (see pages 155-156), including the recommendations for the relief of blocked sinuses, can be applied when necessary. However, it is better not to apply warm towels to your child's head or neck while he is experiencing fever.

Chills, Fatigue, or Body Aches

Rubbing your child's body with a warm towel or warm ginger towel can help in relieving these conditions. Hot towels are best *not* applied to the whole body during an active fever.

Diarrhea

A WARM ROASTED SALT PACK can be applied to the abdomen to help relieve looseness in the bowels. (Make sure the pack is not uncomfortably hot and do *not* apply it to infants.)

Cough or Congestion

Warm towels can be applied to the chest in order to loosen stagnated mucus. Apply warm towels repeatedly for ten to fifteen minutes. They can also be applied to the sinuses to help relieve stagnation in the nasal passages.

Croup

See Sore Throats and Tonsillitis.

Earaches

Excess frequently gathers in the middle or inner ear. These excessive factors come primarily from the overconsumption of fruits, fruit juices, sugar and concentrated sweeteners, oily foods, spices, and other extreme yin items. Animal fats, including those in dairy foods, meats, poultry, and eggs, can also cause excess to accumulate in the ears.

The ears are especially sensitive to the effects of cold or iced foods or beverages, as are the kidneys. The overconsumption of ice cream, soft drinks, Popsicles, and similar frozen items is a frequent contributor to problems in the ears and kidneys. Too much salt or extremely salty foods in the diet can also contribute to ear and kidney problems.

Children who consume the modern diet frequently have earaches. One or two earaches a year is not unusual for children today. On the other hand, children who eat a more natural, balanced diet rarely experience earaches. When they do, the underlying dietary causes can usually be readily identified and corrected.

In some cases, the accumulation of excess in the ear contributes to the growth of viruses or bacteria and to infection. Ear infections are more common when the natural immunity is weakened through the overconsumption of sugar, tropical fruits, drugs and medications, and fatty animal foods. When younger children develop ear infections, they often have fever. Fever is less common among older children with earaches.

The most common site for an ear infection is the region behind the eardrum. Infection here is called *otitis media,* or middle ear infection. Pain frequently results when accumulated excess, including fluid, mucus, or infection, hampers the normal drainage of the ear through the eustachian tubes.

Some children still feel pressure and experience blockage in the ears for several weeks after an earache has disappeared. They may even experience some temporary loss of hearing. This is often the result of the buildup of liquid and mucus in the middle ear. The eustachian tubes often become blocked as a result.

In some cases, earaches are caused when children put some type of small object into their ears, including beans, stones, paper, and so on. If the object can be seen and grasped easily, it can be carefully and gently removed. If it cannot be easily grasped, or if trying to reach it could result in its being pushed further in, medical assistance is needed. It is also advisable to seek assistance if a child punctures the eardrum with a pencil or other sharp object.

Some children experience a chronic buildup of wax in the ears. Wax is often caused by excessive fats, oils, and sugars in the diet. Milk and other dairy foods, candy, sugared soft drinks, tropical fruits, and oily or greasy foods are often the underlying cause.

Tympanotomy, or the surgical puncturing of the eardrum to allow drainage of fluid, is widespread today. Tympanotomy is now the most common operation among children, and has surpassed removal of the tonsils. This procedure is often done in cases of recurrent middle ear infection. It does not address the underlying cause of the condition, however, and can cause such side effects as scarring of the eardrum, hearing loss, and acute middle ear infection. It is recommended that such a drastic procedure be used only in emergencies and *after* dietary changes and home care have been tried.

DIETARY CHANGES

As with the other conditions presented in this book, simple adjustments in diet can often help in bringing relief. Children who experience an earache can adopt the standard macrobiotic diet—with a selection of foods and cooking methods appropriate for their age and condition. Avoiding or minimizing the foods that contribute to the swelling of the mucous membranes of the middle ear—dairy products, sugar, and tropical fruits, for example—helps eliminate the underlying cause.

Specific adjustments, such as those recommended for colds and fever, may also be helpful when necessary (see the appropriate sections in this chapter).

RECOMMENDATIONS

GREEN VEGETABLE PLASTER or TOFU AND GREEN VEGETABLE PLASTER can be applied to the painful ear. It is recommended that the cool plasters be used together with WARM SESAME OIL DROPS. Several drops of warm, specially filtered sesame oil are put in the ear with an eyedropper. It is better not to use these drops, however, if the ear is already draining.

Absorbent cotton can be put on the ear if a thin, clear liquid is discharged. Ear discharges or leakages usually occur when the eardrum tears from the pressure of infection. The tear is usually tiny and will normally heal quickly. It does not necessarily indicate a more serious infection.

Middle ear problems often occur together with stagnation in the kidneys. Mucus, fat, or liquid may accumulate in the kidneys at the same time that middle ear pain is being experienced. Repeatedly applying warm towels to the middle back can help loosen and dissolve stagnation in the kidneys. Towels can be warmed under a hot faucet or in a pan of hot water. Adjust the temperature of the towels by waving them back and forth after wringing them out. Younger children should receive a milder, not-so-hot application, while older children can tolerate hotter towels. Do not make the towel so hot that your child squirms or cries each time it touches the skin. The purpose of the application is to help swollen tissues relax and become more activated. If your child becomes tense or fearful, the effectiveness of the application will be diminished.

PALM HEALING can be very helpful in comforting an earache or in helping to loosen stagnated mucus in the middle ear.

Eczema

See Skin Disorders.

Fever

When children eat a naturally balanced diet, they rarely experience fever. Children who eat properly run a fever only when their diet or environment becomes extreme. Measles, which represents a normal discharge, is the only exception.

Simple fevers represent the discharge of excessive factors. Depending upon the type of excess being discharged, the fever may or may not be accompanied by other discharge symptoms, such as coughing, runny nose, or sore throat.

In most cases, fevers are not serious and respond to simple home remedies and therapies. Fevers that indicate serious illness are usually accompanied by other symptoms, such as difficulty breathing, extreme listlessness, or behavioral disturbance. Fevers that are more serious are usually those resulting from obvious medical emergencies such as heatstroke or poisoning. Parents suspecting an emergency condition are, of course, advised to seek appropriate medical attention.

Simple fevers result when the discharge of vibration from metabolic activity becomes excessive. This discharge may take many forms, one of which is heat. In Oriental medicine, the generation of heat from metabolic activity is coordinated by what is referred to as the body's triple heater function. The name triple heater comes from the three energy centers, or chakras, where this function is coordinated. The generation of heat in the upper body is centered around the heart energy center, or chakra; in the mid-section, around the stomach energy center; and in the abdomen, around the small intestine energy center, also known as the hara chakra. These chakras can also be referred to as "energy furnaces."

Fevers result when the energy within these furnaces becomes excessive. The body receives energy from the environment in the form of food, light, heat, and other types of radiation. In normal circumstances, a child discharges unused factors through urination, bowel movements, and breathing, as well as through the skin. Children also constantly discharge through activity and the maintenance of normal body temperature, through which a great deal of heat is continually generated.

When the child's intake becomes excessive, then a variety of abnormal discharge mechanisms may take place. Fever is one of the more common mechanisms for the discharge of excess. In many cases, simple fevers occur when children become constipated. When the abdominal energy center becomes blocked or stagnated, excess begins to accumulate and discharge through other channels, including fever.

As we have already mentioned, fever is a mechanism through which the body releases excess and maintains harmony with the environment.

It is not, as is commonly thought, a "defense" against disease. The body does not "fight" illness in the way that opposing armies clash on the battlefield. Bacteria and viruses are not our enemies but are the natural results of excess. Fever helps the body discharge these and other excesses. For example, fever is associated with the release of chemicals known as pyrogens, which stimulate white blood cells to eliminate viruses and bacteria. The white blood cells do not "fight" viruses and bacteria, rather they eat them. Physiologists refer to this function as phagocytosis, from the Greek, *phagein*, "to eat." One part of the body's immune response is actually an internal eating mechanism; it is no more violent than a plant's drawing nutrients from the soil or a person's enjoying a meal. If we eat excessively, then the white blood cells are kept busy eating the products of our excess, including viruses and bacteria. The concept of the immune system "fighting" infection is actually a profound misconception. The presence of fever is a positive thing. It shows that a child's power to discharge is strong and functioning properly.

DIETARY CAUSES

The intake of extreme yang foods, such as meat, eggs, salt, poultry, and fish, can produce fever. Fever can also result from the intake of extreme yin food items, such as sugar, tropical fruits, soda, honey, and other concentrated sweeteners, ice cream, spices, chocolate, and soft drinks. Foods that cause constipation, such as creamy flour cereals, oily, greasy or sticky foods, nut butters, and baked flour products, can also produce fever.

DIETARY CHANGES

When your child experiences a fever, first assess his overall condition to determine the possible causes and hopefully rule out a specific disorder or emergency such as heatstroke. Also, please note that if your child has not had the measles, it is better to deal with a fever as if it is the first sign of this illness. If measles is treated improperly, more serious complications may result in some cases, especially if the fever is mistakenly suppressed. When this is done, rather than discharging naturally, the condition goes deep inside the body. The risk of a more serious complication is increased when this happens. Please refer to Measles for suggestions on handling the condition properly. Additional information is also included in *Macrobiotic Pregnancy and Care of the Newborn.*

Children with fevers can eat according to the standard macrobiotic diet with appropriate adjustments for their age and condition. The dietary extremes that underlie the condition can be reduced or eliminated. If, for example, your child drinks several cups of fruit juice daily or often eats sweetened desserts or oily snacks, you may need to eliminate these items from his diet or at least limit them until your child's fever subsides. Even after the fever disappears, it may be necessary to limit your child's intake of these items to prevent discharges from occurring in the future. If you determine that the fever is due to too many salty or baked foods or a lack of fresh foods, your child may temporarily need to be put on a salt-free diet, or the amount of salt used in cooking may need to be substantially reduced. You may also want to reduce your child's intake of dishes that require much cooking or baking. Try to include quickly steamed greens, boiled salads, and other lightly cooked vegetable dishes on a daily basis.

As we have already mentioned, fevers often result from constipation. Foods such as whole grain breads or muffins with peanut or sesame butter can cause stagnation in the digestive tract and lead to constipation. When this occurs, cooked whole grain dishes, including snacks such as sushi and rice balls, are best substituted for bread or flour products, while nuts and nut butters are best avoided until the condition improves. Occasional snacks of udon or other whole grain noodles are easiest to digest and may be preferable to flour products, while sweet rice mochi or arepa made with whole corn can also be eaten as snacks.

Special Dishes and Preparations

In addition to modifying your child's overall diet, the following special dishes and beverages are often helpful in relieving simple fevers:

- *Special Rice Cream*
- *Dried Daikon Tea*
- *Shiitake Tea*
- *Dried Daikon/Shiitake Tea*
- *Grated Daikon Tea*
- *Cereal Grain Tea*
- *Grated Sour Apple*

RECOMMENDATIONS

Giving aspirin or other fever-reducing medications routinely for simple fevers weakens the body's natural discharging powers. Aspirin is extremely yin and paralyzes the power to expel excess, so discharge symptoms such as coughing or fever disappear. The entire body becomes weaker as a result, and it takes more time to recover and return to a normal, healthy state.

In general, it is better *not* to suppress the fever. It makes more sense to allow the excess to be eliminated from the body. Natural applications such as PLASTERS can help ease discomfort. At the same time, they do not weaken or interfere with the process of discharge. Plasters can be used if your child's fever goes higher than 103°F. GREEN VEGETABLE PLASTER, TOFU AND GREEN VEGETABLE PLASTER, and TOFU PLASTER are effective in reducing fevers. If you are unfamiliar with these applications, contact a macrobiotic center or instructor before using them.

As mentioned previously, it is better not to apply plasters if a child has not yet had the measles. After a child has had the measles, however, external applications can be used when a simple fever becomes uncomfortably high.

A child with a fever may lose fluid through perspiration. It is better to keep your child's room slightly moister and warmer than usual. The air can be moistened by putting a pot or two of steaming water in a corner of the room. Water can be heated on an electric hot plate, or moist towels can be put on a radiator. Humidifiers or electric steam vaporizers can also be used.

Children can drink *Rice, Barley*, or *Bancha Teas* to make up for fluid loss. It is important to prevent chilling. Keep your child well-dressed with cotton clothing and covered with blankets. For fevers that are localized in the head and neck, keep the rest of the body covered and warm. If your child develops chills, apply a WARM SALT PACK to his abdomen. It is usually better to avoid cold water baths or alcohol rubs as a normal practice. These methods can shock the child's system and can produce chilling. They can also cause the excess to be directed toward the inside. If your child develops cold hands or feet, rub them gently with a washcloth that has been dipped in warm water. PALM HEALING can help reduce discomfort by allowing excessive energy to discharge more smoothly.

If a child experiences fever due to constipation, a simple ENEMA often brings relief. In many cases, an enema will lower the fever and make

make other special applications unnecessary. MASSAGE can also be helpful if your child runs a fever due to constipation. Use this method only if your child is over the age of two.

Flu

See Colds and Flu.

Gastroenteritis

See Stomachaches.

Headaches

Headaches are not common among children who eat well. If they do occur, it is usually because of some dietary excess; headaches are a symptom of discharge. In some cases, headaches arise together with other discharge symptoms, such as sore throat, fever, or abdominal pain. Headaches often accompany colds and the flu. Some headaches occur along with emotional stress, while others are the result of an injury to the head.

DIETARY CAUSES

The dietary causes of headaches vary, and depend upon the region of the head that is most affected. Headaches in the front of the head arise from the excessive intake of extremely yin foods, such as sugar, candy, ice cream, chocolate, spices, tropical fruits, soft drinks, iced beverages, and drugs and medications. Pain in the side of the head usually results from the overintake of more yin foods that are less extreme, such as ketchup, potatoes, oily chips, mustard, too many fresh fruits, tomatoes, fruit drinks, and nuts and nut butters. Oily or fried foods especially affect this region. Of the various sweeteners, the ones that tend to affect the front of the head are the more extreme: sugar, honey, and maple syrup. Rice honey and barley malt, which are yin but somewhat less so, tend to affect the side of the head when eaten in excess.

Children who eat meat, poultry, eggs, or more salty dishes are more prone to tension headaches in the back of the neck and head. These foods also produce tension in the shoulders. The regular consumption of very extreme foods like smoked salmon, bacon, liver, caviar, or eggs can cause headaches deeper inside the head, together with tension in other parts of the body.

Sinus Headaches

Headaches that occur together with the discharge of mucus from the nose or blocked nasal passages often indicate inflammation of the sinuses, or sinusitis. The sinuses can easily become blocked or inflamed when a child eats an unbalanced diet. Mucus in the sinuses often results from eating too many fatty or oily foods, including milk, ice cream, and other dairy products, oily desserts, or dishes that have a very greasy quality. Excessive sugar intake—whether in the form of refined sugar, honey, maple syrup, and other concentrated sweeteners or in the form of fruits—can also contribute to this condition, and to sinus inflammation. Too much fluid or too many watery foods can promote nasal blockage by causing the tissues in the sinuses and nasal passages to become swollen.

Migraines

Some children experience migraines, which are more severe than the types of headaches previously discussed. Migraines result when the arteries on the surface of the brain become more yin or swollen and cause pressure to build up. Migraines are often accompanied by nausea and vomiting, and tend to occur in families.

The dietary cause of migraines is the overconsumption of extreme yin foods and beverages. The repeated overconsumption of extremely expansive items causes the peripheral regions of the brain to swell, including the arteries just below the surface of the skull.

When children experience headaches, they may require a period of quiet rest. Headaches are often associated with psychological and emotional stresses that result from dietary imbalances. The intake of more extreme foods weakens the pain control mechanisms in the brain and causes oversensitivity to the normal stresses of daily living. Children who are frequently tired, anxious, or stressed by dietary imbalances are more prone to headaches. Children who frequently experience low-level headaches are often depressed as a result of chronic overconsumption of more extremely yin foods and beverages.

When the overall condition becomes unbalanced, factors such as simple pressure changes within the sinuses, changes in blood pressure that produce expansion or contraction in the arteries in the brain, or tension in the neck or shoulders can create a headache.

DIETARY CHANGES

As with other common conditions covered in this chapter, you should first check your child's overall condition when a headache develops and, hopefully, rule out a medical emergency. You can also ask your child what he has been eating. Any of the extreme foods that underlie the disorder are best avoided. Parents usually have a good idea of what younger children are eating, and can spot their imbalances relatively easily. When children get older, they may eat outside the home more frequently. Questioning them about what they have been eating is therefore helpful when seeking the underlying causes.

Dietary Adjustments for Specific Head Pains

Children with headaches can follow the standard macrobiotic diet with the appropriate adjustments for their age and condition. General adjustments in diet for the most common types of headaches are presented here, together with special dishes and preparations for use in each case. Since the recommendations vary slightly according to the location of the pain, it is important to ask your child where his head hurts.

Pain That Is Localized in the Front of the Head

More yin items—concentrated sweeteners, fruit juices, carbonated beverages, icy cold foods or drinks, and others—contribute to front headaches and are best avoided during a headache in this area. Oily chips and fried foods are also best avoided if this type of headache is being experienced. Children can eat a standard macrobiotic diet appropriate for their age and condition, with care not to overdo the intake of more yin foods and beverages.

Children who experience more yin headaches need to be careful about their intake of fruit, concentrated sweeteners such as rice honey and barley malt, and raw salads. They should also make sure that they do not consume too much liquid. The overconsumption of flour products can produce stagnation in the intestines and contribute to this condition, as can the intake of nuts, nut butters, and oily foods. Sinus headaches are often the result of excess milk, ice cream, cheese, sugar, and fruit.

Pain in the Sides of the Head

The less extremely yin items mentioned above are best reduced or avoided, together with foods to the far-yin and far-yang. The standard macrobiotic diet—with appropriate adjustments for age and condition— can form the basis of the child's way of eating.

Oily foods or snacks frequently contribute to this problem. It is better to minimize the use of oil in cooking until the condition improves. Nuts, nut butters, and chips are included in this category, as are oily baked goods. Herbal teas with an aromatic and stimulant effect can also produce pain in the side of the head, and are best avoided.

Tension Headaches in the Back of the Head

Animal foods and heavily salted foods or dishes are best reduced or avoided, as are more extremely yin items. The standard macrobiotic diet can be adopted with the necessary modifications for age and condition.

When children become too tight, it is important that they not use too much salt, and that you not serve them heavily salted foods, including snacks and processed items. Overly cooked dishes and baked foods can also contribute to a tight condition.

In general, the cooking for this condition can be light and fresh. Lightly steamed or boiled vegetables, plus plenty of sweet-tasting dishes are appropriate. A small volume of cooked fruit dessert can be enjoyed from time to time, and concentrated grain sweeteners can be added occasionally.

Pain Deep Inside the Head

Excessive yang foods are best reduced or avoided for this condition, and the standard macrobiotic diet with appropriate considerations can be adopted. The suggestions for pains in the back of the head can also be considered.

RECOMMENDATIONS

Along with correcting your child's physical condition through dietary change and home care, you also need to provide emotional support and reassurance. You need to search for any factors in your child's life that may contribute to emotional or psychological unhappiness. If your child is old enough, discussing this matter can be helpful.

PALM HEALING is especially helpful in easing headaches. Aside from restoring a more normal balance of energy, it establishes a soothing emotional bond between parent and child. It helps to relieve stress, tension, and anxiety and helps children relax and calm down. Palm healing methods are safe and effective and do not expose your child to artificial substances. If headaches persist, see your health care professional.

Home Care for Specific Head Pains

Traditional methods for treating head pain have been used safely and effectively for generations. Below, you will find home care techniques that are designed for specific types of head pains.

Pain in the Front or the Sides of the Head, Including Migraine Headaches

When headaches arise in this region, dilation of brain cells and blood vessels is the most frequent cause. Cold applications, such as a cold towel, can be applied to the forehead or top and sides of the head. Cold towels can be repeatedly applied for ten to fifteen minutes.

Tension Headaches in the Back of and Deep Inside the Head

Tension headaches caused by tension in the neck and shoulders can often be eased by applying warm towels to the back of the head and neck. Tension headaches deep inside the head—often the result of constriction of the arteries that nourish the brain, and of the brain tissues—can frequently be helped by wrapping a warm towel around the neck. Warm towels can be applied repeatedly for ten to fifteen minutes.

Sinus Headaches

Sinus blockage can often be relieved by applying a warm towel or washcloth to the forehead—above the eyes and nose—and to each of the cheekbones. Warm towels can be applied repeatedly for ten to fifteen minutes. Severe, chronic sinus blockage in older children can be loosened by applying a LOTUS ROOT PLASTER.

Hyperactivity and Behavioral Problems

There is no rigid standard for human behavior. Every child is unique, with differences in constitution, diet, environment, and upbringing. These influences produce an endless variety in behavior and appearance. It is because of these differences that life is so interesting, joyful, and amusing.

Food and environment are primary in determining behavior. Both influence the child long before conception. They determine the quality of the parental reproductive cells. They also determine the general pattern of the culture or society the child is born into, which in turn will influence how he will think and act. The child's constitution and condition, therefore, are a product of diet and environment. Behavior is simply the expression of the child's constitution and daily condition.

Today, many children have problems with learning, perception, and behavior. Many children have trouble learning basic reading, writing, spelling, and arithmetic. Some are consistently erratic in behavior. They cannot pay attention, are extreme in their emotions, and are unable to sit still. These children are often labeled hyperactive or hyperkinetic. They may or may not have specific learning disabilities, although many children who are considered hyperactive are actually quite bright. Hyperactivity is actually a comprehensive term that usually includes many traits.

It is important to remember, however, that children are normally active and energetic. They do not behave like adults, nor should they be expected to. It is necessary to be careful before labeling a child hyperactive, hyperkinetic, or learning disabled. All children learn at different rates. It is not test scores that are important, but whether children put forth their best efforts.

DIETARY CAUSES

Behavior and learning problems are related to the modern highly processed, artificial diet and to an increasingly unnatural lifestyle, including the use of synthetic materials in the home and at school. An extreme diet often interferes with the normal processes of learning and of normal or balanced behavior. An excessive intake of more yang items—meat, eggs, poultry, or refined salt, for example—can produce emotional characteristics such as overly aggressive behavior, extreme stubbornness, or an overly self-centered attitude. These food items tend to narrow the child's scope of vision and reduce patience, endurance, and sociability. The body and mind become less flexible when more yang extremes are overconsumed.

The excessive intake of yin extremes also contributes to behavioral and learning disabilities. Refined sugar, artificial sweeteners, milk, ice cream, refined flour, chocolate, and additives and preservatives can cause more yin disintegrative symptoms such as an inability to focus on visual images, sounds, or thoughts, a poor memory, a poor sense of balance, and a lack of self-discipline. Unfortunately, more than five thousand additives have been used in foods over the last twenty years.

In general, the symptoms of hyperactivity can be classified into two general categories, according to the primary foods that promote them. These include (1) symptoms influenced primarily by the overconsumption of yang extremes; and (2) those that are influenced primarily by the excessive intake of yin extremes. The most common symptoms of hyperactivity are classified by yin and yang factors in Table 5.1.

Table 5.1 Symptoms of Hyperactivity

More Yin Symptoms	More Yang Symptoms
Inability to focus on one thing at a time, or to think concretely.	Rigidity in body and mind, including extreme stubbornness or literal-mindedness.
Confusion, or inability to make order out of vibrations received by the brain.	Continual movement, especially involving large muscles of the body, such as continually getting up from a chair, always running rather than walking, jumping up and down, or rocking back and forth.
No sense of direction or purpose.	Overly rapid development, such as walking, crawling, or talking earlier than normal; or skipping stages of development.
Mixing up common yin and yang distinctions such as left and right, vertical and horizontal, inside and outside, front and back, or beginning and ending.	Impatience or lack of inhibition.

Table 5.1 Symptoms of Hyperactivity (cont.)

More Yin Symptoms	More Yang Symptoms
Being out of touch with the body, including not being aware of certain parts of the body, a lack of coordination, or a loss of control over body functions.	Overly rough or destructive behavior, including violent outbursts of temper.
Continual movement, especially involving small, nervous movements of the hands, fingers, or other parts of the body, including minor twitching or shaking.	Aggressiveness towards others, including bullying, harassing, or fighting with other children, or cruelty toward pets or others in a defenseless position.
Slow development, such as learning to walk, talk, or read later than normal.	Extreme ego-centeredness, to the point of being unaware of or insensitive to others.

The diet of most hyperactive children is generally extreme at both ends—meat, eggs, and poultry on one hand, and plenty of sugar, tropical fruits, chemicals, and refined and processed foods on the other. Their actions and behavior, therefore, tend to swing unpredictably back and forth between both extremes. Underlying both extremes is often the excessive overconsumption of milk and other dairy products.

When children have a tendency toward hyperactivity, artificial substances in the immediate environment often trigger symptoms. They frequently react to products ranging from chemicalized toothpaste to felt-tipped markers. A list of substances that can trigger extreme reactions in hyperactive children is presented in Table 5.2. As mentioned previously, we recommend using more natural materials in the home. Clothing, home fixtures, toys, soap, shampoo, toothpaste, laundry detergents, and kitchen utensils made from natural materials are preferred over those made from synthetic substances. Natural materials are less likely to trigger a reaction.

CURRENT APPROACHES

Current approaches to hyperactivity include nutritional management, behavior modification, counseling, special education programs, and drug therapy.

Dietary Changes

The management of hyperactivity through diet includes a variety of

Table 5.2 Examples of Environmental Irritants That Can Trigger an Increase in the Hyperactivity of an Exposed Child

Clothing
any polyester fabric or item
polyester bedding
permanent-press clothes not yet washed
TRIS flame retardant in clothes

House fixtures
blown-in insulation with
  urea formaldehyde
smell from new carpeting
fluorescent lighting
oil, natural gas, and coal heating systems
propane appliances
vinyl wallpaper
interior of new mobile homes
glue used in flooring, wallpaper,
  and paneling

Playthings
ball-point ink on skin
invisible ink on skin
flet-tip marker on skin
colored chalk
chalk dust in the air
finger paint
scratch and sniff books
putty-like, slimy, and clay-like
  modeling compounds
caps and fireworks
white powder inside balloons
Easter-egg dye

Toiletries
alcohol on skin
hand lotion
colored and perfumed soap
facial powder
eye shadow
fingernail polish
lipsticks to prevent chapping
perfume
after-shave lotion
hair spray
toothpaste
bubble bath
dental cleaning agents
fluoride treatment

adhesive bandages
colored and flavored medicine

Cleaning and polishing agents
disinfectant containing methyl salicylate
pine fragrance soap
furniture and floor wax
oven cleaner
pine fragrance liquid cleaner
rug shampoo
colored dishwasher detergent
fabric softener sheets for dryer

Paper products
colored or scented paper towels
colored or scented facial tissue
colored or scented bathroom tissue
colored cupcake liners
paper wiping rags

Workshop chemicals
fumes of paint, varnish, etc.
glue (including postage stamps and
  envelope seals)
gasoline fumes
gasoline or oil leak
chlorine in swimming pool
airborne particles of paint or varnish
  from sanding finished wood
freshly poured blacktop

Aromatics
mothballs
incense
scented candle
air freshener
dog and cat repellent
aerosol spray cans
smoke from a fire
smoke from a menthol cigarette

Plastics
old teflon pans, flaking
polyurethane food-storage bowls
plastic food wrap
waterbeds

Reprinted from *The Hyperactive Child and the Family* by John F. Taylor, Dodd, Mead & Company, 1980, pp. 54–55, with permission.

approaches, most notably that developed by the late Dr. Benjamin Fein-gold. Dr. Feingold reported success in reducing hyperactivity in about 50 percent of the cases under his care. The Feingold Diet involves primarily reducing or eliminating the intake of extreme yin items, including preservatives such as BHT and BHA, refined sugar, and chemical additives, including artificial flavors and colors. Products such as aspirin, bell peppers, chili powder, coffee, oranges, spearmint and peppermint, commercial tea, and tomatoes, all of which contain salicylates—acidic compounds found in fruits and other more yin foods—have also been associated with hyperactive reactions and are often eliminated from the diet.

The avoidance of more yin foods and other substances can lessen the more yin symptoms of hyperactivity; however, at least 50 percent of hyperactive children do not respond to this approach. This seems to indicate that many cases of hyperactivity result from the overconsumption of extreme yang foods or from the combined effect of both extremes. A dietary approach that takes both aspects into consideration is therefore necessary.

Drug Therapy

The other common approach to hyperactivity involves giving children amphetamine drugs such as Dexedrine and Ritalin. Like coffee, these drugs are often used as mental stimulants, and when taken regularly, they weaken the motion centers of the brain, and cause the child to become less hyperactive. They tend to activate the front portions of the brain, artificially stimulating the ability to focus thinking.

For the most part, drugs are an unsatisfactory response to behavioral problems. They are purely symptomatic, and do not address nor change the underlying causes of the problem. There have been no long-term studies of the side effects of the psychoactive drugs given for hyperactivity. In the macrobiotic view, these drugs are classified as extremely yin. Being extreme, they weaken the nervous system and internal organs. The long-term effects of chronic drug use include:

- *Dulling of the body's automatic functions.* Drugs such as amphetamines initially activate the autonomic nervous system and its two complementary branches: the orthosympathetic and parasympathetic systems. However, chronic usage weakens the parasympathetic system and results in a loss of quickness and accuracy in adapting to the environment. Many parents have reported that medicated children frequently act drugged or overmedicated. Impairment of motor functions makes a child more accident prone.

- *Decreased sensitivity.* The continual use of drugs causes the cells of the nervous system to become semipermanently expanded, thus diminishing their reactive powers and leading to decreased sensitivity.

- *A loss of clarity.* The intake of extremely yin stimulant drugs weakens the inner area of the brain, especially the midbrain, while activating the more yin surrounding cortex. The more yang motion centers of the brain are also weakened. The midbrain represents the focal point for gathering information from the entire nervous system in the form of stimuli. It simultaneously relays information outward to appropriate parts of the body in the form of various responses such as speech and decisions to act. In hyperactivity, "gatekeepers" that control input to the midbrain do not function properly. Information comes in without being properly ordered. The relay of information from the midbrain to the various parts of the body is also disrupted. Instead of a more orderly or controlled relay of information, the brain of the hyperactive child sends a variety of poorly coordinated, uncontrolled, and contradictory signals to the various parts of the body.

  In order for this key function to operate well, the innermost orbit of the nervous system, which is situated at the midbrain, must be tightly coiled and highly energized, with its cells compact. The habitual expansion produced by drugs has a damaging effect on mental clarity after a period of time, although the initial impression may be one of relaxation and heightened clarity.

- *Weakening of internal organs.* Certain of our internal organs rely primarily on contraction for their normal activity, and others depend more on relaxation, although both tendencies exist in each organ. Like the midbrain and the motion centers of the brain, the major organs that are relatively more yang tend to be weakened by the habitual use of drugs. They include the spleen, pancreas, heart, lungs, liver, and kidneys. Which of these are affected to a noticeable extent depends on a number of individual considerations, including constitution, previous illnesses, former diet, and so on.

- *Decline of reproductive ability.* Giving children drugs during childhood might impair their future reproductive abilities. The reproductive organs—the ovaries and testes—are more yang and compact. They are easily debilitated by the intake of extremely yin substances. Infertility and reproductive disorders are approaching epidemic proportions in modern society. Many of these problems can be traced to the use of medications during childhood or adolescence.

Continual drug use creates imbalances in the quantity and quality of hormones, such as testosterone, due to abnormal stimulation of adrenal, gonadal, and pituitary glands. This imbalance in the hormone system, when combined with general weakening of the nervous system, leads to debility and irregular functioning of the reproductive system. These debilitating effects of drugs are particularly acute during puberty and adolescence when the hormonal functions connected with sexual maturation become operative.

- *Degeneration of blood quality and weakening of natural immunity.* Drugs such as those given for hyperactivity tend to destroy the intestinal flora, which are essential for smooth absorption of food into the bloodstream. The liver, spleen, and bone marrow, involved in the continued regeneration of red blood cells, are adversely affected by prolonged drug use. Therefore, children who already suffer from illnesses associated with lowered blood quality, such as leukemia, anemia, diabetes, asthma, allergies, and skin disorders, may experience a worsening of their condition after prolonged drug use.

  Drugs also weaken the body's autoimmune system. Functions such as the ability of the liver to detoxify poisons and the ability of specialized cells in the lymphatic system and bloodstream to identify and ingest foreign substances are especially weakened. The cooperative functioning of T cells and B cells as part of the body's immune response is disrupted by the intake of drugs. Drug use is a contributive factor in many cases of AIDS and other immune deficiency disorders.

- *Psychological and social impairment.* These various manifestations of lessened physical and mental vitality combine to impede both the individual and social development of the children burdened with them. Children who are given drugs for hyperactivity may very easily develop psychological dependence on drugs and on artificial or superficial methods of dealing with problems.

Aside from these possible long-term consequences, there are many documented short-term side effects associated with the drugs given for hyperactivity. For example, Ritalin, a drug recommended for a variety of emotional problems, has the potential to produce such immediate side effects as skin rash, fever, scaling or itching of the skin, blood clotting disorders, nausea, dizziness, irregular heartbeat, drowsiness, headache, loss of appetite, stunting of growth, and others.

An approach that carries the risk of potentially damaging side effects—both short- and long-term—while ignoring the underlying cause of hyperactivity is obviously unsatisfactory. Many parents are justifiably distrustful of the use of behavior-modifying drugs to control hyperactivity. Most people tend to favor nutritional approaches to behavioral problems.

THE MACROBIOTIC APPROACH

A more holistic approach to hyperactivity involves changing the underlying causes. As a first step, parents need to reflect on their way of eating and on the family's way of eating as a whole, together with their overall manner of living and relating to each other. Hyperactivity is the product of the lifestyle of the family as a whole, including daily dietary practice. Approaches that isolate the hyperactive child without considering other members of the family are at best partial and cannot be thought of as solutions.

As a first step toward overcoming hyperactivity, therefore, we recommend that all members of the child's family change their way of eating toward the standard macrobiotic diet described in Chapter 1. Appropriate modifications are, of course, required for each person. The daily life recommendations presented in Chapter 4 can also be applied to the whole family, especially the substitution of more natural products for more artificial ones in the home.

If your child has not been placed on medication, the transition to a macrobiotic diet can proceed in a smooth and straightforward manner. As you learn how to cook and the family as a whole changes its diet, your child can begin to eat according to general macrobiotic guidelines appropriate for his age, condition, and activity. Children who have been placed on medication will need a more gradual period of moderate transition.

An overly rapid or inflexible approach to adopting macrobiotics is not recommended. The following guidelines may be applied whether or not your child is using medication:

- Whole grains may account for 40 to 60 percent of food intake. Grains may include both whole grains and flour products such as high-quality traditional sourdough breads, noodles, seitan (a wheat gluten product often used as a meat substitute), fu, and others, and may be prepared in a variety of styles—pressure-cooked, boiled, and served in soups, casseroles, pancakes, muffins, crackers, and so on.

- Soups may be included daily. Light miso or tamari broth soups may also be served once a day. Whole grain, vegetable, and bean soups may also be included if desired.

- Vegetables may account for 20 to 30 percent of daily intake, and may be prepared in a variety of styles. In addition to cooked vegetables, a small portion of raw salad and pickles may be included regularly if desired.

- Beans, cooked in a variety of styles, may account for about 10 percent of daily intake. Traditionally-processed soy products such as tempeh, tofu, dried tofu, and natto may be eaten daily in addition to beans.

- Cooked sea vegetables may account for about 5 percent of daily intake. Because of their high mineral content, they are particularly useful in restoring those parts of the nervous system damaged by drugs and other extremely yin items.

- Fish and seafood, nuts and seeds, snacks, and seasonal fruits may account for roughly another 5 percent of daily intake, varying with individual desire and needs and with the time of year. For example, more fruit is consumed in the warmer summer months as the body seeks refreshment. Fish should be consumed on a more regular basis during the autumn and winter months.

- Liquids may be consumed as much as desired, although sugared or artificial soft drinks, milk, and tropical or semitropical fruit juices are best avoided.

- Guidelines for seasonings, use of condiments, cooking styles, variety of foods, etc., generally follow those presented in chapters 1 and 3.

These general suggestions, if followed in a common-sense manner with appropriate adjustments and guidance from an experienced macrobiotic adviser, can lead to a gradual diminishing of hyperactive behavior. Macrobiotic dietary and way-of-life suggestions may be combined with other approaches such as behavior modification, family counseling, and remedial teaching programs for academic deficiency. The effectiveness of these approaches will be greatly enhanced when combined with the practice of macrobiotics.

As the new dietary pattern becomes more well established, parents will notice gradual improvement in behavior. The child will become able to sit still, to concentrate, to be more steady in thought and emotion. The child will gradually become more self-controlled and more responsive to parents, teachers, and others.

In many cases, the condition may improve to the point where it is possible to reduce or discontinue the use of medication, without any worsening of behavioral symptoms or decline in learning abilities. The question of when or how the child should gradually discontinue medication is a highly individual issue and is best approached with care and in consultation with the appropriate medical professional. As a general rule, reliance on drugs or medications is best withdrawn slowly rather than all at once, in stages that follow the gradual improvement of condition and that permit a regular reassessment of dosages and their effects. Depending on how successful the family is in adopting the macrobiotic guidelines, the drugs that are commonly given for hyperactivity can be gradually withdrawn over several months. Again, this is a matter that should be discussed with a health-care professional.

It is important to remember that once drugs are discontinued, their effects do not disappear overnight, even though the overall condition is steadily improving. Hyperactive children are often given drugs for extended periods. The estimated amount of time needed to recover from the effects of these medications is listed in Table 5.3.

Until the period of recovery is complete, it is recommended that the complete range of foods recommended as a part of macrobiotic practice be included on a regular basis. The percentage of grains is best kept within the general 40 to 60 percent range, while other foods may be increased according to need and personal desire. For example, sea vegetables may be 10 percent instead of 5 percent, or beans and bean products may be 15 percent instead of 10 percent. If your child experiences problems with the withdrawal from drugs, the percentage of vegetables, fruits, and/or fish may be increased and the percentage of grains decreased slightly until the symptoms improve.

During the period of recovery from the previous use of drugs, improvement is gradual but may be interrupted by occasional recurrence of symptoms associated with the effects of drugs. These minor relapses may include periodic strange or disturbing dreams, occasional overexcitement or depression, hypersensitivity, general anxiety or feelings of fear, laziness or sloppiness, irregularity in writing or speaking or difficulty with schoolwork, frequent changes of mind and difficulty in making decisions or thinking clearly, low resistance to cold weather or infection, slow rate of healing from injuries, periodic drowsiness or loss of appetite, and difficulty going to sleep or sleeping soundly.

Which of these symptoms will appear depends on your child's former medical history, but none is necessarily cause for serious concern since they generally disappear as the healing process proceeds. However,

**Table 5.3   Estimated Recovery Period
From Hyperactivity Medications**

Duration of Daily Medication	Period to Recover From the Effects
1–4 weeks	4 months
1–3 months	1 year
4–6 months	2 years
6–12 months	3 years
1–2 years	4-5 years
3–5 years	6-7 years

until the period of recovery is complete, children who were placed on drugs may experience any of these symptoms.

When your children experience behavioral problems, and while they are recovering a more natural balance, you need to devote time and energy to creating a loving, patient, and supportive atmosphere at home. You can also meet with teachers and others with whom your child has regular contact, such as a minister or rabbi, or the parents of classmates or friends. Explain your situation to them whenever necessary, including your child's dietary practice, and ask for their support and encouragement.

The macrobiotic approach, when combined with a loving, warm, and understanding attitude on the part of parents, teachers, and other members of the family, offers a sane and humane approach to hyperactivity and other behavioral disorders. It offers children with these problems an opportunity to become healthy and productive members of society and to realize their fullest potential.

Impetigo

See Skin Disorders.

Insect Bites

See Skin Disorders.

Laryngitis

See Sore Throats and Tonsillitis.

Lice

See Skin Disorders.

Measles

In the macrobiotic view, measles is not an illness in the usual sense of the word. Rather, it is a natural discharge of unnecessary factors accumulated in the womb. Through the measles, a baby discharges some of the yang quality that remains from the embryonic period.

At one time, measles was a common childhood disorder. Practically every child experienced it. Now, however, it is relatively rare for a child to have the measles.

There are several possible reasons for this decline in incidence. The measles vaccine is one factor that inhibits discharging abilities. The vaccine has the potential to cause many serious complications, and stimulates the production of antibodies that interfere with the natural discharge of the measles. Another factor is the widespread use of mass-produced, chemicalized, artificial foods, many of which are extremely yin. Items such as ice cream, sugared cereals and sweets, soft drinks, processed fruit juices, cow's milk, and artificial infant formulas weaken a child's ability to discharge effectively. When children eat a large volume of these and other modern foods, or if they are consumed during pregnancy, the child's capacity for discharging excess, including the measles, is diminished. The incidence of measles started to decline before the vaccine was widely introduced. This was due largely to the shift from a more natural to a more artificially processed diet, and the corresponding decline in natural discharging power. Many children who receive the vaccine develop measles anyway, indicating that the vaccine is frequently ineffective.

If a normally healthy child with measles is cared for properly by parents, the risk of complications is slight. It is actually beneficial for children to discharge excessive factors in the form of measles. The attempt to prevent measles through vaccination may cause excess to be stored deep within the body, contributing to more serious degenerative conditions in the future.

The first symptoms of measles are often similar to those of a cold. Red, watery eyes, fatigue, loss of appetite, and a dry cough are common. A fever starts to develop, usually becoming higher with each passing day. A rash usually appears within three or four days, in the form of faint pink dots on the head and neck. It eventually spreads over the whole body, during which time fever and coughing normally continue. The temperature often returns to normal once the rash reaches the feet.

RECOMMENDATIONS

Special dishes or external applications, including those for reducing fevers, are usually not used as part of the macrobiotic approach to measles. It is better not to interfere with the natural discharge. Provided no serious complications arise, it is far wiser to encourage it to come out. The rash and fever indicate that a child's discharging abilities are functioning normally.

It is important for a child with measles to eat as well as possible, avoiding extremes that can prolong the discharge or increase the likelihood of complications. Children with measles can generally eat according to the standard macrobiotic diet, with appropriate adjustments for age and physical makeup. The special dietary modifications for colds and flu, such as making daily foods with a softer consistency, may also be tried.

In normal circumstances, do *not* apply mashed tofu or chlorophyll plasters or prepare any of the daikon or other special teas that are often used to reduce a fever. The discharge of measles can be gently and naturally encouraged to come out by utilizing the following simple adjustments at home:

- Let your child rest quietly in his room. Pull down the shades or close the curtains to darken the room slightly.
- Moisten the air by placing one or two pots of steaming water in your child's room. Humidifiers or electric steam vaporizers may also be used, or moist towels may be placed on radiators.
- Keep your child comfortably warm. Windows can normally be kept closed. However, open them slightly from time to time to allow fresh air to circulate when the weather is warm.
- Keep your child indoors. If children go outside in the fresh air and sunshine before the discharge is complete, excess may be driven inside toward the internal organs. A high fever or some other type of discharge may occur later, or complications such as pneumonia may arise. It is better to keep your child indoors for about a week

after the measles appear to be over so as to allow the discharge to fully run its course.

If, however, the fever becomes dangerously high (above 104° F), some measures should be employed to lower it. A chlorophyll plaster such as the GREEN VEGETABLE PLASTER made from finely chopped, mashed greens can be applied for a short while until the temperature begins to drop.

You need not fear the measles. With the proper dietary and lifestyle approach, your children will shed their embryonic excess smoothly and begin a new stage of growth and development. (For further information about measles, including a discussion of complications that occur in rare cases, refer to *Macrobiotic Pregnancy and Care of the Newborn.*) *Parents who suspect complications are advised to seek appropriate medical care.*

Mumps

Unlike measles, which represents a natural constitutional discharge, mumps comes about when a child discharges excessive factors that were eaten after birth or later in childhood. Mumps is very common among children who eat the modern diet. A primary cause of mumps is the overconsumption of extreme yin foods and drinks, including ice cream, candy, sugared soft drinks, artificial sweeteners, tropical fruits, acidic vegetables such as potatoes and tomatoes, spices, and oily or greasy foods. Mumps may develop suddenly after a child goes to a party or social gathering and eats foods such as cake, ice cream, chips, or soda.

Mumps represents the accumulation and discharge of excess in the throat, particularly in and around the salivary glands. There are several sets of salivary glands in the throat, and among them, a particular set of glands known as the parotids is most commonly affected. In the majority of cases, the swelling is located on one side of the throat, although the glands on the other side of the throat may also begin to swell.

Aside from swollen glands, the other symptoms of mumps include headache, loss of appetite, and a mild fever. The symptoms normally last for about a week, or until the excessive factors that the body seeks to eliminate are discharged.

At present, it is believed that mumps is caused by a virus; however, not everyone who is exposed to the virus develops the condition. Some exposed people develop a very mild, or subclinical, form of the illness, some develop full-blown mumps, while others are not affected at all. Therefore, the underlying cause of mumps is an imbalance in the daily diet that leads to abnormal discharge and susceptibility to the virus.

Modern medicine has now developed a mumps vaccine that is routinely given to children. The vaccine suppresses the body's ability to discharge toxins and does not correct the underlying imbalances that produce susceptibility to mumps. Suppressing a discharge such as mumps can result in retaining of toxic excess inside the body where it can lead to another form of discharge or eventual deterioration and weakening of the internal organs. The vaccine may actually contribute to development of a degenerative condition later in life.

DIETARY CHANGES

Children with mumps can eat according to the standard macrobiotic diet, with appropriate adjustments for their age and condition. It is important for children to avoid sugar, ice cream, milk, soft drinks, tropical fruits, and other extreme yin items that can aggravate their condition.

If necessary, you can prepare your child's food with more water. Grains may be soft-cooked or served in soups; vegetables may be lightly steamed, boiled, cooked nishime style, water sautéed, or served in soups and stews.

Since the condition is caused largely by the overconsumption of more yin foods and beverages, it is important for your child to limit or avoid intake of fruits, fruit juices, carbonated beverages, flour products (which can cause stagnation in the intestines), chips and other snack foods, oils, nut butters, and concentrated sweeteners. We recommend using cooked or dried fruits rather than fresh fruits or juices, and limiting your child's intake of concentrated sweeteners to an occasional small volume of rice syrup or barley malt until he recovers. Children with mumps can also enjoy moderate consumption of *Bancha Tea*, *Cereal Grain Tea*, or other macrobiotic beverages.

Special Dishes and Preparations

The fever that a child runs with mumps is usually not very high. If it does become uncomfortably high, however, any of the special macrobiotic drinks used to reduce fever can be used, with appropriate considerations for the age and overall condition of your child. See the section on fever for further instructions.

If loss of appetite occurs, *Special Rice Cream* or *Soft Brown Rice* may be given daily until it returns to normal. A mild *Ume-Sho-Kuzu Drink*, given once a day for several days, helps neutralize an overly acidic blood condition and aids digestion. This drink should be milder than that taken by adults and should not be given to children who have not yet begun to use salt.

Very mildly seasoned *Kinpira Carrots and Burdock*, prepared without oil, can be included along with other vegetable dishes every couple of days for a week or so, until the child regains normal strength. (Kinpira refers to the method of cooking in which root vegetables are cut into matchsticks or shaved into slices and sautéed in a little sesame oil or water.)

RECOMMENDATIONS

Unless the child complains of fever, or unless the fever becomes uncomfortably high, home applications such as Tofu Plaster need not be used. If the fever does become uncomfortably high, however, the external applications used to draw out fever may be used (see section on fever in this chapter).

For the swelling in the throat, TOFU AND GREEN VEGETABLE PLASTER or any of the cool applications recommended for tonsillitis may be applied to the throat. The plaster can be employed several times a day for several days until the swelling is reduced. Leave each application in place for about an hour before removing it or replacing it with a fresh plaster.

If your child complains of a headache, the applications used to relieve headache pain can be used, depending upon the location of the pain. See the headache section of this chapter for further instructions.

A variety of PALM HEALING techniques can be used to ease discomfort. These techniques are used to relieve pain and discomfort in the throat, as well as headaches and fever; apply the ones that are applicable.

The child with mumps can rest or play at home until the swelling returns to normal and his strength and appetite are regained.

Orthopedic Problems

Many common bone and joint problems correct themselves when appropriate adjustments are made in the child's diet and activity. The most common orthopedic problems can be classified into two broad categories: those caused by an excess of more yin items in the diet, and those caused by an excess of more yang items. A lack of balance in the child's daily environment can also produce developmental problems, as the development of rickets illustrates.

More yin orthopedic problems include bowed legs, pigeon toes (toeing in), flat feet, pigeon chest (the breastbone and front of the chest are pushed outward), congenital hip displacement, and scoliosis (the spine curves outward). More yang orthopedic problems include knock-knees and funnel chest (the breastbone and front of the chest are pushed inward). Orthopedic problems caused by the combined effects of both extremes include lateral scoliosis (the spine curves to the left or right), rickets, and wryneck (torticollis).

RICKETS

Rickets results largely from a lack of sunshine. Ultraviolet radiation from the sun is needed by the body for the production of calciferol, a hormone that promotes normal calcification in the bones. If the body does not produce enough calciferol, a variety of bone deformities occur. Severely affected children may develop thickened joints, deformed legs, an enlarged head, and spinal deformities.

Rickets is often thought of as a disease of industrial civilization. The earliest cases were reported in England in the mid-1600s, at about the time that the burning of soft coal began to become widespread, thickening the atmosphere and blocking the sun's rays. It was also around that time that people started living in dark, narrow streets within the larger cities. By 1889, the British Medical Association found rickets to be most prevalent in "large towns and thickly peopled districts, especially where industrial pursuits are carried on." Very few cases were found in the countryside.

In the late 1800s, a British medical missionary by the name of Theobald Palms visited Japan. He noted an "absence of rickets among the Japanese as compared with its lamentable frequency among the poor children of the large centers of population in England and Scotland." The traditional Japanese diet at that time consisted largely of brown rice and other whole grains, sea vegetables, beans and soy products, and occasional fish. However, Japan enjoys a bright, sunny climate, in comparison to the more overcast climate of northern Europe. Japanese children also spent a great deal of time out-of-doors, even in winter.

If your children eat a well-balanced macrobiotic diet, with ample variety, and are taken outside on a regular basis, preferably every day, then you need not worry about rickets. Children who have a tendency toward this disorder can include regular servings of fish in their diets. Special efforts must also be made to encourage them to play outside in the sunshine. In addition to the appropriate standard macrobiotic diet—with a wide range of foods and cooking methods, including regular servings of cooked white-meat fish—children with more serious conditions may require fish-liver oils as dietary supplements. It is recommended that children with more serious conditions also consult with physicians in addition to employing macrobiotic suggestions.

DIETARY CAUSES

More yin conditions can result from overconsumption of fruits—especially tropical fruits—sugar and other concentrated sweeteners, fluids, milk, ice cream, soy milk, tofu, soft drinks, and oily snacks. Too many watery foods and flour products may also contribute to more yin conditions, as can overeating. Overly yang conditions can result from overconsumption of meat, eggs, fish, or other forms of animal protein, salt, and baked foods. A lack of variety—not enough fresh or lightly cooked vegetables, for example—or an overly restricted diet can also produce more yang developmental problems. Conditions that result from the combination of both extremes are often caused by excessive intake of sugar, milk, fruits, and other more yin items, plus meat, animal foods, salt, and baked foods. A lack of variety can also contribute to the development of these problems.

DIETARY CHANGES

As already mentioned, minor orthopedic problems often improve with time and the practice of a balanced natural diet. When a specific imbalance is found to exist, minor dietary adjustments can often help correct it. Conditions caused by overeating or by consuming too many yin items can be improved when the overall volume of food is kept moderate and the intake of more yin extremes is reduced or stopped. Within the standard diet, too many fruits, juices, concentrated sweeteners, oily snacks, or overly watery dishes can interfere with recovery. The regular intake of soy milk, which contains plenty of fat, can also interfere.

More yang developmental problems can be improved when your child isoffered more variety in the diet, including a variety of whole grains, a wide selection of vegetables—including those which are lightly cooked, such as quick, steamed greens and boiled salad—and the normally wide range of foods and cooking methods within standard macrobiotic practice. If your child becomes overly contracted, be especially careful about his intake of salt and baked flour products, including bread, muffins, chips, and crackers.

When children have an unbalanced condition caused by both extremes, a centrally balanced diet—with plenty of variety in the selection of foods and cooking methods—would be appropriate. Extremes of yin and yang are best minimized or avoided.

Of course, in every case, the standard macrobiotic approach must be adapted to suit your child's age and condition.

RECOMMENDATIONS

Daily activities are also important. Appropriate exercise and outdoor play—with frequent exposure to sunlight—help your child maintain a healthy balance. This is especially important in the case of rickets.

Scrubbing the body daily with a warm moist towel is also beneficial for developmental problems. Special attention can be paid to the areas of the body where the main problem exists. For example, you may concentrate on your child's feet if he has pigeon toes or on the spine if he has scoliosis. A towel that is dipped in warm ginger water can also be used for body scrubbing from time to time.

If your child is experiencing pain, you can apply PALM HEALING directly to the painful region. Warm, moist towels can be applied repeatedly to the painful area for five to ten minutes as well.

Supplementary approaches, including acupuncture, shiatsu massage, and physical therapy, can also be helpful in some cases. It is recommended that children with more serious developmental disabilities be referred to the appropriate medical professional, in addition to applying the general dietary and lifestyle modifications presented in this section.

Parasites

See Pinworms; and Skin Disorders.

Pinworms

Pinworms are the most common type of worms affecting children. They look like tiny pieces of white thread and live in the large intestine. They migrate through the colon and come out at night through the rectum to lay their eggs. They can often be found at night between the buttocks or in the child's bowel movements. The most common symptom is itching that becomes more noticeable at night.

Other symptoms of pinworms (and other varieties of worms) include:

- Fatigue or laziness.
- Cravings for certain foods or a feeling of unsatisfied hunger. Children with worms sometimes stay thin even when they are eating a great deal.
- Irritability, short temper, and crying. Children with worms may suddenly become hysterical without any apparent reason.
- Periodic anemia.
- Occasional nausea or stomach pain arising an hour or so after eating.
- Nail biting.
- A consistently loose or fragmented bowel movement.
- Tiny pinpoint indentations in the fingernails.

DIETARY CHANGES

Children with worms can begin the standard macrobiotic diet, with appropriate considerations for their age and condition. It is recommended that raw fruits, nuts, and raw vegetables be reduced temporarily or sometimes avoided until the condition improves. Children who are old enough can eat several pieces of mochi every day for several weeks along with soba (buckwheat noodles) several times per week. Try *Soba with Light Tamari Broth and Scallions*. Various types of seeds can also help improve the condition. *Roasted pumpkin, squash,* or *sunflower seeds* can be given as snacks or over rice or other dishes.

In addition to their regular beverages, children with worms can also be given mild *Corsican Sea Vegetable Tea*. (Corsican sea vegetable is available in many natural foods stores.) A cup or two can be taken daily in addition to their usual beverages for a week or so.

RECOMMENDATIONS

The soreness and itching produced by pinworms can often be relieved by applying a WARM SESAME OIL AND GINGER APPLICATION directly to the anus.

If macrobiotic children develop worms, the cause is often excess consumption of oily, fatty, or floury foods. Keeping their intake of these items to a minimum helps prevent worms. Cleanliness is also helpful in preventing the spread of worms. Make sure your children wash their hands after going to the bathroom and keep their nails properly cleaned and trimmed.

Unlike the medications given to control worms, these natural approaches do not produce undesirable side effects or disrupt your child's overall condition.

Rheumatic Fever

See Sore Throats and Tonsillitis.

Poison Ivy

See Skin Disorders.

Prickly Heat

See Skin Disorders.

Rickets

See Orthopedic Problems.

Roseola

Unlike measles, roseola (which is sometimes referred to as "one-day measles") is not necessary for further growth and development. It is more of a conditional problem caused by excesses in the diet, especially the overconsumption of extreme yin items such as sugar, soft drinks, ice cream, and tropical fruits, together with fats and oils, including those in milk and other dairy products, eggs, meat, poultry, and other animal foods.

When children eat a more centrally balanced diet, they usually do not develop roseola. Since the symptoms of roseola often resemble those of measles, if your child has not yet had the measles, it is generally better not to do anything to reduce the fever and to deal with the condition as if it were the measles.

In roseola, the fever may come on suddenly and rapidly rise to 103°F to 105°F. Some children experience convulsions, known as febrile-seizures, as a result of this sudden rise in temperature. If the fever climbs above 103°F to 104°F, a chlorophyll plaster such as GREEN VEGETABLE PLASTER can be applied for a short time until the temperature begins to go down. The fever may last three to four days, after which a rash appears, usually covering the whole body except for the face and legs. The rash usually lasts for twenty-four hours.

In general, children with roseola can rest in bed until they feel well enough to be up and about; however, it is better to wait until you are sure they do not have the measles before letting them go outside. Children with roseola can eat according to the standard macrobiotic diet, with emphasis on any of the more simple foods that they prefer. Refer to the section on measles and make the simple home adjustments recommended until you are sure that your child does not have the measles. At that time, your child can simply rest at home until he recovers.

Scabies

See Skin Disorders.

Scoliosis

See Orthopedic Problems.

Skin Disorders

The skin is one of the major pathways for the discharge of excess. When excess accumulates in the bloodstream, the body may discharge it in the form of a skin disease. Skin disorders are often related to problems in two of the other primary organs of discharge: the kidneys and the intestines. The foods that underlie skin conditions are usually those that weaken these internal organs and diminish their capacity to discharge excess.

The more common conditions that affect the skin include: prickly heat, eczema, and diaper rash, as well as scabies, impetigo, and ringworm. Some children also experience poison ivy, warts, and head lice. The underlying dietary factors that promote these conditions are presented in this section. (For a discussion of skin problems in the newborn, including diaper rash, cradle cap, and birthmarks, refer to *Macrobiotic Pregnancy and Care of the Newborn.*)

ECZEMA

The underlying dietary cause of eczema is overconsumption of fats and oils, including those in milk and other dairy products, animal foods, and vegetable oils. An excessive intake of simple sugars, including those in refined sugar, corn syrup, honey, and fruits, is often a contributing cause. Overconsumption of baked flour products can also contribute to eczema and other skin conditions.

Eczema takes the form of a rash with patches of red, rough skin. The rash tends to occur on certain areas of the body. For example, babies are often affected on the cheeks while in older children, the rash often appears behind the knees, in the folds of the elbows, or on the forearms and neck. The location of the rash shows which of the internal organs is primarily being affected by accumulations of mucus and fat. The cheeks, for example, reflect the condition of the lungs. Eczema on the cheeks shows that mucus is accumulating in the lungs. Eczema on the arms and legs normally occurs along the meridians, and reveals dysfunction in the corresponding organs and functions. Eczema on the front or back of the body frequently reflects dysfunction in the organs located in the same general area. The condition is often chronic and produces itching. When children continually scratch the area, the skin may become hard and thick. Children with eczema also have a tendency to develop asthma and allergies, both of which are frequently caused by the overconsumption of milk, dairy products, and other more yin items.

HEAD LICE

Lice, or tiny parasitic insects, are more likely to be a problem when the blood quality becomes more acidic. The overconsumption of meat and other animal proteins, simple sugars, tropical fruits, spices, and other more yin items contributes to a more acidic blood quality. Lice will often disappear once these items are reduced and a centrally balanced diet is adopted. Common-sense practices in regard to bathing, washing the hair, and overall cleanliness also help prevent infestation and complement a more balanced dietary approach.

IMPETIGO

The overconsumption of animal fats, especially those in poultry, cheese, and eggs, is the primary cause of impetigo. Too many oily or greasy dishes, including French fries and chips that are prepared with vegetable oils, also contribute to the condition, as do too many simple sugars. The main symptom in older children is scabs or crusty skin with a brownish-yellow color. These markings often start on the face and spread elsewhere. In infants, the condition usually takes the form of small blisters with yellowish fluid and pus. The blisters usually break and leave an exposed raw sore.

INSECT BITES

Children are more prone to mosquito bites, bee or wasp stings, and other insect bites when they eat excessive amounts of sugar, concentrated sweeteners, tropical and other fruits, ice cream, and soft drinks. Children who eat a more centrally balanced diet tend to have more alkaline blood and thus tend to be bitten less frequently. Mosquitoes seem to know intuitively to avoid more yang quality blood, since it often coagulates before reaching the mosquito's stomach. This is fatal to the mosquito; hence, they seem to prefer thinner, sweeter, and more yin blood.

POISON IVY

Exposure to poison ivy (or such plants as poison oak or sumac) can trigger a skin eruption. The rash usually develops within two days after contact with the leaves of the plant. As it develops, the skin becomes red and swollen, and clusters of small blisters appear. The rash normally disappears in two to three weeks. It usually causes itching and burning. The irritation is caused by a chemical called oleoresin, which is found in the leaves, stems, and roots of the plant.

Overconsumption of sugar, fruit—especially tropical varieties— soft drinks, juices, milk, spices, and highly acidic vegetables makes the skin more susceptible to poison ivy, and can make the symptoms more severe.

PRICKLY HEAT

Prickly heat occurs with babies, often in hot weather. The underlying dietary cause includes overconsumption of simple sugars, in combination with oils and fats, including those in dairy products. Overconsumption causes fat and oil to accumulate in the sweat glands, leading to blockage and inflammation. The condition usually becomes worse when the weather is hot and the child perspires. It can also result when a mother consumes too many of the aforementioned foods while nursing.

SCABIES

Scabies are clusters of pimples that develop scabs. They can cause severe itching, and children frequently scratch them to the point that these scabs break open. They are caused primarily by the overconsumption of animal fats and oils, including those in milk and dairy products, and by excessive simple sugars such as those in concentrated sweeteners and tropical fruits. The location of the scabies correlates with the internal organs that are primarily affected.

WARTS

Warts represent the discharge of excess. The most common cause is the overconsumption of animal protein. Many people experience the disappearance of warts once they reduce their intake of animal products. Warts are often located along meridians that correspond to internal organs.

RECOMMENDATIONS

The macrobiotic approach to skin problems is based on correcting the underlying dietary imbalances that lead to chronic imbalances in the blood and to skin discharges. A variety of natural home remedies can also help in relieving discomfort; however, instead of trying to interfere with the body's natural discharge of excess, it is far better to allow the excess to come out while simultaneously removing the underlying cause.

Children with skin conditions can begin the standard macrobiotic diet with appropriate adjustments for their age and condition. It is, of course, important to reduce or avoid foods that contribute to each particular condition.

Within the standard macrobiotic diet, it is often helpful to reduce or limit the intake of animal foods, buckwheat products, raw fruits, concentrated sweeteners, flour products, nuts, nut butters, and oil, including vegetable oils. Again, these are general recommendations and need to be adapted to each circumstance. It is, therefore, helpful to contact an experienced macrobiotic advisor when implementing these or other dietary suggestions.

External applications that utilize natural products in the home can also be used to relieve discomfort and to aid in improving the condition. These applications include the following:

- RICE BRAN (NUKA) SKIN WASH OR BATH.
- DRIED DAIKON LEAVES AND SEA SALT SKIN WASH.
- DAIKON JUICE WASH.
- SESAME OIL. Sesame oil often helps soothe skin discomfort. It can be applied directly to the affected area. Either light or dark oil can be used.
- TOFU AND GREEN VEGETABLE PLASTER. A tofu-chlorophyll plaster can be applied when an insect bite or other skin disorder produces swelling.

When children develop a skin condition, it is important to be careful about selecting natural fabrics for their clothing and sleeping materials. Cotton is preferable to wool or synthetics. Rice bran, oats, or natural vegetable soaps are preferable to chemical soaps or shampoos for regular use.

It can also be important to treat the intestines and kidneys, which respond to easy-to-use home therapies along with proper eating. Warm towel compresses may be applied repeatedly to the middle back (kidneys) and abdomen (intestines) to strengthen these organs. These applications can be done for five to ten minutes in each region, every day or every other day while a child is recovering from a skin condition. PALM HEALING is also helpful in stimulating these organs.

Sore Throats and Tonsillitis

The throat is a frequent site for the accumulation of excess, which tends to gather here in order to be discharged. These accumulations may or may not be accompanied by the growth of viruses or bacteria. The underlying cause of these discharges is the intake of extremes. Extreme yin foods and beverages—sugar, ice cream, cookies, soft drinks, and orange juice—can often lead to accumulation in the throat. The intake of eggs, meats, poultry, and dairy products—extreme yang foods—can also result in throat inflammation.

Children who adhere to a macrobiotic diet that is balanced in terms of yin and yang rarely experience sore throats or inflammation of the tonsils or adenoids.

In some cases, sore throats occur together with other symptoms of colds or flu. In many cases, especially when the daily diet is more extreme, excessive factors accumulating in the tissues and glands in the throat create a medium for the growth of viruses. The symptoms of a viral sore throat include a slight tingling in the back of the throat that is especially noticeable when the child swallows, followed by the appearance of pain one or two days later. Pain may occur with other symptoms of a cold. The lymph glands in the neck may also become swollen.

In a minority of cases, bacteria, especially the *Streptococcus* bacilli, begin to develop. These infections are commonly referred to as "strep throat." When bacteria develop, the symptoms generally appear more rapidly. Children may develop a high fever, pain in the throat, and swollen glands in several hours. Other symptoms of a cold may or may not be present.

In general, viruses are more yin, while bacteria are more yang. Antibiotics, which are extremely yin, are effective in neutralizing the more yang bacteria, but have no effect on more yin viruses. Yin and yang attract and neutralize each other, while yin and yin repel. Although they are effective against bacteria, antibiotics do not address the underlying cause.

LARYNGITIS AND CROUP

Laryngitis, or inflammation of the voice box, may occur together with a cold. The inflammation is usually a virus type and disappears within forty-eight hours. Croup is a more severe form of laryngitis, in which the inflamed larynx blocks the normal passage of air. Croup usually appears in the evening, when the lungs and respiratory passages become more active in discharging mucus and other excessive factors. The symptoms of croup include difficulty breathing, and a hard, ringing cough. A child with croup will often suck in the chest with each breath and make a strange noise that sounds like barking.

TONSILLITIS AND ADENOIDITIS

The tonsils are small, oval bodies located at the top of the throat on either side. The adenoids are located in the upper part of the throat, opposite the nasal passageways. They are both part of the lymphatic system and are frequent sites for the localization of excess. Tonsillitis is the enlargement and inflammation of the tonsils as a result of accumulation of excess. When inflammation occurs in the adenoids, the condition is known as adenoiditis.

It is not uncommon for children who eat the modern diet to regularly experience both conditions. Many children have three or four episodes of tonsillitis per year.

The tonsils play an important role in natural immunity. When excess accumulates in the body, the tonsils and adenoids help localize it. They also localize viruses and bacteria, and this is why they become inflamed.

Tonsillitis and adenoiditis are rare in children who do not consume dairy products, sugar, tropical fruits, and meats, eggs, and other animal products containing saturated fats. The underlying cause of these conditions is the extremes in diet that produce excess in the blood and lymph streams and throughout the body.

Removing the tonsils does not solve the underlying problem. What it does do is weaken the person's overall vitality and ability to resist infection. At one time, removal of the tonsils was almost routine. More than a million and a half tonsillectomies were performed every year during the 1930s; however, in the face of growing criticism, the number of yearly operations has dropped by about two-thirds.

Relationship Between the Tonsils and Adenoids and the Reproductive Organs

The relationship between these lymphatic tissues and the body as a whole can be understood when we consider their embryonic origins. The glands that develop in the throat are similar in structure and quality to the reproductive organs. The uvula at the back of the throat is similar to the penis and the clitoris. These organs receive a strong external charge from heaven's more yang, descending force. The uvula is surrounded on either side by the adenoids. The penis is surrounded by the testes. The adenoids and testes are similar in structure and quality.

The tongue is charged primarily by an opposite quality of energy— the expanding energy of the Earth—and its structure and quality are very similar to the vagina. The ovaries also receive an external charge primarily from the Earth, and their quality is similar to the tonsils.

Inflammation of the tonsils and adenoids is an indication that the overall condition of the body has become unbalanced. The reproductive organs, in particular, have become weaker. The wide incidence of tonsillitis and adenoiditis over the last several generations corresponds to the large number of reproductive disorders, including infertility, that are being reported today.

Sexual vitality and reproductive ability are further weakened when the tonsils and adenoids are removed. As a consequence, these operations are contributing to the modern increase in sexual frustration, unhappiness, and disorders, and to the decline in fertility and reproductive ability.

Removing the tonsils and adenoids does not solve the underlying problem that causes inflammation and enlargement of these areas. When these organs are removed, other lymphatic organs must take over their function. People who have had their tonsils and adenoids removed have less resistance to toxic excess, and are also less able to eliminate excess than are people who still have these organs intact. Because they are more susceptible to illness, individuals who have had these organs removed need to eat well throughout life.

The symptoms of tonsillitis may include high fever, vomiting, headache, and a general feeling of malaise. The tonsils become red and swollen, and tiny white spots or larger patches of white pus may develop. Pain in the throat is usually more severe in older children.

Excess may also accumulate in other lymph glands in the neck, causing them to become enlarged and infected. Enlargement of the glands may also occur after the tonsillitis (or other throat infection) has subsided, and may last for weeks.

The use of antibiotics to treat throat infections, including tonsillitis, is now being questioned. Antibiotics are recommended in cases where the streptococcus bacteria is found. The primary reason for using antibiotics is to prevent the infection from leading to more serious consequences, including rheumatic fever and inflammation of the kidneys. However, most sore throats do not involve streptococcus, while the possibility of rheumatic fever, even when streptococcus is present, is normally very slight.

RHEUMATIC FEVER

Rheumatic fever, a more yin condition, is rarely seen among adequately nourished children. It occurs among children who receive a chronically unbalanced diet—one lacking in whole grains, fresh vegetables, and other complex carbohydrate foods—or whose diet lacks a wide enough variety and selection of foods. The intake of simple sugars, including soft drinks, refined sugar, white bread or flour, poor-quality oils or fats, and highly acidic vegetables such as potatoes and tomatoes also contributes to this condition. These imbalances weaken the natural immunity and can allow bacteria to flourish.

It is important to note that many children have streptococcus bacteria in their throats yet do not develop an infection. Infections result when the natural immunity is compromised through an inadequate diet. If you suspect that the infection exists, see your health care provider.

DIETARY CHANGES

When your child experiences a sore throat, you need to assess his overall condition, including diet and activity, so as to discover the underlying cause. As with the other common conditions that affect children, the underlying cause of a throat discharge can be the repeated intake of more excessive foods—too much fruit or juice, oily snacks, or simple sugars—or from the one-time intake of some extremely unbalanced food, such as birthday cake made with sugar or ice cream. Like other common discharges, sore throats normally clear up once the excessive factors have been eliminated from the body. However, if the child continues to eat more extreme foods as a regular part of the diet, sore throats and infections normally recur with regularity.

Therefore, the most fundamental way to eliminate sore throats is to avoid extreme or excessive foods and beverages. The intake of sugar and concentrated sweeteners, oily or greasy foods, spices, tropical fruits, iced or chilled beverages, and poor-quality fats and oils is best reduced or avoided. Children can eat according to the standard macrobiotic diet, with the appropriate adjustments for their age and condition.

The adjustments in daily diet presented earlier for colds and flu can also be applied in cases of sore throat. If children have difficulty swallowing, their grain, vegetable, bean, and other dishes can be cooked with more water and mashed into semi-solids in a suribachi or baby food mill.

RECOMMENDATIONS

If the air in a heated home or apartment is especially dry, the atmosphere in the child's room can be kept moist by placing a pot or two of steaming water in a corner. Electric steam vaporizers or humidifiers can also be used. An electric hot plate can be used to heat a pot of water as well.

In many instances, a mild sore throat develops together with other symptoms of a cold or flu. If your child develops symptoms such as fever, headache, or general fatigue, see the appropriate sections in this chapter for recommendations and home remedies that can be used.

For tonsillitis or other throat inflammations, cool applications are often helpful. You may apply either cold towels, GREEN VEGETABLE PLASTER, TOFU AND GREEN VEGETABLE PLASTER, or TOFU PLASTER. PALM HEALING can also help ease the discomfort of a sore throat.

Rickets

See Orthopedic Problems.

Stomachache

When children eat a naturally balanced diet, stomachaches seldom occur. If they do arise, it is usually because the child ate some type of extreme or unbalanced food, or perhaps ate too rapidly or too much.

DIETARY CAUSES

Stomachaches can be caused by the intake of too many constrictive items, such as eggs, poultry, fish, meat, and baked foods, or by a lack of freshness or variety in the diet. Extreme yang foods can cause the stomach energy center, or chakra, to become tight and contracted. The stomach, liver, gallbladder, spleen, and pancreas often become tighter, and their function may stagnate. The intake of these excessive yang foods tends to affect the contracted lower portion of the stomach and the duodenum more than the expanded body of the stomach.

The intake of extreme yin items can also cause stomach pains or cramps. Overindulgence in cold or iced foods or beverages, raw fruits, oily snacks or chips, fried foods, concentrated sweeteners, spices, and vegetables such as tomatoes and potatoes may produce this reaction.

Two foods commonly found in children's diets today can be especially troublesome:

• *Cow's Milk.* The consumption of cow's milk and its products frequently causes stomach and digestive upset. Lactose intolerance, or the inability to digest milk products, is a common cause of stomach and intestinal discomfort. Common symptoms include stomachache, bloating, and diarrhea. Repeated overconsumption produces an overall weakening of the stomach and intestines.

- *Refined Sugar.* Stomach problems are also produced by refined sugar, including concentrated sweeteners such as honey and maple syrup. When sugar enters the stomach, it temporarily paralyzes the organ. As little as a quarter teaspoon of sugar can cause this reaction. Refined sugar is an extremely alkaloid substance and causes the stomach to secrete a large amount of acid in order to maintain a normal balance. An overacidic stomach is a frequent cause of discomfort.

GASTROENTERITIS

The intake of extremes of either yin or yang can sometimes produce an inflammation in the digestive organs, a condition known as gastroenteritis. This condition can result in cramplike pains in the stomach or intestines, which are sometimes accompanied by vomiting and diarrhea.

Abdominal pain can occur by itself or together with other symptoms. Children with sore throats or colds may also complain of stomachaches. Emotional factors, including stress and anxiety, also play a role; however, dietary imbalances usually underlie many stress-related conditions, including stomachache. (You may wish to refer to *Macrobiotic Pregnancy and Care of the Newborn* for a discussion of diarrhea, constipation, colic, and other digestive disorders.)

DIETARY CHANGES

When children experience stomachaches, it is helpful to review their overall condition. In this way, the underlying cause can more easily be determined. Hopefully, a specific emergency requiring medical attention such as appendicitis, poisoning, or the presence of a foreign object in the stomach can be ruled out.

For a child who normally eats macrobiotically, stomachaches can arise from recurring excesses in the diet, as from regularly binging on sugared snacks, perhaps at school or with friends; or from the occasional or one-time intake of some extreme or unbalanced food, such as the child's eating too much cake or too many snacks at a birthday party.

You may need to ask your child questions to find out the cause of the problem. In most cases, the condition will improve once the problem food or foods are identified and removed from the diet. Recovery is usually fairly rapid once your child begins to eat the appropriate standard macrobiotic diet, perhaps with the addition of a few special dishes or teas.

Another type of disorder comes about when children eat an extremely unbalanced diet as a normal practice. In these cases, changing the cause of the condition involves reorienting the diet as a whole. Recurring stomachaches, headaches, colds, or other chronic health problems are the result of repeated dietary imbalances. In these cases, it is recommended that you consider changing your family's way of eating toward the standard macrobiotic diet, with appropriate adjustments for each member of your family.

For stomach disorders in general, millet can frequently be served. Of course, brown rice and other whole grains can be eaten as well. Millet can be pressure-cooked together with rice, prepared with vegetables such as squash or carrots, or served in soups or as a soft breakfast cereal. Round, sweet-tasting vegetables such as fall or winter squash, onions, and cabbage can also be helpful and soothing for stomach discomfort. These vegetables can be served nishime style, or in soups or stews. Millet-squash soup is often useful in soothing stomach discomfort.

A small volume of such items as umeboshi plum, sauerkraut, or sour pickles—like those made with umeboshi vinegar—can help quiet an overactive stomach. A small amount can be given to your child in the form of condiments. Remember, however, that they contain salt, so use them in very small quantities and only for children who have already begun to eat a small amount of salt in their diets.

Special Dishes and Preparations

Among special macrobiotic drinks, several can be useful in relieving discomfort in the stomach and digestive organs, including the small and large intestines. These preparations are especially helpful in neutralizing an overly acidic condition. The following beverages should be given only to children who have already begun to use a small amount of salt in their diets:

- *Baked Umeboshi Plum Drink*
- *Ume-Bancha Tea*

- *Ume-Sho-Bancha*
- *Ume-Sho-Kuzu (Kudzu)*

Other special dishes, including soft cooked cereals—such as soft rice or millet—can be substituted for regular grains for several days until the condition improves. *Special Rice Cream* can also be used.

In some cases, the specific dietary cause of stomach or intestinal discomfort can be pinpointed. If you are able to trace the condition to the toxic effects of a specific food or category of foods, you can then prepare macrobiotic dishes to help offset these effects. These special dishes can be added to the daily diet, with the appropriate considerations for age and condition. Again, the use of salt should be consistent with our earlier suggestions. Dishes that contain salt should not be given to children who have not yet begun to include salt in their diets.

Easing Stomachaches Caused by Dairy Products

When dairy products are the cause of stomachaches, try the following dishes:

- *Light Miso Soup*
- *Squash with Onions*
- *Nori Condiment*
- *Daikon, Daikon Leaves, and Kombu*

Easing Stomachaches Caused by Meat, Poultry, or Fish

If you suspect your child's stomachaches are caused by meat, poultry, or fish, add *Pearl Barley Soup* and *Light Miso Soup* to the diet. Shiitake mushroom can be added to soups and vegetable dishes as well, or can be used in making *Shiitake Tea*. Give children several cups of tea over the course of several days.

An older child (over six) with stomach or intestinal pain caused by eating meat or poultry can receive a small amount (several teaspoons) of grated raw daikon with one or two drops of tamari added. It can be given once a day for three days. You can give younger children the milder *Dried Daikon Tea*.

Green leafy vegetables are also beneficial for stomach upsets. Kale, watercress, daikon, or turnip greens can be quickly steamed or boiled and served every day as a part of your child's diet.

Easing Stomachaches Caused by Overconsumption of Eggs

For stomach or digestive pains caused by eating too many eggs, a small amount of either sauerkraut, umeboshi vinegar, cooked daikon, or daikon pickles will often help bring relief. Again, please remember the appropriate considerations about giving children salt or salty foods. A small volume of *Light Miso Soup* can also be included in the diet for several days.

Easing Stomachaches Caused by Fish and Shellfish

Digestive upsets caused by eating shellfish can be offset by adding a small amount of grated ginger to vegetable dishes or to soups, or, for older children, by giving them several tablespoons of grated raw daikon or raw radish with one or two drops of tamari. A small amount of brown rice or other grain vinegar can be used for several days in salad dressing or as a condiment to help offset the effects of shellfish.

Stomachaches caused by eating fish can be offset by serving several dishes of cooked daikon or mustard greens, or by seasoning one or two dishes with a small amount of grated ginger or umeboshi or grain vinegar. Shiso (beefsteak) leaves are also helpful in relieving stomachaches caused by eating too much fish.

Easing Stomachaches Caused by Sugar

The following special drinks are recommended for stomachaches caused by sugar. Give only to children who are old enough to be using salt in their diets.

- *Mild Tamari/Bancha Tea*
- *Mild Ume-Sho-Bancha Tea*
- *Umeboshi teas*

As discussed earlier, these beverages should be very mild. Use only several drops of tamari or a small piece of umeboshi plum when preparing them. Use *only* one of these teas once a day for several days.

Sea vegetables can be added to your child's diet if he is suffering from stomachaches caused by sugar. Again, remember to consider whether the salt content is appropriate for your child. *Hijiki* is especially recommended. Children can receive a small, mildly seasoned side dish for several days. Arame, wakame, kombu, and nori can also be used in a variety of dishes. The minerals in sea vegetables help to offset the effects of sugar. Children's sea vegetables should be very mildly seasoned.

Azuki beans served with kombu and squash is also effective in relieving stomachaches caused by sugar. Children can receive a small serving of this dish once a day for several days. It should be more mildly seasoned than that eaten by adults.

RECOMMENDATIONS

Since stomachaches frequently occur with emotional problems or upsets, it is important to provide children with a loving, supportive, and warm home environment. If a specific problem or situation is bothering them, discuss it and help them to find a solution. Love and reassurance can be powerful forces in keeping children healthy.

Your child can be scrubbed daily with a warm towel or warm ginger towel. Scrub gently until the skin becomes slightly red. Repeated warm towels may be applied to the abdomen for ten to fifteen minutes, or a hot water bottle or a WARM ROASTED SALT PACK may be applied instead. Make sure applications are not too hot.

When the stomach or intestinal energy centers become overly tight or contracted, applying the palms can help loosen and energize them. The right palm, which conducts more of Earth's expanding force, is generally more effective for this purpose. When the digestive energy centers become overly expanded or weak, applying the palms can help strengthen and consolidate them. The left palm conducts more of heaven's descending energy and is generally more effective for this purpose. In addition to PALM HEALING, MASSAGE can ease discomfort in the stomach and intestines.

Tonsillitis

See Sore Throats and Tonsillitis.

Warts

See Skin Disorders.

Whooping Cough

Whooping cough is known in the Orient as "100 days cough." Whooping cough, or pertussis as it is known medically, is a form of discharge. Susceptible individuals may develop whooping cough after exposure to pertussis bacteria. The severity of the illness varies, from a light cough and mild symptoms to severe coughing with a whooping sound on each inhalation. Children with a more severe form of this disease sometimes cough repeatedly with every breath, and their faces may turn blue or purplish in color. Choking and vomiting may accompany severe coughing. Whooping cough can last for more than three months; hence the name "100 days cough." Children with healthy autoimmune systems resulting from a balanced, natural foods diet do not experience this condition.

DIETARY CAUSES

The underlying dietary cause of whooping cough is the overconsumption of extreme yin foods, including sugar, honey, tropical fruits, carbonated beverages, and refined flour products, along with fats such as those found in milk and other dairy products. People of all ages develop whooping cough, but more than half of those who do are under two. In cases where newborns or young children are afflicted, the primary dietary cause is the type of food eaten by the mother during pregnancy or the infant's use of cow's milk or artificial formulas.

When infants develop this condition, medical advice should be sought due to the possibility of complications such as pneumonia. Children with severe coughing are also best referred to appropriate medical care.

A great deal of controversy—much of it within the medical community—now surrounds the immunization given for pertussis, as part of the DPT (diptheria, pertussis, tetanus) inoculation. The vaccine has the potential to cause damaging side effects and in many cases has been found to be ineffective in preventing the disease. In his book *How to Raise a Healthy Child in Spite of Your Doctor,* Dr. Robert S. Mendelsohn suggests pertussis had already begun to decline before the vaccine came into use. The most frequently noted side effects of the vaccine include fever, crying, emotional upset, swelling, soreness, and redness in the area of the injection. More serious side effects, including convulsions and brain damage, have also been reported. Dr. Mendelsohn reports that some researchers have begun to suspect a connection between the vaccine and Sudden Infant Death Syndrome (SIDS).

DIETARY CHANGES

A child with whooping cough can eat according to the standard macrobiotic diet, with appropriate adjustments for age and condition. (In cases where a nursing infant develops whooping cough, it is recommended that the mother avoid extremes and eat according to the standard macrobiotic diet appropriate for her needs.) In general, yin extremes such as sugar, tropical fruits and juices, ice cream, spices, soft drinks, and milk and milk products are best avoided. Even within the standard diet, a child with this condition must be careful not to overindulge in fruits, especially raw fruits or fruit juices, salads, concentrated sweeteners, and oily or greasy snacks.

Brown rice may serve as the principal grain. When desired, it may be served softly cooked or in soups. Other grains may be used regularly as supplements to brown rice. Children may also take a cup or two of *Special Rice Cream* from time to time. An appropriate volume of condiments may also be eaten with grain dishes. Lotus root seeds, which can be beneficial to the lungs and respiratory passages, may be added to brown rice prior to cooking. *Light Miso Soup* or tamari broth may also be served when appropriate.

Root vegetables, cooked along with their green tops, can also be helpful in relieving lung problems. Daikon and their greens, or carrots and turnips with their tops, can be served often, along with other vegetable dishes. Root vegetables and their green tops are especially nourishing for the lungs and their complementary partner, the large intestine. Lightly boiled salads or quickly steamed greens are preferable to raw salads during recovery. Lotus root—either fresh or dried—may also be included in vegetable or sea vegetable dishes or in soups.

A small piece of white-meat fish may be eaten by older children on occasion if desired. It is better to limit the intake of fruit to occasional small servings of cooked northern fruit. Concentrated sweeteners are best reduced or avoided during recovery, as are nuts and nut butters.

Brown rice tea may be used alternately with bancha and other macrobiotic beverages. It is recommended that all beverages be served hot or at room temperature. Your child may return to the appropriate standard macrobiotic diet once the condition returns to normal.

Special Dishes and Preparations

Any of the following dishes and teas may be given for whooping cough when appropriate:

- *Arame with Lotus Root*
- *Fish and Vegetable Stew*
- *Light Miso Soup*
- *Nishime Vegetables with Lotus Root*
- *White-Meat Fish*

Easing Coughing and Nasal Discharge

Try *Lotus Root Tea*. Tea made from grated fresh lotus root can be helpful in easing chest congestion and coughing. Small children can receive one-third to one-half cup; older children can drink a full cup. Lotus Root Tea can be given once a day for three days or periodically during the time that your child is coughing.

Easing Digestive Discomfort, Fatigue, and Aches and Pains

Try *Ume-Sho-Kuzu Drink*. This powdered kuzu root drink can be used to restore vitality and ease digestive upset, including diarrhea. The drink can be given for one to three days. Small children can have one-quarter to one-third of a cup; older children, one-half to one cup. (Children who have not yet started to use shalt should not be given this preparation.) The drink should be milder than for adults. Ume-Sho-Kuzu can also help restore the appetite.

Reducing Fever

The following teas can help reduce fever:

- *Dried Daikon Tea*
- *Dried Daikon and Shiitake Tea*
- *Grated Daikon Tea*
- *Shiitake Tea*

RECOMMENDATIONS

Children with whooping cough can rest at home and, when necessary, in bed. Because of concern over the possibility of spreading the illness, children are often kept at home for five weeks after the beginning of the sickness. If children with whooping cough have no fever and feel up to it, they can play quietly around the house, provided they are properly dressed to prevent chilling.

The air in your child's room can be kept slightly cooler than normal, and windows can be opened to allow cool air to circulate. Again, make sure that your child is properly dressed and covered.

If your child's cough makes him uncomfortable, the air in the room can be kept slightly moist by placing a pot or two of steaming water in a corner. Electric steam vaporizers or humidifiers can also be used. An electric hot plate can be used to heat a pot of water.

Warm towels can be applied to the chest in order to loosen stagnated mucus. Apply warm towels repeatedly for ten to fifteen minutes. They can also be applied to the sinuses to help relieve stagnation in the nasal passages. A warm towel body rub can be especially helpful. Hot or warm towels should not be applied during a fever.

PALM HEALING can be used to ease discomfort in the lungs and chest region.

Home Care for Specific Symptoms Accompanying Whooping Cough

Fever

When your child's whooping cough is accompanied by fever that exceeds 103° F, you may wish to use natural external applications such as GREEN VEGETABLE PLASTER, TOFU AND GREEN VEGETABLE PLASTER, and TOFU PLASTER. These plasters do not weaken or interfere with the process of discharge. If you are unfamiliar with these applications, contact a macrobiotic center or instructor before using them.

As mentioned previously, it is better not to apply plasters if a child has not yet had the measles. After a child has had the measles, however, external applications can be used when a simple fever becomes uncomfortably high.

You may also wish to apply a WARM ROASTED SALT PACK to the abdomen.

Headaches

The compresses and massage described in the discussion of headaches, including the recommendations for the relief of blocked sinuses, can be applied when necessary. However, it is better not to apply warm towels to your child's head or neck while he is experiencing fever.

Chills, Fatigue, or Body Aches

Rubbing your child's body with a warm towel or warm ginger towel can help in relieving these conditions. Hot towels are best *not* applied to the whole body during an active fever.

Diarrhea

A WARM ROASTED SALT PACK can be applied to the abdomen to help relieve looseness in the bowels. (Make sure the pack is not uncomfortably hot and do *not* apply it to infants.)

Chapter 6
Recipes for Health

Macrobiotics is concerned with keeping people well through a wholesome diet, moderate exercise, and a balanced lifestyle. Although a balanced diet of whole foods is the best and safest path to good health, we must still be prepared for those times when the body may get out of balance. As mentioned in Chapter 5, these imbalances may be due to past abuses, extreme environmental conditions, or other factors. The recipes that follow are recommended for use as part of your child's daily diet during the natural recovery from illness or discomfort, and not as a substitute for appropriate medical attention when necessary.

The recipes in this chapter are not intended to make up a complete meal plan. Included are general recipes to help your child achieve optimum health, as well as recipes to help your child recover from an unbalanced condition. These recipes are generally appropriate for children living in a temperate, four-season climate. Variety is important when cooking for children. We recommend a wide selection of foods and cooking methods. Boiling, steaming, pressure cooking, sautéing, and nishime are desirable methods for preparing foods. The recipes presented here are only a small sampling of the infinite possibilities that you may explore in the world of macrobiotic cooking. More complete guidelines for family cooking are presented in *Aveline Kushi's Complete Guide to Macrobiotic Cooking, Introducing Macrobiotic Cooking,* and other cookbooks listed in the Recommended Reading List.

Step-by-step guidelines for preparing complete meals for children are presented in this book's companion volume, *Macrobiotic Family*

Favorites: Cooking for Healthy Children. Please consult this source for ideas when planning meals for children.

In the following recipes, it is advisable that, whenever possible, ingredients such as grains, beans, and vegetables be organic. When a recipe calls for processed items like miso, tamari soy sauce, and tofu, use only those of the highest quality. Please note that tamari soy sauce should be used sparingly and only in cooking. Many of these items can be found at a natural foods store. In addition, it is recommended that spring or well water be used in the preparation of foods and beverages.

DISHES TO ENSURE OPTIMUM HEALTH

The following recipes are grouped according to their primary ingredients. Their order is determined by a food's place in the macrobiotic diet: whole grains followed by vegetables, and then beans and bean products.

Grains

Fu (Dried Seitan)

Dried seitan, or fu as it is called, is an easily digested food that children can eat quite often. It is a flour product, but because it is moist and does not make children tight or contracted, it is highly recommended for children. Fu should be soaked first and then cooked very soft with vegetables or in soups. There are many varieties of fu from which to choose.

1 kombu strip, 1–2 inches long, soaked and thinly sliced
½ cup onions, sliced in thick half-moons
¼ cup carrots, sliced on a thin diagonal
1 cup fu, soaked and sliced
2 cups water, approximately
1 cup broccoli flowerettes
½ cup fresh tofu, cubed
tamari (optional)

Place kombu in a heavy pot. Add onions, carrots, and fu. Add approximately 2 cups of water. Cover and bring to a boil. Reduce flame to low and simmer until vegetables are tender, about 5–7 minutes. Add broccoli and tofu, and simmer another 5 minutes or so until soft. Season with a small amount of tamari if your child is old enough for it, and continue to simmer about 5 minutes longer. Stir well, remove from heat, and serve.

Mochi

Mochi may be steamed, baked, sautéed in a little oil for older children, added to soups and stews, deep-fried, broiled, or roasted in a dry skillet as above. Serve plain or with a strip of toasted nori wrapped around it, or dip in a little warm barley malt or rice honey. For older children, mochi can also be topped with a couple of drops of tamari.

1 cup sweet brown rice, washed and soaked 6–8 hours
$1\frac{1}{4}$ cups water
pinch of sea salt (optional)

Place rice and water in a pressure cooker, and add sea salt if you are preparing this dish for older children. Cover, turn flame to high, and bring cooker up to pressure. Reduce flame to medium-low, place flame deflector under cooker, and cook for 50 minutes. When rice is done, remove cover after the pressure comes down and place rice in a thick wooden bowl. Pound rice with a heavy wooden pestle until all grains are crushed and rice becomes very sticky. Texture should be quite smooth. Good mochi takes at least 30–45 minutes of pounding.

Pack mochi firmly to form squares, cakes, or rectangles about $\frac{1}{2}$-inch thick and place them on a lightly floured (use brown rice flour) baking sheet. Allow mochi to dry, uncovered, for 1–2 days. After mochi is dry, store in refrigerator until needed.

To toast mochi after it has been dried properly, place squares in a dry skillet. Turn flame to medium-low and cover skillet. Toast until mochi is golden brown; then turn it over and toast other side until golden brown.

Noodles in Broth

Children can eat noodles often for meals or snacks, as they are moist and easily digested. The best types for children are whole wheat spaghetti, elbows, shells, whole wheat udon, or whole wheat somen.

Soba can be used very occasionally for older children but is usually not recommended for babies under one year old.

4 ounce package somen
3 cups water
1 kombu strip, 1–2 inches long, soaked 3–4 minutes
1 shiitake mushroom, soaked
tamari (optional)
$\frac{1}{2}$ cup Chinese cabbage, sliced on a thick diagonal
$\frac{1}{2}$ sheet nori, toasted and cut into 1-inch squares

Cook somen as you would any noodle for several minutes until done. Please test by sampling. Rinse under cold water and drain. In another pot, add 3 cups of water for broth. Add kombu and shiitake, cover, and bring to a boil. Reduce flame to low and simmer for about 10 minutes. Remove kombu and shiitake and set aside for future use. Season broth with a small amount of tamari if appropriate for your child's age, and simmer several minutes longer.

Place Chinese cabbage in a pot with about $\frac{1}{4}$ inch of boiling water, cover, and simmer about 4–5 minutes, until tender.

Place noodles in a bowl. Pour broth over them. Garnish with Chinese cabbage and several squares of nori. Serve hot.

Rice and Lotus Seeds

1 cup brown rice
$\frac{1}{2}$ cup lotus seeds, soaked 3–4 hours
2 cups water
pinch of sea salt

Put rice, lotus seeds, and water in a pressure cooker. Place pressure cooker, uncovered, on a low flame and cook for about 10–15 minutes. Add sea salt if cooking for older children. Cover, raise flame to medium-high, and bring cooker up to pressure. Reduce flame to medium-low, place a flame deflector under cooker, and cook for 50 minutes. Remove cooker from flame and allow pressure to come down. Remove cover and let rice sit in cooker for 4–5 minutes. Place rice in a wooden bowl and serve.

Soft Grain Cereal

Such items as root vegetables, squash, or round vegetables can be cooked with grain from time to time to add variety to the baby's diet.

1 cup grain (rice, millet, barley)
5 cups water
1 kombu strip, 1 inch long, soaked 3–4 minutes

Wash grain and place in a bowl. Add water and soak 6–8 hours or overnight. Place grain and liquid in pressure cooker. Add kombu. Cover cooker and bring up to pressure. Reduce flame to medium-low, place flame deflector under cooker, and cook for approximately 1 hour.

Remove from flame and allow pressure to come down. Remove cover and let cereal grain sit in cooker for 4–5 minutes.

For babies, place the grain in a suribachi and grind to a smooth consistency. For children over one year old, either grind grain slightly or serve as is. If desired, sweeten this dish occasionally with a little barley malt or rice honey. Place cereal in a wooden bowl and serve.

Special Rice Cream

Children can be given one or two small bowls of Special Rice Cream, served hot, in addition to their regular rice and other foods. In cases where the child's condition has become overly yang–that is, tight and contracted–a small amount of rice syrup or high-quality barley malt can be added. If the child's condition is overly yin, a tiny piece ($^1/_4$ or $^1/_3$) of an umeboshi plum or a small amount ($^1/_4$ teaspoon) of children's gomashio may be added. The use of salt or salty condiments should, of course, be consistent with our earlier recommendations for adding salt to children's diets.

1 cup brown rice (short grain), soaked 6–8 hours
7–10 cups water
1 kombu strip, 1 inch long, soaked 3–4 minutes
barley malt (optional)
rice honey (optional)

$\frac{1}{4}$ or $\frac{1}{3}$ umeboshi (optional)
$\frac{1}{4}$ teaspoon gomashio (optional)

Wash rice well in cold water. Put kombu in a pressure cooker. Place rice and water in the pressure cooker. Set aside and soak for 6–8 hours. (If your baby is very young—2 to 6 months—use 10 cups of water instead of 7 to make the rice cream moister and easier for the baby to swallow.) Cover cooker and bring up to pressure. Place flame deflector under cooker and cook for approximately $1\frac{1}{2}$ hours. Remove cooker from flame and allow pressure to come down. Remove cover.

Use sterile cotton cheesecloth to make a sack, and place cooked rice and rice liquid inside. Squeeze out all of the creamy liquid. Rice pulp remaining in sack can be set aside and used in making bread.

Place Special Rice Cream in a saucepan. Add a little sweetener such as barley malt or rice honey to rice cream if desired (about $\frac{1}{2}$ teaspoon sweetener per cup of rice cream). Heat rice cream and serve. Put leftover rice cream in a tightly sealed glass bottle or jar and store in a cool place or refrigerator. Reheat before serving.

Vegetables

Arepa

1 cup dried corn
1 kombu strip, 1 inch long, soaked 3–4 minutes
1 cup wood ash
2 cups water

Wash corn, place in a bowl, cover with water, and soak overnight. Remove corn and drain. Place corn, kombu, wood ash, and water in a pressure cooker, and bring up to pressure. Reduce flame to low and place flame deflector under cooker. Cook until corn is soft, about 80–90 minutes. Remove from flame and allow pressure to come down. Remove cover.

Place corn in a strainer or colander, and wash it very well to remove wood ash. Place corn in a pressure cooker. Cover and pressure cook for 1 hour. Remove and place in a grinder. Mash cooked corn to a thick paste or dough. Corn should be moist enough to make patties; if necessary, add a little more water. Take 1 handful of corn paste and shape into a patty about $\frac{1}{2}$-inch thick and 3 inches in diameter. Repeat until all corn is used.

Place cakes in a dry, heated skillet and fry or toast until golden brown on each side. (If a hard skin on the outside is not desired, steam the Arepa instead of pan-frying. Steamed Arepa become very soft and are especially good for children.) Remove from heat and serve.

Dried Daikon

It is better not to give Dried Daikon to very young children,
as its harder texture may make it a little difficult to digest.
Instead, give them the sweet juice left over from cooking it.
After the child is about two years old, he can begin eating
Dried Daikon, but be sure to cook the daikon until it is very soft.
Daikon may also sometimes be cooked with vegetables, in soups,
or in grain dishes.

1 kombu strip, 2 inches long, soaked 5 minutes
and cut in 1-inch squares
$\frac{1}{2}$ cup dried daikon, soaked 5–7 minutes and cut in 1-inch chunks
$\frac{1}{4}$ cup buttercup or butternut squash, cut in 1-inch chunks
$\frac{1}{4}$ cup carrots, cut in 1-inch chunks
water
pinch of sea salt (optional)
tamari (optional)

Place kombu in a pot and set daikon on top. Next, layer celery, squash, and carrots in that order on top of daikon. Place about $\frac{1}{2}$ inch of water in a pot and add a very small pinch of sea salt if the child is old enough. Cover pot and bring to a boil. Reduce flame to low and simmer for approximately 25–30 minutes, or until vegetables are very soft. Season with a small amount of tamari at this point if appropriate for your child's age. Continue to cook until almost all liquid is gone. Mix and place in a serving dish.

Beans and Bean Products

Azuki Beans with Chestnuts and Raisins

1 kombu strip, 2 inches long, soaked and sliced in 1-inch cubes
$\frac{1}{2}$ cup azuki beans, soaked 6–8 hours
$\frac{1}{2}$ cup dried chestnuts, soaked 6–8 hours
$\frac{1}{4}$ cup raisins
$2\frac{1}{2}$–3 cups water (include azuki and chestnut soaking water)
pinch of salt (optional)

Place kombu in a heavy pot and set azuki beans, chestnuts, and raisins on top. Add water and bring to a boil. Cover and reduce flame to low. Simmer for about 2 hours. At this point, add sea salt if cooking for an older child, and continue to simmer 30 minutes longer. Additional cold water may be added from time to time if necessary to keep the beans from burning or becoming too dry.

If necessary, beans, chestnuts, and raisins may occasionally be pressure-cooked for about 50 minutes. If prepared in pressure cooker, season dish when done.

Dried Tofu

*Young children may find it a little difficult to digest dried tofu unless
it is properly cooked. Also, unless cooked together with vegetables
and a little tamari, dried tofu is somewhat tasteless.
Not having a particular taste of its own, it absorbs the flavors
of whatever else is cooked with it.
To properly prepare dried tofu for children, soak it several minutes
in warm water, rinse it under cold water, and then pressure-cook it
together with whatever vegetables are desired.
For children over two years old, season with a little tamari.*

1 kombu strip, 2 inches long, soaked and sliced into 1-inch squares
$\frac{1}{4}$ cup onions, sliced in thick half-moons
$\frac{1}{4}$ cup carrots, sliced in 1-inch chunks
$\frac{1}{2}$ cup cabbage, sliced in thick chunks
3 slices dried tofu, soaked, rinsed, and cut into 1-inch cubes

water
tamari

Place kombu in a pot. Add onions, carrots, and cabbage. Place dried tofu in the pot. Add about $\frac{1}{2}$ inch of water, a small amount of tamari, and cover. Bring to a boil on a high flame. Reduce flame to low and cook for approximately 15–20 minutes. Remove from flame and serve.

RECIPES FOR SPECIFIC CONDITIONS

Acidic Conditions

Bancha Tea

1 quart water
1–2 tablespoons bancha twigs

Place water and twigs in a teapot and bring to a boil. Reduce flame to low and simmer for 5–10 minutes. For milder tasting tea, simmer for 3–4 minutes. (Children may enjoy tea brewed to this strength.) Bancha Tea is good any time of day, especially after meals.

Anemia, Iron, and Calcium Deficiencies

Hijiki

Hijiki is a good source of potassium. It is useful in strengthening the blood and immune system and in restoring intestinal flora.

$\frac{1}{2}$ cup onions, cut into thin half-moons
$\frac{1}{2}$ cup carrots, cut into matchsticks
$\frac{1}{2}$ cup tempeh, cubed
$\frac{1}{2}$ cup hijiki, washed, soaked, and sliced
water
tamari

Place about $\frac{1}{4}$ inch of water in a skillet and bring to a boil. Add onions and sauté 1–2 minutes. Add carrots and tempeh. Place hijiki on top of tempeh. Add enough water to half cover hijiki and vegetables. Bring to a boil, reduce flame to low, and cover. Simmer about 35 minutes. Season with a very small amount of tamari and continue to cook another 5 minutes, until almost all remaining liquid is gone.

Bed-wetting

Applesauce

2 apples, washed, peeled, and sliced
$\frac{1}{2}$ cup water
small pinch of sea salt

Place water, apples, and sea salt in a saucepan. Cover and bring to a boil. Reduce flame to medium-low and simmer for about 7–10 minutes, until apples are soft and tender. Place apples and water in a food mill or suribachi and grind.

Baked Apple

1 baking apple, washed
water

Place apple in a baking dish with about $\frac{1}{8}$ inch of water. Cover and bake at 350°F for about 30 minutes. Remove and slice. You may wish to remove skin and seeds for younger children.

Hot Apple Cider

1 cup apple cider
1 grain sea salt

Heat cider and salt in a saucepan. Remove cider from heat and serve warm or at room temperature.

Kanten

1 cup apple juice
1 cup water
1 apple, with or without skin, washed, sliced

small pinch of sea salt
$2\frac{1}{2}$–3 tablespoons agar-agar flakes (read package directions)

Place all ingredients in a saucepan and bring to a boil. Cover, reduce flame to low, and simmer 2–3 minutes. Remove from flame and pour into a glass baking dish or ceramic bowl. To jell quickly, place in the refrigerator. Kanten can also be left out at room temperature to jell more slowly.

Coughs

Lotus Root Tea

Lotus Root Tea is especially helpful in relieving coughs and dissolving mucus in the lungs. This tea can be given once a day for three days or periodically during the time that your child is coughing.

1 piece lotus root, 3–4 inches long
several grains of sea salt

Grate lotus root on a fine grater. Wrap in a piece of sterile cotton cheesecloth and squeeze out lotus juice into a measuring cup. Add an equal amount of water to the juice. Place water and juice in a saucepan, and add sea salt. Bring to a boil, stirring constantly. Reduce flame to low and simmer for several seconds. Drink warm.
Give small children $\frac{1}{3}$ to $\frac{1}{2}$ cup, older children 1 cup.

Digestive Upsets Accompanying a Cold or Flu

Ume-Sho-Kuzu

Ume-Sho-Kuzu is especially beneficial for digestion and helps to normalize and tone the intestines.

For very small children:
$\frac{1}{2}$ teaspoon kuzu
1 cup water
small piece umeboshi

For older children:
1 teaspoon kuzu
1 cup water
$\frac{1}{4}$–$\frac{1}{2}$ umeboshi plum
1–2 drops of tamari

Dissolve kuzu in about 1 teaspoon of cold water and stir. Add remaining water and umeboshi. Cook on a high flame, stirring constantly to prevent lumping. When mixture begins to boil, reduce flame to low. If preparing for older children, season with tamari if desired. Simmer for about 1 minute. Drink hot or warm. For digestive discomfort including diarrhea that accompanies a cold or flu, give small children $\frac{1}{4}$ to $\frac{1}{3}$ cup. Older children may have $\frac{1}{2}$ to 1 cup.

Fever

Cereal Grain Tea

This tea, made from brown rice or barley, can be given to children in place of (or as one of) their normal beverages.

$\frac{1}{4}$ cup brown rice
1 quart water

Wash, then dry-roast rice in stainless steel skillet over a medium flame until rice is golden brown, stirring constantly to prevent burning. Place water in a teapot or saucepan. Add roasted rice and bring to a boil. Reduce flame to low and simmer for 10–15 minutes.

Grated Sour Apple

Raw green apple can help offset fever by releasing stagnated energy, especially in the stomach and intestines. The juice helps to dissipate stagnation in the stomach; the grated applesauce releases stagnation in the intestines.

1 sour green apple (Granny Smith)
2 grains sea salt (omit for babies)

Grate half of the sour green apple, including skin, and place in a piece of sterile cheesecloth. Squeeze out all of the juice. Place the juice in a saucepan, add a couple of grains of sea salt—except if beverage is for babies—and heat. Serve warm or hot. (Grate the remaining half apple and make applesauce with it.) Babies may be given a teaspoon or so of the juice, and children can receive $\frac{1}{2}$–1 cup of the juice and gratings from the apple.

Shiitake Tea

Because it helps dissolve excess animal fats, Shiitake Tea is also beneficial for stomachaches caused by consumption of meat, poultry, and fish.

1 shiitake mushroom
2 cups water

Place shiitake and water in a saucepan. Bring to a boil. Cover and reduce flame to medium-low. Simmer until only 1 cup of liquid remains. Remove shiitake and give approximately $\frac{1}{2}$ cup of tea water to small children (over the age of two). Give only 1 teaspoon Shiitake Tea to babies. Older children may have up to 1 cup.

Lung Problems

Fish and Vegetable Stew

This stew is especially recommended for whooping cough.

1 kombu strip, 2 inches long, soaked and diced
1 shiitake mushroom, soaked, stem removed, and diced
2 cups water
1 stalk celery, diced
1 piece fresh daikon, 2 inches long, diced
1 onion, diced
1 carrot, cut in 1-inch chunks
$\frac{1}{4}$ cup white-meat fish (haddock, sole, scrod, etc.)
tamari

Place kombu and shiitake in a pot. Add water and bring to a boil. Cover, and reduce flame to medium-low. Simmer for about 5 minutes. Add celery, daikon, onions, and carrots. Cover and simmer for several minutes until vegetables are very soft and tender. Add fish and simmer 5 minutes longer. Season with a little tamari (very mild) and simmer 10 minutes longer on a low flame. Place stew in individual serving bowls and serve. Makes 2 servings.

Nishime Vegetables with Lotus Root

1 kombu strip, 2–3 inches long, soaked and cubed
$\frac{1}{3}$ cup celery, sliced on a thick diagonal
$\frac{1}{4}$ cup daikon, cut in chunks
$\frac{1}{2}$ cup buttercup squash, cut in chunks
$\frac{1}{4}$ cup carrots, cut in chunks
$\frac{1}{4}$ cup lotus root, cut in $\frac{1}{4}$-inch chunks
water
tamari

Place kombu in a heavy pot. Place celery on top of kombu. Set daikon on top of celery, and place squash on top of daikon. Add carrots and lotus root. Pour $\frac{1}{4}$–$\frac{1}{2}$ inch of water into the pot. Bring water to a boil, cover, and reduce flame to medium-low. Simmer about 30 minutes, until all vegetables are tender. Add a very small amount of tamari and continue to simmer another 10 minutes, until almost all remaining liquid is gone and vegetables are soft. Mix vegetables to coat them with any remaining liquid, remove, and place in a serving bowl.

Mumps

Kinpira Carrots and Burdock

$\frac{1}{2}$ cup burdock, sliced in matchsticks
$\frac{1}{2}$ cup carrots, sliced in matchsticks
water
tamari

Put about $\frac{1}{4}$ inch of water in a stainless steel skillet and bring to a boil. Place burdock in skillet and sauté for 2–3 minutes. Place carrots on top of the burdock, add about $\frac{1}{4}$ cup of water, and cover skillet. Reduce flame to low. Simmer about 10 minutes until burdock and carrots are tender. Season with a small amount of tamari and simmer 5 minutes longer. Remove cover and sauté until remaining liquid is gone. Mix carrots and burdock, remove from flame, and place in a serving bowl.

Pinworms

Corsican Sea Vegetable Tea

This tea should be used for several days only.

2 cups water
$\frac{1}{4}$ cup Corsican sea vegetable, rinsed

Place water and sea vegetable in a saucepan and bring to a boil. Reduce flame to low, cover, and simmer until 1 cup of liquid remains. Remove from heat, allow to cool, and serve $\frac{1}{4}$ cup of tea for children under two, $\frac{1}{2}$ cup for children two to five years old, and 1 cup for children over five years old.

Dried Daikon Tea

When adults or older children experience a fever, a cup or two of tea
made with grated raw daikon with a few drops of tamari
(see Grated Daikon Tea) can be used to help reduce it.
This tea is too strong for infants and children under the age of five.
Dried Daikon Tea can be used instead.

1 tablespoon dried daikon
2 cups water

Place dried daikon and water in a saucepan. Bring water to a boil. Cover and reduce flame to medium-low. Simmer until only 1 cup of liquid remains. Strain liquid to remove daikon. Children over the age of two can drink up to $\frac{1}{2}$ cup of Dried Daikon Tea. Younger children should consume no more than 1 or 2 teaspoons of the tea.

---
*Grated Daikon Tea**
---

1 tablespoon fresh grated daikon
pinch of fresh grated ginger ($\frac{1}{8}$ teaspoon)
1–2 drops tamari
Bancha Tea

*For older children only.

Place daikon, ginger, and tamari in a teacup. Pour hot bancha tea over the mixture. Stir and drink hot or warm.

Children over the age of six can have freshly grated daikon tea for simple fevers. A small cupful should be sufficient.

Roasted Pumpkin Seeds*

$^1\!/_2$ cup pumpkin seeds, rinsed

Heat a stainless steel skillet and add pumpkin seeds. (*Do not add any oil.*) To roast evenly and prevent burning, mix constantly with a wooden spoon or bamboo rice paddle. Lower flame to medium-low. To ensure even roasting, occasionally shake pan to rotate seeds. Continue roasting for several minutes until seeds begin to pop and turn golden brown. Remove immediately to prevent burning and place in a bowl.

Roasted Squash Seeds*

$^1\!/_2$ cup squash seeds, pulp removed, washed

Set oven at 350°F, spread squash seeds on a baking sheet, and bake seeds for about 20 minutes. Every few minutes, stir seeds with a wooden spoon to prevent burning and to roast evenly. When seeds are golden brown, remove and place in a bowl to cool. The seeds can be chopped for smaller children to make them easier to digest.

Roasted Sunflower Seeds*

$^1\!/_2$ cup sunflower seeds, rinsed

Follow recipe for *Roasted Pumpkin Seeds.*

Soba with Light Tamari Broth and Scallions

This soup should be used only by older children and is for occasional use only.

*No salt.

1 cup soba noodles, cooked and rinsed
1 teaspoon scallions, sliced

Broth
1 cup water
1 kombu strip, 1–2 inches long, soaked
tamari

Place water and kombu in a pot. Cover and bring to a boil. Reduce flame to low and simmer about 7–10 minutes. Season very lightly with a couple of drops of tamari, and simmer about 5 minutes longer. Place rinsed noodles in the broth and warm them slightly. Place noodles and broth in a bowl, and garnish with sliced scallions.

Severe Stomach Problems

Baked Umeboshi Plum Drink

Older children (above the age of six) can be given Bancha Tea in which one-quarter to one-third of a teaspoon of baked, powdered umeboshi plum or pits are dissolved. This special tea can be given only once in two days.

umeboshi plum
water

Preheat oven to 300° F. Place a whole umeboshi plum in a cast iron skillet and cover. Bake until plum is completely black and brittle. Place the baked plum in a suribachi and grind to a fine powder. Place about 1 teaspoon powder in a cup and pour 1 cup of hot water over it. Mix and drink while warm.

Sinus Conditions

Nishime Vegetables with Lotus Root

1 kombu strip, 2–3 inches long, soaked and cubed
$\frac{1}{3}$ cup celery, sliced on a thick diagonal
$\frac{1}{4}$ cup daikon, cut in chunks
$\frac{1}{2}$ cup buttercup squash, cut in chunks
$\frac{1}{4}$ cup carrots, cut in chunks

¼ cup lotus root, cut in ¼-inch chunks
water
tamari

Place kombu in a heavy pot. Place celery on top of kombu. Set daikon on top of celery, and place squash on top of daikon. Add carrots and lotus root. Pour ¼–½ inch of water into the pot. Bring water to a boil, cover, and reduce flame to medium-low. Simmer about 30 minutes, until all vegetables are tender. Add a very small amount of tamari and continue to simmer another 10 minutes, until almost all remaining liquid is gone and vegetables are soft. Mix vegetables to coat them with any remaining liquid, remove, and place in a serving bowl.

Stomachaches

Ume-Bancha Tea

This tea can help relieve stomach or intestinal discomfort.

1 cup hot *Bancha Tea*
¼–½ umeboshi plum

Place umeboshi plum in a teacup. Pour hot *Bancha Tea* over it and stir. Drink hot or warm.

Ume-Sho-Bancha

A small teacup of Ume-Sho-Bancha can be given in place of Ume-Sho-Kuzu for stomach upset. Ume-Sho-Bancha strengthens the blood and overall condition by normalizing digestion.

1 cup hot *Bancha Tea*
¼–½ umeboshi plum
1–2 drops tamari

Place umeboshi plum and tamari in a teacup. Pour hot *Bancha Tea* over mixture and stir. Drink hot or warm.

Stomachaches Caused by Dairy Products

Arame with Lotus Root

$\frac{1}{2}$ cup onions, cut into thin half-moons
$\frac{1}{2}$ cup carrots, cut into matchsticks
$\frac{1}{4}$ cup lotus root, quartered and thinly sliced
$\frac{1}{2}$ cup arame, washed and sliced
water
tamari

Heat about $\frac{1}{4}$ inch of water in a skillet. Place onions in skillet and cook 2–3 minutes. Put carrots and lotus root on top of onions. Place arame on top of vegetables. Do not mix. Add enough cold water to almost cover vegetables but not arame. Cover skillet and bring water to a boil. Reduce flame to medium-low and simmer about 30 minutes. Season with a small amount of tamari and cook another 5 minutes. Remove cover, turn flame up to medium-high, and cook until almost all remaining liquid is gone. Remove from heat, mix, and serve.

Daikon, Daikon Leaves, and Kombu

Daikon helps dissolve stagnant fat and mucous deposits that have accumulated in the body. Freshly grated raw daikon is especially helpful in the digestion of oily foods. This dish can be prepared nishime style and served along with meals several times per week.

1 kombu strip, 1–2 inches long, soaked and cubed
$\frac{1}{2}$ cup daikon, sliced into $\frac{1}{2}$-inch-thick rounds and quartered
water
$\frac{1}{2}$ cup daikon greens, chopped
tamari

Put kombu in a saucepan. Set daikon on top of kombu. Add enough water to half cover daikon. Bring to a boil. Reduce flame to low, cover, and simmer for about 25–30 minutes. Add greens and a few drops of tamari. Simmer for 4–5 minutes until the greens are done. If too much liquid remains, it may be thickened with kuzu for a sauce or used in soup.

Light Miso Soup

*Miso, which aids digestion, comes in many varieties. Mugi miso—
made from barley, soybeans, and sea salt—is usually best for daily use,
although other varieties may be used occasionally. This particular
soup can be served along with meals for several days.*

2 cups water
2 tablespoons wakame, soaked and sliced
1/2 cup onions, sliced in thin half-moons
1/2 teaspoon barley (mugi) miso

Place water in a saucepan and bring to a boil. Add wakame and
simmer for 1–2 minutes. Add onions and cook 3–5 minutes or
until very soft. Reduce flame to very low. Purée the miso with a
little water or soup broth and add to the soup. Simmer for 2–3
minutes. Place soup in individual serving bowls, and garnish
with a few finely sliced scallions. Children may drink 1/2–1 cup
per day.

Nori Condiment*

*Nori is rich in vitamins and minerals. Children can eat one-half
teaspoon of nori condiment for several consecutive days
or several times over the course of a week.*

2 sheets nori
water
tamari

Pull nori apart into approximately 1-inch squares and place in a
saucepan. Add just enough water to cover nori. Bring to a boil,
reduce flame to low, cover, and simmer until almost all liquid is
gone. Season with a couple of drops of tamari and simmer for 3–4
minutes longer.

Squash with Onions

You can serve this dish with meals for several days.

*For older children only.

1 kombu strip, 2 inches long, soaked and cubed
$\frac{1}{2}$ cup onions, quartered
$\frac{1}{2}$ cup winter squash (buttercup or Hokkaido pumpkin),
cut into chunks
water
sea salt

Put kombu in a pot. Place onions and squash on top of kombu. Add about $\frac{1}{2}$ inch of water and a couple of grains of sea salt. Bring to a boil, then cover and reduce flame to low. Simmer until squash is very soft, approximately 20 minutes.

Stomachaches Caused by Meat, Poultry, or Fish

Dried Daikon Tea

*When adults or older children experience a fever, a cup or two of tea
made with grated raw daikon with a few drops of tamari
(see Grated Daikon Tea) can be used to help reduce it.
This tea is too strong for infants and children under the age of five.
Dried Daikon Tea can be used instead.*

1 tablespoon dried daikon
2 cups water

Place dried daikon and water in a saucepan. Bring water to a boil. Cover and reduce flame to medium-low. Simmer until only 1 cup of liquid remains. Strain liquid to remove daikon. Children over the age of 2 can drink up to $\frac{1}{2}$ cup of Dried Daikon Tea. Younger children should consume no more than 1 or 2 teaspoons of the tea.

Dried Daikon and Shiitake Tea

1 tablespoon dried daikon
1 shiitake mushroom
2 cups water

Place daikon, shiitake, and water in a saucepan. Bring water to a boil. Cover, and reduce flame to medium-low. Simmer until only 1 cup of liquid remains, then strain to remove shiitake and daikon.

Babies may be given only 1 teaspoon; small children, $\frac{1}{2}$ cup; older children, 1 cup.

Grated Daikon Tea*

Children over the age of six can have freshly grated daikon tea for simple fevers. A small cupful should be sufficient.

1 tablespoon fresh grated daikon
pinch of fresh grated ginger ($\frac{1}{8}$ teaspoon)
1–2 drops tamari
Bancha Tea

Place daikon, ginger, and tamari in a teacup. Pour hot bancha tea over the mixture. Stir and drink hot or warm.

Light Miso Soup

Miso, which aids digestion, comes in many varieties. Mugi miso—made from barley, soybeans, and sea salt—is usually best for daily use, although other varieties may be used occasionally. This particular soup can be served along with meals for several days.

2 cups water
2 tablespoons wakame, soaked and sliced
$\frac{1}{2}$ cup onions, sliced in thin half-moons
$\frac{1}{2}$ teaspoon barley (mugi) miso

Place water in a saucepan and bring to a boil. Add wakame and simmer for 1–2 minutes. Add onions and cook 3–5 minutes or until very soft. Reduce flame to very low. Purée the miso with a little water or soup broth and add to the soup. Simmer for 2–3 minutes. Place soup in individual serving bowls, and garnish with a few finely sliced scallions. Children may drink $\frac{1}{2}$–1 cup per day.

Nori Condiment*

Nori is rich in vitamins and minerals. Children can eat one-half

* For older children only.

teaspoon of nori condiment for several consecutive days or several times over the course of a week. A small amount of fresh grated ginger can be added when the digestive upset is the result of eating cheese.

2 sheets nori
water
tamari

Pull the nori apart into approximately 1-inch squares and place in a saucepan. Add just enough water to cover the nori. Bring to a boil, reduce flame to low, cover, and simmer until almost all liquid is gone. Season with a couple of drops of tamari and simmer for 3–4 minutes longer.

Pearl Barley Soup

This soup can be served daily for several days in addition to the other soups included in your child's diet.

1 kombu strip, 2–3 inches long, soaked and diced
$\frac{1}{4}$ cup diced onions
2 tablespoons diced celery
1 shiitake mushroom, soaked and diced
$\frac{1}{4}$ cup diced carrots
$\frac{1}{2}$ cup pearl barley, soaked 6–8 hours
3 cups water
tamari
chopped parsley or scallions

Place kombu in a saucepan and layer onions, celery, shiitake, carrots, and pearl barley on top. Add water and bring to a boil. Cover and reduce flame to low. Simmer about 45 minutes, until barley is soft. Season with a little tamari and continue to simmer for another 10–15 minutes. Place soup in individual serving bowls and garnish with a pinch of chopped parsley or scallions.

Shiitake Tea

1 shiitake mushroom
2 cups water

Place shiitake and water in a saucepan. Bring to a boil. Cover and reduce flame to medium-low. Simmer until only 1 cup of liquid remains. Remove shiitake and give approximately $\frac{1}{2}$ cup of tea water to small children (over the age of two). Give only 1 teaspoon Shiitake Tea to babies. Older children may have up to 1 cup.

Stomachaches Caused by Sugar

Tamari/Bancha Tea

2–3 drops tamari
1 cup hot *Bancha Tea*

Add the tamari to a cup of hot *Bancha Tea.*

Tense Muscles and Nerves

Shiitake Tea

1 shiitake mushroom
2 cups water

Place shiitake and water in a saucepan. Bring to a boil. Cover and reduce flame to medium-low. Simmer until only 1 cup of liquid remains. Remove shiitake and give approximately $\frac{1}{2}$ cup of tea water to small children (over the age of two). Give only 1 teaspoon Shiitake Tea to babies. Older children may have up to 1 cup.

Whooping Cough

Fish and Vegetable Stew

1 kombu strip, 2 inches long, soaked and diced
1 shiitake mushroom, soaked, stem removed, and diced
2 cups water
1 stalk celery, diced
1 piece fresh daikon, 2 inches long, diced

1 onion, diced
1 carrot, cut in 1-inch chunks
$\frac{1}{4}$ cup white-meat fish (haddock, sole, scrod, etc.)
tamari

Place kombu and shiitake in a pot. Add water and bring to a boil. Cover and reduce flame to medium-low. Simmer for about 5 minutes. Add celery, daikon, onions, and carrots. Cover and simmer for several minutes until vegetables are very soft and tender. Add fish and simmer 5 minutes longer. Season with a little tamari (very mild) and simmer 10 minutes longer on a low flame. Place stew in individual serving bowls and serve. Makes 2 servings.

Nishime Vegetables with Lotus Root

1 kombu strip, 2–3 inches long, soaked and cubed
$\frac{1}{3}$ cup celery, sliced on a thick diagonal
$\frac{1}{4}$ cup daikon, cut in chunks
$\frac{1}{2}$ cup buttercup squash, cut in chunks
$\frac{1}{4}$ cup carrots, cut in chunks
$\frac{1}{4}$ cup lotus root, cut in $\frac{1}{4}$-inch chunks
water
tamari

Place kombu in a heavy pot. Place celery on top of kombu. Set daikon on top of celery, and place squash on top of daikon. Add carrots and lotus root. Pour $\frac{1}{4}$–$\frac{1}{2}$ inch of water into the pot. Bring water to a boil, cover, and reduce flame to medium-low. Simmer about 30 minutes, until all vegetables are tender. Add a very small amount of tamari and continue to simmer another 10 minutes, until almost all remaining liquid is gone and vegetables are soft. Mix vegetables to coat them with any remaining liquid, remove, and place in a serving bowl.

White-Meat Fish

white-meat fish
fresh lemon juice
tamari

Place a small piece of white-meat fish on a baking sheet, squeeze a little fresh lemon juice on top, and add a couple of drops of tamari. Place in a broiler and cook several minutes until fish is soft and tender. Do not cook too long as the fish may become tough.

Chapter 7

Home Care Guide

The Macrobiotic home remedies and therapies are based on traditional techniques that have been used for thousands of years in many parts of the world to alleviate symptoms brought on by dietary and lifestyle imbalances. If you have any doubts about the advisability of any of these home remedies, consult an experienced macrobiotic counselor before using them. The special preparations and applications are especially helpful for children during their natural recovery from illness or discomfort. Persons with serious illnesses are, of course, advised to seek appropriate medical, nutritional, and psychological care.

Macrobiotic counselors and others who already have some familiarity with macrobiotic home remedies will find the following to be a useful reference. For each remedy, instructions for preparation follow a brief description of the item's purposes. If you are a newcomer to macrobiotics and you are interested in using these home remedies, consult an experienced macrobiotic counselor first.

Home remedies are often derived from foods on the macrobiotic diet. Understanding the effects of these foods on our health and using them to create balance and harmony is the key to a healthy and happy future. The therapies discussed in this chapter are specifically designed for external use.

ENEMAS

There are two types of enemas, cleansing and retention. The cleansing enemas are not retained or held in the body; they are used to flush out the colon.

If a child experiences fever due to constipation, a simple enema often brings relief. In many cases, an enema will cause the fever to drop and make other special applications unnecessary. Additional information about the use of enemas can be found in various child-care books (see Recommended Reading). Since this is a potentially invasive procedure, seek the advice of your child's pediatrician in regard to administering an enema.

COOL OR WARM APPLICATIONS

In macrobiotics, the use of external applications is based on the understanding of energy. External applications are used to adjust the abnormal energy arising from various symptoms. When energy becomes overactive, for example, such as in a fever or inflammation, applying mild cold, which draws off excessive energy, can help ease the discomfort of symptoms. Cool applications, such as a cabbage leaf or other green leafy plaster, a tofu plaster, a tofu and leafy greens plaster, or plasters made from various cooked grains and green vegetables, are suitable for this purpose.

These simple applications work on the principle of applying an opposite type of energy to neutralize symptoms. Overactive energy can be counterbalanced and made more quiet by using a cool application with more inert energy. Conversely, stagnant or condensed energy in the body, such as that in constipation, can be counteracted by applying an energy-activating treatment such as warm towels or a mild ginger compress. Always remember that very young children or infants should not be given strong external applications. Stronger external applications are best used only on older children.

MASSAGE

Massage is one of the most important elements of holistic, natural healing. Like acupuncture and palm healing, it involves stimulating and unblocking the meridians and points along which electromagnetic energy flows throughout the body. Energy flow becomes blocked or stagnated through accumulation of mucus, fats, or toxins in the blood, organs, or joints, which in turn causes stiffness or pain along the meridians. These blockages and accumulations are caused by dietary imbalances and a lack of proper activity. These blockages interfere with the flow of energy along the meridians and can contribute to illness. Basic massage uses only the hands and fingertips and can be learned in several hours. With practice, you can develop your ability to give a healing massage. Massage can be used as a regular part of family health care.

For Constipation and Fever

Gentle stimulation of the large intestine point on the outside of the hand (see Figure 7.1) can be helpful in bringing relief from constipation. Press the point gently with your thumb and rub with a circular motion. Massage the points on each hand off and on for about 5 minutes. Remember, however, that children are much more sensitive than adults. Use only very light pressure. It is recommended that massage normally be used only after children have reached the age of two, and even then, only very gently.

For Headaches

Simple, light massage is often helpful in relieving the discomfort of headaches, especially when it is given in combination with warm or cold compresses. One of the most effective ways to restore balance in the flow of energy in the head is to massage points or regions on the energy meridians that run along the face, head, and front of the body. The stomach meridian runs down the front of the body from the face to the second and third toes. It can be massaged when children experience frontal headaches, including sinus and migraine headaches. The gallbladder meridian runs along the side of the head down to the fourth toe. It can be massaged to relieve side headaches. The bladder meridian runs along the back of the head down either side of the spine and along the back of the legs to the fifth toe. It can be used to release tension in the back of the head or neck. Tension or pressure in the center of the head can be relieved through massage on the liver or spleen meridians that run up along the inside of the legs and the front of the body from the first toe.

Stimulating the peripheral areas of the meridians is especially effective in releasing excessive energy in the head. The most peripheral regions of the aforementioned meridians are located on the toes. As we have seen, the fifth toe is an extension of the bladder meridian; the fourth, an extension of the gallbladder; the third and second, extensions of the stomach; and the big toe, an extension of the liver and

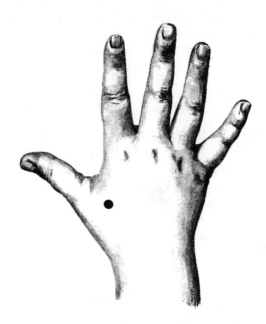

**Figure 7.1 The Large Intestine Point (Go-Koku, or
"Meeting Valley") on the Outside of the Hand**

spleen meridians. (You may refer to *The Book of Do-In: Exercise for
Physical and Spiritual Development* by Michio Kushi for a complete
explanation of the meridians and organs.)

- *For pain in the front of the head, including migraine and sinus headaches.*
  Your child can lie comfortably on his back and relax. Repeatedly
  apply cold cotton washcloths to his forehead for 5 to 7 minutes. Then
  gently massage the second toe for several minutes by gently pulling
  it outward. Do the third toe in a similar manner, and then do both
  toes at the same time. After finishing one foot, repeat the same
  procedure on the other one.

- *For pain in the side of the head.* Have your child lie comfortably on his
  back and relax. Repeatedly apply cold cotton towels to the painful area
  for 5 to 7 minutes. Then massage the fourth toe of each foot for several
  minutes by gently pushing it outward.

- *For tension headaches in the back of the head.* Your child can lie
  comfortably on his front with his head turned to the side. Repeatedly

apply warm towels or a cotton washcloth to the painful region as above. Then massage the fifth toe of each foot in the same manner as you would in the preceding procedure.

- *For tension headaches deep inside the head.* Your child can lie comfortably on his back. Dip a towel or washcloth in hot water, squeeze out excess water, and wrap the cloth around your child's neck. Replace with a fresh application as the first one cools and continue for 5 minutes. Then massage the large toe of each foot as described previously.

These applications are safe and effective and do not expose children to artificial substances. The majority of simple childhood headaches can be relieved through natural applications such as these, along with attention to proper diet.

For Stomachaches

Gently stimulating the stomach meridian can help ease discomfort in that organ. When energy is excessive, massage can help to discharge it more smoothly. When energy is deficient, it can help in supplying energy.

Have your child lie comfortably with feet on the floor and knees raised. The stomach meridian runs down the outside-front of both legs to the second and third toes.

Sit facing your child's legs. Gently grip the leg with your thumb on the inside and your fingers opposite to it on the outside. Beginning just below your child's knee, use your fingers to press the stomach meridian down on the leg and then across the top of the foot to the second and third toes. Use your thumb to support your fingers. Your child's legs and feet can be massaged simultaneously or one at a time.

When massaging the stomach meridian, stop in the area of the *San-Ri* point located on the outside of the leg below the knee as shown in Figure 7.2. With your index and middle fingers, give extra massage at this point. Use a rotating, circular motion and massage the point for several minutes before proceeding down the meridian.

The second and third toes can be massaged once the meridians have been treated. To do this, straighten your child's leg and hold the foot by placing one hand under the heel. Use the thumb and index finger of your other hand to gently grasp each toe. Begin at the base of the toe and with a gentle, pinching motion, work outward to the tip. Next, pull and rotate the toe, then pull again, snapping your fingers gently off the tip of each toe. Repeat this procedure on each foot on the two toes that are part of the stomach meridian.

Figure 7.2   San-Ri

PALM HEALING

Palm Healing can help reduce discomfort by allowing excessive energy to discharge more smoothly. In our other family health volume, *Macrobiotic Pregnancy and Care of the Newborn,* we introduce the use of Palm Healing in a variety of childhood disorders. Also included are exercises to generate healing power. Please refer to this book for further information.

When practicing Palm Healing, it is important to keep a straight but comfortable posture. It is not necessary to press the palms firmly on the area that you wish to treat. A light, gentle touch is better.

Methods to Alleviate Coughing and Lung Congestion

If your child has a cold or the flu, the following methods can help alleviate coughing and lung congestion:

1. Have your child lie on his back. Place one hand across the chest

region. Breathe naturally and quietly and keep your hand in place for 10 to 15 minutes. Your palms can be applied to each lung separately, or place one hand on your child's upper back or chest and cover both lungs at the same time.

2. As a variation, one palm can be placed on the chest and the other on the abdomen in the region of the transverse colon. Breathe naturally and quietly and keep your hands in place for 10 to 15 minutes. In this way, problems in the lungs and large intestine can be dealt with simultaneously.

If your child has whooping cough, any of the following methods can be used to ease discomfort in the lungs and chest region:

1. *Applying the palm to the front of the chest.* This application can be done with your child lying comfortably on his back. Place one hand gently over his chest, covering both lungs. Breathe with a normal rhythm, and remove your hand after 15 to 20 minutes. The sound of "Su" may be added when you are exhaling.

2. *Applying palms to the chest and upper back.* This application can be done with your child sitting up. Place one hand on his chest, covering the region of the lungs with your other palm opposite, on your child's upper back. Breathe with a normal rhythm, and remove your hand after 15 to 20 minutes. The sound of "Su" may be added when you are exhaling.

3. *Applying palms and fingers to the lungs and lung meridian.* The lung meridian runs down along the inside of both arms to the thumbs. To treat both regions, have your child lie comfortably on his back. Sit on one side of your child. Gently hold one of your child's thumbs between your thumb and index finger, and place the palm of your other hand lightly over his chest. Breathe and continue as in number one above for 10 to 12 minutes. After applying your hands in the above manner, sit on the other side of your child and gently hold the opposite thumb with one hand and place the other on his chest. Breathe and continue as before for 10 to 12 minutes before removing your hands.

Methods to Alleviate Earaches

If your child suffers from earaches, the following simple techniques can help relieve pain and loosen stagnated mucus in the middle ear:

Figure 7.3 Applying Palms to the Chest and Upper Back

1. *Applying the palms to the affected ear.* To comfort your child's affected ear, place one hand gently over it so that the center of your palm covers the opening of the ear. Breathe quietly and gently. The sound of "Su" may be added when you are exhaling. Remove your hand after 15 to 20 minutes.

2. *Applying palms to both ears.* This method may be used instead of the preceding one. Simply place your palms over both ears so that the center of the palm covers the ear opening. Breathe and continue as in number one.

3. *Applying palms to the kidneys.* Relieving stagnation or tightness in the kidneys can often be helpful in easing discomfort in the inner ear. To comfort the kidneys, place one hand gently across the child's back in the kidney region. Breathe and continue as in number one.

4. *Applying palms to the ears and kidneys.* The ears can be comforted

at the same time that you relieve stagnation in the kidneys. Place one hand gently over your child's ear as described above. Place your other hand on the same side of your child's back in the kidney region. (When comforting the right ear, apply your hand to your child's right kidney; when comforting the left ear, apply it to the left kidney.) Breathe and continue as in number one.

Methods to Alleviate Fever

Following are several simple methods for easing the discomfort of a fever:

1. *Applying palms to the forehead.* To help release energy in the forehead, have your child lie on his back, covered as usual. Place one hand lightly on his forehead. Close your eyes and breathe quietly and gently, keeping your hand lightly on his forehead. The sound of "Su" may be added when you are exhaling. Slowly remove your hand after 15 to 20 minutes.

2. *Applying palms to the front and back of the head.* As a variation of the preceding method, place one hand on your child's forehead and the other directly opposite to it on the back of his head. Breathe as above and hold your hands lightly in this position for 15 to 20 minutes.

3. *Applying palms to the intestines.* Have your child lie on his back. Sit near him with a straight but relaxed posture. Breathe normally and quietly, and place one hand lightly on your child's abdomen so that the center of your palm covers the area just below his navel. Make sure that your child remains properly covered. Breathe as above and apply your palm for 15 to 20 minutes.

   This method is effective for easing the discomfort of a fever. Many fevers are related to blockage in the intestines. Applying palms to the intestines can help relieve stagnation or help excessive energy to discharge.

4. *Applying palms to the forehead and intestines.* Place one hand on your child's forehead, as in number one, and the other hand on the lower abdomen, as in number three. Breathe as described previously and continue for 15 to 20 minutes.

   The lower regions of the body coordinate with the upper regions. An imbalance in one region affects the other. Stagnation in the intestines, for example, often produces elevated temperatures in the forehead or, in some cases, headache and tension in the shoulders and neck. (For the same reason, menstrual problems also frequently cause headaches or emotional tension.) The palms can be applied to both regions in order to release stagnation and harmonize the flow of energy in both regions and the body as a whole. This method is especially helpful for fevers caused by intestinal disorders. Be careful to prevent your child from becoming chilled.

Methods to Alleviate Headache Pain

Palm Healing is especially effective in relieving headache pain. In addition to restoring a more normal balance of energy, it establishes a warmth between parent and child. It helps to ease stress, tension, and anxiety, and soothes and relaxes the child.

1. *For pain in the front of the head.* This application can be done with your child sitting in a comfortable, relaxed position. Sit facing your child's side. Keep a straight but relaxed posture. Extend your arms and place one palm directly in front of you on the back of your child's head. Close your eyes and breathe with a quiet, gentle rhythm. The sound of "Su" may also be added when you exhale. Remove your hands after 15 to 20 minutes.

2. *For headaches caused by blocked sinuses.* This application is divided into two procedures. In the first, the palms are applied to loosen stagnation in the general area of the sinuses. In the second, energy is focused on specific points within the sinuses.

   Begin by placing one hand gently over your child's eyes so that the center of your palm covers the bridge of his nose. Place your other hand directly opposite on the back of his head. Breathe as above and apply the palms for 5 to 7 minutes. (This method can also be used to relieve discomfort due to eyestrain.)

   Next, lightly apply the fingers of one hand to the sinus points illustrated in Figure 7.4. (Use your thumb, index, and middle or ring fingers.) Place your other hand on the back of your child's head, opposite to the cheeks and forehead. Close your eyes and breathe with a gentle, quiet rhythm. The sound of "Su" may be added on the exhalation while you are gently vibrating your fingers. After 10 to 15 minutes, rapidly detach your palms and fingers.

3. *For pain in the side of the head.* Sit or stand (if your child is sitting in a chair) behind your child. Extend your arms and place your

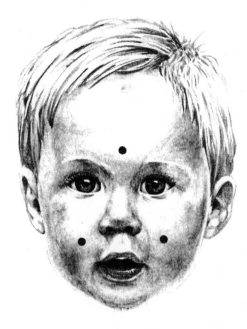

Figure 7.4   Points for Relief of Sinus Blockage

palms lightly on the sides of your child's head or on both sides of the top of the head, if this region is painful. Breathe as above, and apply the palms for 10 to 15 minutes before slowly removing them.

4. *For pain in the back of the head.* Sit next to your child, facing his side. Place one hand gently on the region of the back of his head where the pain is centered, the other on his forehead. Breathe as above and remove the hands after about 10 to 15 minutes.

5. *For pain deep inside the head.* Pain in the inner regions of the head can be approached in several ways.

- Sit behind your child and gently place one hand on top of his head. Breathe as above and remove your hand after 10 to 15 minutes.

- Sit behind your child and gently cover his ears with your palms, so that the center of the palm covers the center of the ear. Breathe and continue as above.

- Sit facing your child's side and place one hand gently on the back of his head and the other on his forehead. Breathe and continue as above. (This method is similar to that used for pain in the back of the head.)

If your child becomes distracted before the application is finished, pause a few minutes and then proceed. It is better, however, for the application to be continuous, without interruption. Therefore, before beginning, try to help your child relax by telling him a story or by singing him a song. Also, when he is old enough, explain to him in simple language how Palm Healing works and how it helps him to feel better. If your child is too active to sit still, you can use Palm Healing while he is sleeping. Posture can be adjusted when necessary.

Methods to Alleviate Pain Caused by Orthopedic Problems

If your child experiences joint pain, place your palm lightly on the affected area. Close your eyes and breathe with a quiet, gentle rhythm. The sound of "Su" may also be added when you exhale. Remove your hand after 15 to 20 minutes.

Methods to Improve Skin Conditions

Because skin disorders are often related to problems in the kidneys and intestines, it is often helpful to apply the palms lightly to the middle back and then to the abdomen. Breathe quietly and gently and apply the hands for 10 to 15 minutes on each region.

Methods to Alleviate Sore Throat

Palm Healing can also help ease the discomfort of a sore throat. Have your child sit in a relaxed position. He may lie comfortably on his back. Place one hand gently across the upper part of your child's neck, immediately under the lower jaw. Place your other hand opposite to this on the back of the neck. Breathe quietly and gently and apply the hands for 15 to 20 minutes before detaching them.

If your child is experiencing other discomforting symptoms along with the sore throat, seek further instructions in the appropriate sections of this chapter.

Methods to Alleviate Stomach and Intestinal Discomfort

Any of the following methods can be applied when children experience discomfort in the stomach and intestines:

1. *Applying palms to the stomach energy center (stomach chakra).* Your child can lie comfortably on his back. You should have a straight

but relaxed posture. Breathe normally and quietly and place one hand lightly on the solar plexus just below the breastbone or sternum. The center of the palm should be placed directly over this spot. Keep breathing normally and quietly, and keep the palm in place for 15 to 20 minutes. Make sure that your child is properly covered during the application.

2. *Applying the palms to the stomach energy center and the second and third toes.* This application is based on the complementary/antagonistic relationship that exists between the inner regions of the body and the periphery.

   Your child can lie comfortably on his back. Place one hand on his abdomen—as in number one—and with the thumb and fingers of your other hand, lightly grasp your child's second and third toes. (Either foot is fine.) You can close your eyes and breathe quietly and gently. The sound of "Su" can be added if desired. After about 5 to 7 minutes, release the second and third toes and gently grasp those of the other foot. Keep your other hand in the same position on the abdomen. Continue for another 5 to 7 minutes and then remove both hands.

3. *Applying the palms to the intestines.* Have your child lie on his back. Sit near him with a straight but relaxed posture. Breathe normally and quietly, and place one hand lightly on your child's abdomen so that the center of your palm covers the area just below his navel. Make sure that your child remains properly covered. Breathe as above and apply your palm for 15 to 20 minutes.

   Applying palms to the intestines can help relieve stagnation or help excessive energy to discharge.

4. *Applying palms to the intestines and forehead.* To help release energy in the intestines and forehead, have your child lie on his back, covered as usual. Place one hand lightly on his forehead. Place your other hand on the lower abdomen so that the center of your palm covers the area just below your child's navel. Breathe as described previously and continue for 15 to 20 minutes.

   This method helps relieve discomfort in the lower digestive tract.

PLASTERS

Plasters can be used to relieve fevers that are uncomfortably high—those that exceed 103°F. These natural applications help ease discomfort and do not weaken or interfere with the process of discharge. They also aid in drawing stagnated mucus from the sinuses, nose, throat, and bronchi, which is especially helpful in relieving headache pain. Some plasters can be applied to painful ears as well. If you are unfamiliar with these applications, contact a macrobiotic center or instructor before using them. Remember not to apply plasters if your child has not yet had the measles. See Figure 7.5 for plaster application.

Green Vegetable Plaster

Green Vegetable Plaster is effective in drawing out fever. Made from finely chopped, raw green vegetables, this chlorophyll plaster is very mild. It can be applied to the forehead for a short while until the temperature begins to drop, or it can be left on until it becomes warm and then replaced with a fresh application. This cool chlorophyll plaster can also be applied to a painful ear. Hold the plaster gently over the ear and replace it with a fresh one when the application becomes warm. Green Vegetable Plaster is also beneficial for a sore throat.

1 bunch leafy greens (collard, kale, watercress)

Chop washed greens very fine and place in suribachi. Grind the greens well. If they are very watery, mix in a little pastry flour to hold the mixture together. To apply, spread $\frac{1}{2}$-inch layer on a piece of cotton cheesecloth or cotton linen, and place the side with the greens directly onto the forehead or other affected area. Change every 2–3 hours.

Lotus Root Plaster

Lotus Root Plaster helps draw stagnated mucus from the sinuses, nose, throat, and bronchi. This is especially effective in relieving headache pain.

freshly grated lotus root
pastry flour
freshly grated ginger

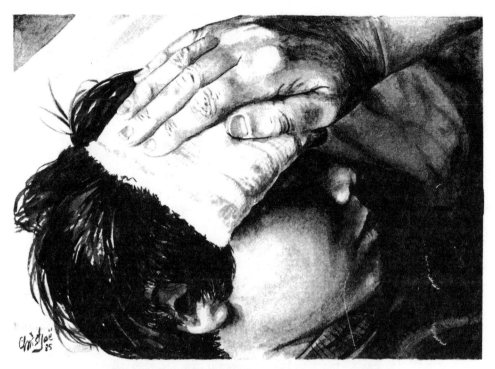

Figure 7.5 Applying Tofu Plaster for Fever

Mix 16 parts freshly grated lotus root with 3 parts pastry flour and 1 part freshly grated ginger. To apply, spread ½-inch layer on a piece of cotton linen, and place the side with the lotus root directly onto the affected area. Leave the plaster on for several hours.

Tofu Plaster

A plaster made with fresh tofu is somewhat stronger than the preceding plaster applications, which include greens. For this reason, we do not recommend using it on children under the age of two. Milder applications are usually sufficient to draw out fever in younger children. Tofu plasters can also be used to ease the discomfort of a sore throat. Apply in the same manner as described above.

½ pound tofu, drained
pastry flour
fresh grated ginger

Place tofu in a suribachi and grind. For every 6 parts tofu, add 1 part freshly grated ginger and 3 parts pastry flour. Mix ingredients to make a paste, then spread $\frac{1}{2}$-inch layer onto a clean piece of cotton cheesecloth or cotton linen. Apply directly to the forehead or other affected area. Change every 2–3 hours.

Tofu and Green Vegetable Plaster

A plaster combining raw green vegetables and fresh tofu can be applied to the forehead instead of the Green Vegetable Plaster to reduce fever. It can be left on until the temperature drops or until it absorbs heat and becomes warm. A fresh plaster can be applied if needed. This plaster can also be applied to a painful ear in place of the Green Vegetable Plaster if your child is suffering from an earache. Apply the plaster to the region of the head directly behind the ear. Hold the plaster gently in place and replace it with a fresh application when the first one becomes warm. Tofu and Green Vegetable Plaster is also recommended for sore throats. In addition, this chlorophyll plaster relieves swelling caused by an insect bite or other skin disorder. Apply directly to the affected area until the tofu becomes warm. Replace with a fresh application if necessary.

$\frac{1}{2}$ pound fresh tofu
several leafy greens (collard, kale, watercress)
pastry flour (optional)

Chop greens very fine and grind well in a suribachi. Place tofu in a suribachi and grind to a thick paste. Add pastry flour to thicken if desired. Spread $\frac{1}{2}$-inch layer on a clean piece of cotton cheesecloth or cotton linen, and apply directly to the forehead or affected area. Change every 2–3 hours.

WARM THERAPIES

Heat is often used to alleviate problems, especially pain. By increasing the temperature in a selected area of the body, warm therapies such as the Warm Sesame Oil Drops will enhance blood circulation and increase mobility in that area. Moist heat is effective in reducing stiffness and relaxing muscles, in addition to its other benefits described in this section. Warm towels are often helpful in relieving tension. See also the section on poultices in this chapter.

Warm Roasted Salt Pack

Warm Roasted Salt Packs are beneficial for children who are running a fever and experiencing chills.

1 cup sea salt

Place sea salt in a skillet and dry-roast for several minutes on a medium-low flame. Continue roasting until the salt turns slightly off-white and releases a strong chlorine smell. To prepare pack, place the hot salt in thick cotton linen or put it in a pillowcase and wrap a thick towel around it to prevent burns. Use enough salt to cover the affected area with a half-inch layer. Allow the pack to cool slightly before applying to the abdomen or other affected area. Replace the pack with another when it begins to cool.

Warm Sesame Oil Drops

For an earache, place 1–2 drops of warm oil in the affected ear with an eyedropper. (The oil can be heated by placing the jar in hot water.) Do not use Warm Sesame Oil Drops, however, if ear drainage is occurring.

¼ cup light sesame oil

Place sesame oil in a saucepan. Turn flame to low, and heat oil. Strain the hot oil through sterile cotton cheesecloth into a small bottle. Cover tightly to store.

Warm Sesame Oil and Ginger Application

This application can be used to relieve soreness and itching caused by pinworms. Apply mixture directly to the anus, and follow the application with a warm towel.

$\frac{1}{4}$ cup sesame oil
$\frac{1}{4}$ teaspoon ginger juice

Place oil in a saucepan on a low flame. Add ginger juice and heat slowly. Remove and place in a tightly sealed glass jar to store, or, if using immediately, dip sanitized cotton into the oil and apply to the affected area.

SKIN WASHES

Natural products such as rice bran and daikon leaves can be applied directly to the skin to relieve discomfort and to aid in improvement of skin disorders, rashes, and insect bites.

Daikon Juice

The juice from freshly grated daikon is often helpful in relieving itching. Grate several tablespoons of fresh daikon. Dip sanitized cotton into the gratings, allowing the cotton to absorb the juice. Apply the juice directly to the area of the skin that itches.

Dried Daikon Leaves and Sea Salt

This application is helpful in extracting excess fat and oil and in helping the skin return to normal. Dry fresh daikon leaves away from sunlight until they become brown and brittle (or purchase dried leaves at a natural foods store). Boil 4 to 5 bunches of leaves with 4 to 5 quarts of water until the water turns brown. Add a medium-sized handful of sea salt and stir well. Dip a cotton cloth or towel into the liquid and squeeze it lightly. Apply it to the affected area, making repeated applications until the skin becomes red. The hair can be washed frequently with this liquid in cases of head lice. This application may also be applied for insect bites or poison ivy.

Rice Bran (Nuka)

Nuka, or rice bran, can be purchased at most natural foods stores. To prepare a skin wash, wrap nuka in cheesecloth. Place in warm water, squeeze, and shake. The nuka will dissolve, the water will turn a yellowish color, and a white foam may form on the surface. Lightly wash the affected area several times with a towel or face cloth that has been dipped in the nuka water.

Children with skin problems can also be given a bath in which nuka has been dissolved. Put about 3 to 5 tablespoons of nuka into a white cotton sock or a sack made of thin cotton cloth or cheesecloth. Tie the sack so that the nuka does not fall out. Place the sack in the bath water and squeeze it until a milky liquid comes out. Mix the milky liquid in the water and use it to wash the skin, including the areas where the disorder is present. Rice bran contains natural oil that helps the skin return to a smooth and healthy condition. The hair can also be washed in nuka water.

If you cannot find rice bran, rolled oats can be substituted. About $\frac{1}{4}$ cup can be used. Nuka or oat applications may also be used to ease the itching and discomfort of poison ivy or insect bites.

Sesame Oil

Sesame oil often helps soothe skin discomfort. It can be applied directly to the affected area. Either light or dark oil can be used.

Conclusion

The future exists today. Long after we leave this planet, our children and descendants will continue. Providing them with the basis for a healthy and productive life is our most important priority as parents.

Creating a healthy family is the work of God. The family is a replica of the universe and the creative process that gives life to everything.

We all cherish the memory of a happy family life. The warmth and love that exist between mother and father, between parents and children, and between brothers and sisters can be found nowhere else. Macrobiotic living makes this type of family life possible for everyone, now and in the future. It is a way of life that is essential for everyone who wishes to create a wonderful, happy family and beautiful, intelligent, and healthy children.

Today, our world is in danger. Degenerative diseases, environmental destruction, and mental illness may destroy the human spirit and undercut the future of life on this planet. Strong and healthy families, and bright, happy children are needed now more than ever. Children who receive the benefit of a macrobiotic upbringing are qualified to guide and inspire humanity toward a bright and positive future.

Macrobiotic child care is a direct method for the eventual realization of planetary health and peace. Those who share a similar quality of food are like members of an extended family, no matter where they live. Beginning with ourselves and our immediate families, let us invite all people to become members of the planetary family of Earth.

In the future, our sense of family unity can be extended to include everyone on the planet. Our spiritual connections can also extend to our ancestors for thousands of generations. Our sense of home and belonging can extend to the entire surface of the planet and beyond. Humanity can share love, understanding, and trust with one another and can be free to realize its most cherished dreams.

The way of health and peace is based on love for nature, for the universe, for other people, and for all beings. Let us hope that in the future, all families embrace it and use it to realize love and peace on our beautiful planet.

Glossary

The following glossary describes macrobiotic foods, cooking methods, kitchen equipment, and ideas that may not be familiar to you. Words that have particular application to the relationship between diet and health are also included.

Aduki. *See* Azuki Beans.

Agar-agar. A white gelatinous substance derived from a sea vegetable. Agar-agar is used in making aspics and kanten. *See also:* Kanten.

Albi. *See* Taro.

Amasaké (Rice Milk). A sweetener or refreshing drink made from sweet rice or koji starter that is allowed to ferment into a thick liquid. Hot amasaké is a delicious beverage on cold autumn or winter nights.

Arame. A dark brown, spaghetti-like sea vegetable similar to hijiki. Rich in iron, calcium, and other minerals, arame is often used as a side dish.

Arrowroot. A starch flour processed from the root of a native American plant. It is used as a thickening agent, similar to cornstarch or kuzu, for making sauces, stews, and desserts.

Azuki. *See* Azuki Beans.

Azuki Beans. Small, dark red beans. Especially good when cooked with kombu, this bean may also be referred to as *adzuki* or *aduki*.

Bancha Tea. The twigs and leaves from mature Japanese tea bushes. Correctly named *kukicha*, bancha aids digestion, is high in calcium, and contains no chemical dyes. It makes an excellent breakfast or after-dinner beverage.

Barley, Pearl. A strain of barley native to China. Pearl barley grows well in cold climates. It is good in stews and soups, or cooked with other grains. Pearl barley helps the body to eliminate animal fats.

Barley Malt. A thick, dark brown sweetener made from barley. Pure

(100 percent) barley malt is used in making desserts, sweet and sour sauces, and a variety of medicinal drinks.

Beefsteak Plant. *See* Shiso.

Black Sesame Seeds. Small black seeds used occasionally as a garnish or to make black gomashio, a condiment. These seeds are different from the usual white or tan variety.

Black Soybeans. *See* Japanese Black Beans.

Bok Choy. A leafy, green vegetable with thick white stems that resemble stalks. Bok Choy is used mostly in summer cooking. It is sometimes called *pok choy*.

Brown Rice. Unpolished rice with only its tough outer husk removed. It comes in three main varieties: short, medium, and long grain. Short grain brown rice contains the best balance of minerals, protein, and carbohydrates, but the other types may also be used on occasion. *See also:* Sweet Brown Rice.

Brown Rice Miso. *See* Genmai Miso.

Brown Rice Vinegar. A very mild and delicate vinegar made from fermented brown rice or sweet brown rice. Brown rice vinegar is not as acid-forming in the body as apple cider vinegar.

Buckwheat. A cereal plant native to Siberia. Buckwheat has been a staple food in many European countries for several centuries. It is frequently eaten in the form of kasha, whole groats, or soba noodles.

Burdock. A hardy plant that grows wild throughout the United States. The long, dark burdock root is delicious in soups, stews, and sea vegetable dishes, or sautéed with carrots. It is highly valued in macrobiotic cooking for its strengthening qualities. The Japanese name is *gobo*.

Chemical Additives. Any of the various artificial flavorings, coloring agents, or preservatives not naturally found in foods that are used in refining and processing. Over three thousand chemical additives have been approved by the United States Food and Drug Administration.

Chinese Cabbage. A large, leafy vegetable with pale green tops and thick white stems. Sometimes called *nappa*, this juicy, slightly sweet vegetable is good pickled or in soups, stews, and vegetable dishes.

Cholesterol. A compound manufactured in the human body, important in the structure of membranes and the formation of certain hormones. Cholesterol is a constituent of all animal products. When consumed in excess in the diet, cholesterol increases the risk of gallstones, heart disease, cancer, and other health problems.

Complex Carbohydrates. Those starches, known chemically as polysaccharides, which provide the body with a high proportion of usable energy over a period of several hours. Complex carbohydrates are the major component of the macrobiotic diet. They are supplied primarily by whole grains, vegetables, and beans.

Condition. An individual's present state of health, rather than his state of health at birth, or *constitution.*

Constitution. An individual's characteristics, determined before birth by the health and vitality of his parents, grandparents, and other ancestors. *See also* Condition.

Couscous. A partially refined and quick-cooking cracked wheat that has a flavor similar to cream of wheat.

Daikon. A long, white radish. Besides making a delicious side dish, daikon helps dissolve stagnant fat and mucous deposits that have accumulated in the body. Freshly grated raw daikon is especially helpful in the digestion of oily foods.

Discharge. The body's elimination of stored mucus, fat, and toxins through a variety of means, including urination, defecation, perspiration, coughing, boils, cysts, and tumors.

Do-In. A form of Oriental exercise and self-massage that works to harmonize and balance the electromagnetic energy flowing through the meridians.

Dried Daikon. Daikon sold in dried and shredded form. Dried daikon is especially good cooked with kombu and seasoned with tamari soy sauce. Soaking dried daikon before use brings out its natural sweetness.

Dried Tofu. Tofu that has been naturally dehydrated by freezing. Used in soups, stews, vegetable and sea vegetable dishes, dried tofu contains less fat than regular tofu. *See also:* Tofu.

Dulse. A reddish-purple sea vegetable used in soups, salads, and vegetable dishes. Dulse is high in protein, iron, vitamin A, iodine, and phosphorus. Most of the dulse sold in America comes from Canada, Maine, and Massachusetts.

Electromagnetic Energy. Energy that flows through all things, including the human body. Electromagnetic energy is generated by the Earth's rotation and orbit.

Fermentation. The act of certain bacteria or enzymes, changing the chemical composition of foods and making them easier to digest. Fermented foods on the macrobiotic diet include sauerkraut, pickles, sourdough breads, and some soyfoods.

Fiber. The indigestible portion of whole foods—particularly, the bran of whole grains and the outer skin of legumes, vegetables, and fruits. Fiber facilitates the passage of waste through the intestines. Foods that are refined, processed, or peeled are low in fiber.

Fu. A dried wheat-gluten product. Available in thin sheets or thick round cakes, fu is a satisfying high-protein food used in soups, stews, and vegetable dishes.

Genmai Miso. Miso made from soybeans, brown rice, and sea salt fermented for approximately twelve months. Also called *brown rice miso,* it is used in making soups and seasoning vegetable dishes.

Ginger. A spicy, pungent, golden-colored root used as a garnish or seasoning in cooking and for various beverages. It is also used in making external home remedies such as the ginger compress.

Ginger Compress. A hot compress made from the juice of ginger root and water. This compress stimulates circulation and dissolves stagnation in the part of the body to which it is applied.

Gluten (Wheat). The sticky substance that remains after the bran has been kneaded and rinsed from whole wheat flour. Gluten is used to make seitan and fu.

Gobo. *See* Burdock.

Gomashio. Also known as *sesame salt.* Gomashio is a table condiment made from roasted, ground sesame seeds and sea salt. It is good sprinkled on brown rice and other whole grains.

Grain Coffee. A non-stimulating, caffeine-free coffee substitute made from roasted grains, beans, and roots. Ingredients are combined in different ways to create a variety of flavors. It is used like instant coffee.

Green Nori Flakes. A sea vegetable condiment made from a certain type of nori, different from the packaged variety. The flakes are rich in iron, calcium, and vitamin A. They can be sprinkled on whole grains, vegetables, salads, and other dishes.

Hatcho Miso. Miso made from soybeans and sea salt and fermented for a minimum of two years. It has a mild salt taste and may be used from time to time in making soup stocks and condiments, and for seasoning vegetable dishes. This dark, rich miso is especially good in cold weather.

Hijiki. A dark brown sea vegetable that turns black when dried. It has a spaghetti-like consistency, a stronger taste than arame, and is very high in calcium and protein. The hijiki sold in the United States is imported from Japan or harvested off the coast of Maine.

Hokkaido Pumpkin. There are two varieties of Hokkaido pumpkin. One has a deep orange color and the other has a light green skin similar to Hubbard squash. Both varieties are very sweet and have a tough outer skin.

Hydrogenation. A process by which vegetable oils are made more saturated, causing them to become denser and more solid.

Japanese Black Beans. A special type of soybean grown in Japan. They can be used to alleviate problems of the reproductive organs. In cooking, these black beans are used in soups and side dishes.

Kanten. A jellied dessert made from agar-agar. It can include seasonal fruits such as melon, apples, berries, peaches, and pears, or amasaké, azuki beans, and other items. Usually served chilled, it is a refreshing alternative to conventional gelatin.

Kasha. Buckwheat groats that are roasted prior to boiling. Kasha is a traditional Eastern European and Russian food.

Kayu. Cereal grain cooked with five to ten times as much water as grain for a long period of time. Kayu is ready when it is soft and creamy.

Kelp. A large family of sea vegetables that grows profusely off both coasts of the United States. Kelp is widely available at natural foods stores, packaged whole, granulated, or powdered. It is an excellent source of minerals, including iodine.

Kinpira. Sautéed root vegetables—usually burdock or burdock and carrots—cut into matchsticks seasoned with tamari soy sauce. This hearty dish is warming and vitalizing, making it ideal for autumn and winter use.

Koji. A grain, usually semi-polished or polished rice, inoculated with bacteria and used to begin the fermentation process in a variety of foods, including miso, amasaké, natto, and saké.

Kokkoh. A porridge especially for babies, made from brown rice, sweet brown rice, azuki beans, sesame seeds, and kombu. A little yinnie (rice) syrup or barley malt may be used to sweeten it.

Kombu. A wide, thick, dark green sea vegetable that is rich in minerals. Kombu is often cooked with beans and vegetables. A single piece may be re-used several times to flavor soup stocks.

Kudzu. *See* Kuzu.

Kukicha. *See* Bancha Tea.

Kuzu. A white starch made from the root of the wild kuzu plant. In this country, the plant densely populates the southern states, where it is called *kudzu.* It is used in making soups, sauces, desserts, and medicinal beverages.

Lotus. The root and seeds of a water lily that is brown-skinned with a hollow, chambered, off-white inside. Lotus is especially good for the sinuses and lungs. The seeds are used in grain, bean, and sea vegetable dishes.

Macrobiotics. A lifestyle approach based on a balanced diet, moderate exercise, harmony with the environment, and an understanding of the philosophic principles of yin and yang. George Ohsawa was the first to recognize how these traditional concepts could be applied to modern living.

Meridian. In Oriental medicine, a pathway through which electromagnetic energy flows in the body. The healing arts of acupuncture, shiatsu, and do-in, along with the martial arts, strive to re-establish the harmony of the energy flow through the many meridians of the body.

Millet. A small, yellow grain that comes in many varieties, with pearled millet being the most common. Millet is used as a cereal and in soups, vegetable dishes, and casseroles.

Miso. A protein-rich fermented soybean paste made from ingredients such as soybeans, barley, and brown or white rice. Miso is used in soup stocks and as a seasoning. When consumed on a regular basis, it aids circulation and digestion. Mugi miso is usually best for daily use, but other varieties may be used occasionally. Quick or short-term misos, which are fermented for several weeks, are less suitable for frequent use; their salt content is higher than that of the longer-term varieties such as mugi and hatcho miso. *See also* Genmai Miso; Hatcho Miso; Mugi Miso; Natto Miso; Onazaki Miso; Red Miso; White Miso; Yellow Miso.

Miso, Puréed. Miso that has been reduced to a smooth, creamy texture so it will blend easily with other ingredients. To purée miso, place it in a bowl or suribachi and add enough water or broth to make a smooth paste. Blend with a wooden pestle or spoon.

Mochi. A heavy rice cake or dumpling made from cooked, pounded sweet brown rice. Mochi is especially good for lactating mothers, as it promotes the production of breast milk. Mochi can be prepared at home or purchased ready-made; it makes an excellent snack.

Mucus. Secretion of mucous membranes, normally serving to protect and lubricate many parts of the body. Illness, environmental pollution, smoking, and the consumption of excess fats, sugar, and flour products can stimulate the overproduction of mucus and clog body passageways, preventing the body from expelling harmful substances.

Mugi Miso. A miso made from barley, soybeans, and sea salt, fermented for about eighteen to twenty-four months. This flavorful miso can be used on a daily basis year-round to make soup stocks, condiments, and pickles, and to season vegetable or bean dishes. Mugi miso is generally suitable for use by individuals with serious illness.

Mu Tea. Tea made from a blend of traditional, non-stimulating herbs. A warming and strengthening beverage, mu tea is especially beneficial for the female reproductive organs. Two popular varieties of mu tea are #9 and #16.

Nappa. *See* Chinese Cabbage.

Natto. Soybeans that have been cooked, mixed with beneficial enzymes, and allowed to ferment for twenty-four hours. Natto is high in easy-to-digest protein and vitamin B_{12}.

Natto Miso. A condiment made from soybeans, barley, kombu, and ginger; not actually a miso.

Natural Foods. Foods that are not processed or treated with artificial additives or preservatives. Some natural foods are partially refined using traditional methods.

Nishime. A method of cooking in which different combinations of vegetables, sea vegetables, or soybean products are slow-cooked with a small amount of water and tamari soy sauce. Also referred to as *waterless cooking.*

Nori. Thin black or dark purple sheets of dried sea vegetable. Nori is often roasted over a flame until it turns green. Rich in vitamins and minerals, it is used as a garnish, wrapped around rice balls in making sushi, or cooked with tamari soy sauce as a condiment. It is sometimes called *laver.*

Palm Healing. A healing art based on stimulating and balancing the flow of electromagnetic energy through the meridians of the body. Palm healing utilizes hand pressure on specific points of the body.

Pok Choy. *See* Bok Choy.

Polyunsaturated Fats. Term used to describe the molecular structure of the fats that are present in vegetable oils and other whole foods, including fish. While polyunsaturates are more healthful than saturated fats, overconsumption may lead to elevated fatty acid (triglyceride) levels in the bloodstream.

Pressed Salad. Very thinly sliced or shredded fresh vegetables, combined with a pickling agent such as sea salt, umeboshi, brown rice vinegar, or tamari soy sauce, and placed in a pickle press. In the pickling process, many of the enzymes and vitamins are retained while the vegetables become easier to digest.

Red Miso. A salty-tasting short-term fermented miso, made from soybeans and sea salt. Also called *aka miso,* it is suitable for occasional use by individuals who are in good health.

Refined Oil. Salad or cooking oil that has been chemically extracted and processed to maximize yield and extend shelf life. Refining strips an oil of its color, flavor, and aroma, and reduces its nutritive value.

Rice Balls. Rice shaped into balls or triangles, usually with a piece of umeboshi in the center, and completely covered with a wrapping of toasted nori or shiso leaves. For variety, different ingredients may be used as filling or for a coating. Rice balls are good for snacks, lunches, picnics, and traveling.

Rice Syrup. *See* Yinnie syrup.

Saké. Japanese rice wine containing about 15 percent alcohol, often used in cooking.

Saké Lees. Fermented residue from making saké (rice wine), used occasionally as seasoning in soups, stews, vegetable dishes, and pickles. Saké lees is especially good for use in winter, as it helps to generate body heat.

Saturated Fats. Term used to describe the molecular structure of most of the fats found in red meats, dairy products, and other animal foods. An excess of these in the diet contributes to heart disease and other illnesses.

Sea Salt. Salt obtained from evaporated sea water, as opposed to rock salt mined from inland beds. Sea salt is either sun-baked or kiln-baked. High in trace minerals, it contains no sugar or chemical additives.

Sea Vegetables. Any of a variety of marine plants used as food. Sea vegetables are a prime source of vitamins, minerals, and trace elements in the macrobiotic diet.

Seitan. Wheat gluten cooked in tamari soy sauce, kombu, and water. Seitan can be made at home or purchased ready-made at many natural foods stores. It is high in protein and has a chewy texture, making it an ideal meat substitute.

Sesame Butter. A nut butter obtained by roasting and grinding brown sesame seeds until smooth and creamy. It is used like peanut butter or in salad dressings and sauces.

Shiatzu. A form of Oriental massage that releases blockages of electro-magnetic energy and harmonizes energy flow through the meridians of the body.

Shiitake. Mushrooms imported dried from Japan and available freshly grown in some parts of the United States. Either type can be used to flavor soup stocks or vegetable dishes, and dried shiitake can also be used in medicinal preparations. These mushrooms help the body to discharge excess animal fats.

Shio Kombu. Pieces of kombu cooked for a long time in tamari soy sauce and used sparingly as a condiment. Shio kombu has a strong salty taste.

Shiso. A red, pickled leaf. The plant is known in English as the *beefsteak plant*. Shiso leaves are used to color umeboshi plums and as a condiment. Sometimes spelled *chiso*.

Shoyu. *See* Tamari and Tamari Soy Sauce.

Simple Sugars. A source of quick but short-lasting energy. Simple sugars include sucrose (table sugar), fructose, glucose (dextrose), and lactose (milk sugar). Up to 50 percent of the carbohydrates consumed in the average modern diet are simple sugars. *See also* Complex Carbohydrates.

Soba. Noodles made from buckwheat flour or a combination of buckwheat and (whole) wheat flour. Soba can be served in broth, in salads, or with vegetables. In the summer, soba noodles are good chilled.

Somen. Very thin white or whole wheat Japanese noodles. Thinner than soba and other whole grain noodles, somen are often served during the summer.

Suribachi. A special serrated, glazed clay bowl used with a pestle, called a surikogi, for grinding and puréeing foods. An essential item in the macrobiotic kitchen, the suribachi can be used in a variety of ways to make condiments, spreads, dressings, baby foods, nut butters, and medicinal preparations.

Sushi. Rice rolled with vegetables, fish, or pickles, wrapped in nori, and sliced in rounds. Sushi is becoming increasingly popular throughout the United States. The most healthful sushi is made with brown rice and other natural ingredients.

Sweet Brown Rice. A sweeter-tasting, more glutenous variety of brown rice. Sweet brown rice is used in mochi, ohagi, dumplings, baby foods, vinegar, and amasaké. It is often used in cooking for festive occasions.

Tahini. A nut butter obtained by grinding hulled white sesame seeds until smooth and creamy. It is used like peanut butter.

Tamari and Tamari Soy Sauce. Tamari soy sauce is traditional, naturally made soy sauce, as distinguished from chemically processed varieties. Original or "real" tamari is the liquid poured off during the process of making hatcho miso. The best-quality tamari soy sauce is naturally fermented for over a year and is made from whole soybeans, wheat, and sea salt. Tamari soy sauce is sometimes referred to as *shoyu*.

Taro. A type of potato with a thick, dark brown, hairy skin. It is eaten as a vegetable or used in the preparation of plasters for medicinal purposes. Also called *albi*.

Tekka. A condiment made from hatcho miso, sesame oil, burdock, lotus root, carrot, and ginger root. Tekka is sautéed over a low flame for several hours. It is dark brown in color and very rich in iron.

Tempeh. A traditional soyfood, made from split soybeans, water, and beneficial bacteria, and allowed to ferment for several hours. Tempeh is eaten in Indonesia and Sri Lanka as a staple food. Rich in easy-to-digest protein and vitamin B12, tempeh is available prepackaged in some natural foods stores.

Tempura. A method of cooking in which seasonal vegetables and fish or seafood are coated with batter and deep-fried in unrefined oil. Tempura is often served with soup and pickles.

Tofu. Soybean curd, made from soybeans and nigari. Tofu is a protein-rich soyfood used in soups, vegetable dishes, dressings, etc. *See also* Dried Tofu.

Toxin. A poisonous compound of animal or vegetable origin that stimulates the production of antibodies.

Udon. Japanese-style noodles made from wheat, whole wheat, or whole wheat and unbleached white flour. Udon have a lighter flavor than soba (buckwheat) noodles and can be used in the same ways.

Umeboshi. Salty, pickled plums that stimulate the appetite and digestion and aid in maintaining an alkaline blood quality. Shiso leaves impart a reddish color and natural flavoring to the plums during pickling. Umeboshi can be used whole or in the form of a paste.

Umeboshi Vinegar. A salty, sour vinegar made from umeboshi plums. Diluted with water, it is used in sweet and sour sauces, salads, salad dressings, etc.

Unifying Principle. The principle of yin and yang, the philosophical foundation of macrobiotics. The Unifying Principle states that everything in the universe is constantly changing and that antagonistic forces complement one another. An understanding of this principle promotes harmony of body and mind and helps individuals to achieve balance with the natural world. *See also* Yang; Yin.

Unrefined Oil. Pressed and/or solvent-extracted vegetable oil that retains the original color, flavor, aroma, and nutritional value of the natural substance.

Unsaturated Fats. *See* Polyunsaturated Fats.

Wakame. A long, thin, green sea vegetable used in making a variety of dishes. High in protein, iron, and magnesium, wakame has a sweet taste and delicate texture. It is especially good in miso soup.

Wheat Gluten. *See* Gluten, Wheat.

Wheatberries. A term for the grains of whole wheat. They are used to make whole wheat flours and noodles. These grains can also be soaked and pressure-cooked with brown rice or other whole grains.

Whole Foods. The edible portions of foods as they come from nature, unprocessed, nutritionally complete, and without chemical additives. Whole foods are not refined at all.

Wild Rice. A wild grass that grows in water and is harvested by hand. Eaten traditionally by native Americans in Minnesota and other areas, these long, dark, thin grains are available at many natural foods stores.

Yang. In macrobiotics, energy or movement that has a centripetal or inward direction. One of the two antagonistic yet complementary forces that together describe all phenomena, yang is traditionally symbolized by a triangle (▲). *See also* Unifying Principle; Yin.

Yellow Miso. A short-term fermented miso made from white rice, soybeans, and sea salt. This miso has a salty but very mellow flavor and is used in making soups, sauces, and vegetable dishes. It is suitable for occasional use by individuals who are in good health.

Yin. In macrobiotics, energy or movement that has a centrifugal or outward direction and results in expansion. One of the two antagonistic yet complementary forces that together describe all phenomena, yin is traditionally symbolized by an inverted triangle (▼). *See also* Unifying Principle; Yang.

Yinnie Syrup. A sweet, thick syrup, made from brown rice and barley, that is used in dessert cooking. This complex carbohydrate sweetener is preferable to simple sugars such as honey, maple syrup, and molasses because the simple sugars are metabolized too quickly. Also called *rice syrup*.

Recommended Reading List

BOOKS BY MICHIO KUSHI

Health and Diet

——. *Cancer and Heart Disease: The Macrobiotic Approach.* New York and Tokyo: Japan Publications, 1986.

——. *Crime and Diet: The Macrobiotic Approach.* New York and Tokyo: Japan Publications, 1987.

——. *How to See Your Health: The Book of Oriental Diagnosis.* New York and Tokyo: Japan Publications, 1980.

——. *Macrobiotic Health Education Series: Diabetes and Hypoglycemia; Allergies; Obesity, Weight Loss and Eating Disorder; Infertility and Reproductive Disorders; Arthritis.* New York and Tokyo: Japan Publications, 1985.

——. *Macrobiotic Home Remedies.* New York and Tokyo: Japan Publications, 1985.

——. *Natural Healing through Macrobiotics.* New York and Tokyo: Japan Publications, 1979.

——. *Your Face Never Lies.* Garden City Park, NY: Avery Publishing Group, 1983.

—— and Martha Cottrell, M.D. *AIDS, Macrobiotics, and Natural Immunity.* New York and Tokyo: Japan Publications, 1990.

—— with Edward Esko. *The Macrobiotic Approach to Cancer.* Garden City Park, NY: Avery Publishing Group, revised edition, 1991.

—— with Alex Jack. *The Cancer-Prevention Diet.* New York: St. Martin's Press, 1983; revised and updated edition, 1993.

—— with Alex Jack. *Diet for a Strong Heart.* New York: St. Martin's Press, 1985.

Philosophy and Way of Life

——. *The Book of Do-In: Exercise for Physical and Spiritual Development.* New York and Tokyo: Japan Publications, 1979.

——. *On the Greater View.* Garden City Park, NY: Avery Publishing Group, 1986.

—— with Stephen Blauer. *The Macrobiotic Way.* Garden City Park, NY: Avery Publishing Group, 1985.

—— with Edward and Wendy Esko. *The Gentle Art of Making Love.* Garden City Park, NY: Avery Publishing Group, 1990.

—— with Edward Esko. *Nine Star Ki.* Becket, MA: One Peaceful World Press, 1991.

—— with Edward Esko. *Other Dimensions: Exploring the Unexplained.* Garden City Park, NY: Avery Publishing Group, 1991.

—— with Alex Jack. *The Book of Macrobiotics: The Universal Way of Health, Happiness and Peace.* New York and Tokyo: Japan Publications, revised edition, 1986.

——————. *The Gospel of Peace: Jesus's Teachings of Eternal Truth.* New York and Tokyo: Japan Publications, 1992.

——————. *One Peaceful World.* New York: St. Martin's Press, 1986.

—— with Aveline Kushi and Alex Jack. *Food Governs Your Destiny: The Teachings of Namboku Mizuno.* New York and Tokyo: Japan Publications, 1986.

—— with Olivia Oredson Saunders. *Macrobiotic Palm Healing: Energy at Your Finger-Tips.* New York and Tokyo: Japan Publications, 1988.

BOOKS BY AVELINE KUSHI

Cooking

——. *How to Cook with Miso.* New York and Tokyo: Japan Publications, 1979.

——. *Macrobiotic Food and Cooking Series–Diabetes and Hypoglycemia; Allergies; Obesity, Weight Loss and Eating Disorder; Infertility and Reproductive Disorders; Arthritis; Stress and Hypertension.* New York and Tokyo: Japan Publications, 1985.

—— with Wendy Esko. *Aveline Kushi's Introducing Macrobiotic Cooking.* New York and Tokyo: Japan Publications, 1987.

————. *Aveline Kushi's Wonderful World of Salads.* New York and Tokyo: Japan Publications, 1989.

————. *The Changing Seasons Macrobiotic Cookbook.* Garden City Park, NY: Avery Publishing Group, 1985.

————. *The Good Morning Macrobiotic Breakfast Book.* Garden City Park, NY: Avery Publishing Group, 1991.

————. *The Macrobiotic Cancer Prevention Cookbook.* Garden City Park, NY: Avery Publishing Group, 1988.

————. *Macrobiotic Family Favorites.* New York and Tokyo: Japan Publications, 1987.

————. *The New Pasta Cuisine: Low-fat Noodle and Pasta Dishes from Around the World.* New York and Tokyo: Japan Publications, 1991.

————. *The Quick and Natural Macrobiotic Cookbook.* Chicago: Contemporary Books, 1989.

—— with Alex Jack. *Aveline Kushi's Complete Guide to Macrobiotic Cooking for Health, Harmony, and Peace.* New York: Warner Books, 1985.

Family Health

————. *Lessons of Night and Day.* Garden City Park, NY: Avery Publishing Group, 1985.

—— with Michio Kushi. *Macrobiotic Pregnancy and Care of the Newborn.* Garden City Park, NY: Avery Publishing Group, 1995.

Philosophy and Way of Life

—— with Alex Jack. *Aveline: The Life and Dream of the Woman Behind Macrobiotics Today.* New York and Tokyo: Japan Publications, 1988.

—— with Wendy Esko and Maya Tiwari. *Diet for Natural Beauty.* New York and Tokyo: Japan Publications, 1991.

OTHER AUTHORS

Aihara, Herman. *Basic Macrobiotics.* New York and Tokyo: Japan Publications, 1985.

Aihara, Cornelia and Herman Aihara with Carl Ferré. *Natural Healing From Head to Toe*. Garden City Park, NY: Avery Publishing Group, 1994.

Benedict, Dirk. *Confessions of a Kamikaze Cowboy*. Garden City Park, NY: Avery Publishing Group, 1991.

Brown, Virginia with Susan Stayman. *Macrobiotic Miracle: How a Vermont Family Overcame Cancer*. New York and Tokyo: Japan Publications, 1985.

Duffy, William. *Sugar Blues*. New York: Warner Books, 1975.

Esko, Edward, editor. *Doctors Look at Macrobiotics*. New York and Tokyo: Japan Publications, 1988.

——. *Healing Planet Earth*. Becket, MA: One Peaceful World Press, 1992.

——. *Notes from the Boundless Frontier*. Becket, MA: One Peaceful World Press, 1992.

—— and Wendy Esko. *Macrobiotic Cooking for Everyone*. New York and Tokyo: Japan Publications, 1980.

Faulkner, Hugh. *Physician Heal Thyself*. Becket, MA: One Peaceful World Press, 1992.

Heidenry, Carolyn. *An Introduction to Macrobiotics*. Garden City Park, NY: Avery Publishing Group, 1987.

——. *Making the Transition to a Macrobiotic Diet*. Garden City Park, NY: Avery Publishing Group, 1987.

Ineson, John. *The Way of Life: Macrobiotics and the Spirit of Christianity*. New York and Tokyo: Japan Publications, 1986.

Jack, Alex. *Let Food Be Thy Medicine*. Becket, MA: One Peaceful World Press, 1991.

——. *The New Age Dictionary*. New York and Tokyo: Japan Publications, 1990.

——. *Out of Thin Air: A Satire on Owls and Ozone, Beef and Biodiversity, Grains and Global Warming*. Becket, MA: One Peaceful World Press, 1993.

—— with Gale Jack. *Amber Waves of Grain: American Macrobiotic Cooking*. New York and Tokyo: Japan Publications, 1992.

——. *Promenade Home: Macrobiotics and Women's Health*. New York and Tokyo: Japan Publications, 1988.

Kohler, Jean and Mary Alice Kohler. *Healing Miracles from Macrobiotics.* West Nyack, NY: Parker, 1979.

Mendelsohn, Robert S., M.D. *How to Raise a Healthy Child in Spite of Your Doctor.* New York: Ballantine Books, 1987.

Nussbaum, Elaine. *Recovery: From Cancer to Health through Macrobiotics.* Garden City Park, NY: Avery Publishing Group, 1992.

Ohsawa, Lima. *Macrobiotic Cuisine.* New York and Tokyo: Japan Publications, 1984.

Sergel, David. *The Macrobiotic Way of Zen Shiatsu.* New York and Tokyo: Japan Publications, 1988.

Sudo, Hanai. *Fire, Water, Wind.* Becket, MA: One Peaceful World Press, 1992.

Tara, William. *Macrobiotics and Human Behavior.* New York and Tokyo: Japan Publications, 1985.

Yamamoto, Shizuko. *Barefoot Shiatzu.* New York and Tokyo: Japan Publications, 1979.

Periodicals

One Peaceful World, Becket, Massachusetts

Macro News, Philadelphia, Pennsylvania

Macrobiotics Today, Oroville, California

Macrobiotic Resources

ONE PEACEFUL WORLD

One Peaceful World is an international information network and friendship society of individuals, families, educational centers, organic farmers, teachers and parents, authors and artists, publishers and business people, and others devoted to the realization of one healthy, peaceful world. Activities include educational and spiritual tours, assemblies and forums, international food aid and development, and publishing. For membership information and a current issue of the *One Peaceful World Newsletter,* including scientific and medical updates and current macrobiotic case history reports, contact:

One Peaceful World
Box 10, Becket, MA 01223
(413) 623-2322
Fax (413) 623-8827

KUSHI INSTITUTE

The Kushi Institute offers ongoing classes and seminars in macrobiotic cooking, health care, diagnosis, shiatsu and body energy development, and philosophy. Programs include the Way to Health Seminar, a seven-day residential program presented several times a month that features hands-on training in macrobiotic cooking and home care, lectures on the philosophy and practice of macrobiotics, and meals prepared by a specially trained cooking staff. The Leadership Training Program offers four- and five-week intensives for individuals who wish to become trained and certified macrobiotic teachers. Michio Kushi Seminars are four- to five-day intensive sessions with Michio on spiritual training, managing destiny, and a new medicine for humanity. Similar leadership training programs are offered at Kushi Institute affiliates in

Europe, and through Kushi Institute Extensions in selected cities in North America and abroad.

The Kushi Institute also offers a variety of special programs including an annual Macrobiotic Summer Conference. For information, contact:

Kushi Institute
Box 7
Becket, MA 01223
(413) 623-5741
Fax (413) 623-8827

GEORGE OHSAWA MACROBIOTIC FOUNDATION

The Foundation conducts a variety of programs and mail-orders certain macrobiotic products. The Vega Study Center, directed by Herman and Cornellia Aihara, offers live-in programs that feature hands-on macrobiotic cooking classes, lectures, home remedies, and more. Programs are designed to meet the needs of all, from those new to macrobiotics to those seeking professional development, and to address all areas of concern, from healing to informal weekends of relaxation and rejuvenation. The center also maintains a current list of other macrobiotic educational centers around the world.

Each July, the Aiharas host the annual French Meadows Summer Camp near Lake Tahoe in the Sierra Nevada. This outdoor camping experience is an excellent way to learn from macrobiotic teachers from around the world. For further information, contact:

George Ohsawa Macrobiotic Foundation
1511 Robinson Street
Oroville, California 95965
(916) 533-7702
Fax (916) 533-7908

Index